BODY TRAPS

BODY TRAPS

Breaking the Binds That Keep You from Feeling Good About Your Body

Dr. Judith Rodin

William Morrow and Company, Inc.
New York

It is the policy of William Morrow and Company, Inc., and its
imprints and affiliates, recognizing the importance of
preserving what has been written, to print the books we
publish on acid-free paper, and we exert our best efforts to
that end.

Library of Congress Cataloging-in-Publication Data

Rodin, Judith.
Body traps : breaking the binds that keep you from feeling
good about your body / by Judith Rodin.
p. cm.
ISBN 0-688-08843-0
1. Body image. 2. Beauty, Personal—Psychological aspects.
I. Title.
BF697.5.B63R63 1992
155.9'1—dc20   90-19885
CIP

Printed in the United States of America

First Edition

1 2 3 4 5 6 7 8 9 10

BOOK DESIGN BY RHEA BRAUNSTEIN

For Alex,
with the hope that he
escapes at least these traps

Acknowledgments

I am deeply indebted to the Guggenheim Foundation for providing a fellowship for the sabbatical year I spent writing this book, and to the National Science Foundation, the National Institutes of Health, and the John D. and Catherine T. MacArthur Foundation for supporting aspects of this line of research for many years. The Yale librarians were extremely helpful in tracking down reference material, and my scientific colleagues were generous in sharing their data with me. My students and Yale collaborators over the years, especially Ruth Striegel-Moore and Lisa Silberstein, contributed to all of the work I have done in this area. My thinking has been enriched by the hundreds of hours we have spent together planning studies, analyzing data, evaluating patients, and discussing our own body traps. Our clinic patients are due thanks for trusting us with their most elemental feelings, from which I learned a great deal.

I owe the idea of doing this book to Suzanne Gluck at ICM, who believed that my knowledge and views had to reach a wider audience and pushed me to make my thinking more accessible. We had a wonderful time bouncing ideas off one another as the nature of the book took form and life. Connie Roosevelt and Liza Dawson at William Morrow were key figures in shaping the material at various stages of the writing.

But this book surely would have never appeared in its current form without the wisdom, taste, and probing of my editor Margaret Blackstone. She felt the impact of the message and helped me to get it across.

My office staff worked tirelessly on several manuscript drafts, especially Lisa Pagliaro, Valerie Vergato, and Barbara Faulkner, and they are saints for putting up with me in these days when most authors sit at the computer themselves. Helen Hayden, a recent Kenyon College graduate, and Nicole Duncan, a recent Yale College grraduate, both worked resourcefully on the reference notes. Their good nature and deep interest in the material were unflagging. I am also grateful to Helen Hayden and to Wendy Bellerman at William Morrow for all their hard work in the last stages of production: getting reprint permissions, making sure credit lines were right, and fixing galleys.

I owe a great debt to my family and friends for putting up with me when the book was absorbing much of my time, attention, and energy, and especially to my son Alex for making the work breaks so much fun.

Contents

Introduction

If the story of Pygmalion were written today, it would not be a story about changing Eliza Doolittle's speech, her clothing, or manners, but rather about changing her face and body. A recent article in *Special Reports* recounts just such a makeover saga, a fairy tale turned into life. The tale's hero is a plastic surgeon who thinks his wife is the perfect woman because he made her what she is today. He has reworked her breast size, removed fat from her abdomen, chemically peeled the sun blotches from her face, performed an eye-lift, and turned up the tip of her nose. And oh how grateful she is to him. "I love having these operations," she confides to the reporter. "After all, I'm a reflection of my husband and his talent. He loves me because I am me, but also because of all he's done to make me look better."

With laser surgery on the horizon and finance companies now lending cash for cosmetic and plastic surgery, you don't need to be married to a plastic surgeon to fulfill your most elemental changeover fantasies. From face-lifts to miracle diets to suction removal of fat, women in increasing numbers are striving—with some degree of panic and often to their own detriment—to match the template of beauty. We are subjecting ourselves and our children to ever more complicated, expensive procedures. As *The Wall Street Journal* recently reported, "Egged on by moms, many teenagers get plastic surgery. Cosmetic surgery is now hardly more exotic than orthodontics among children . . ." The message we are all exposed to is that beauty is a matter of effort. Failure to attain it is the result of not doing enough.

We are living at a moment when society places great value on "looks." Because our appearance affects our sense of self and how other people respond to us, we are all vulnerable to Body Traps. *This book is about those body traps: what they are, what causes them, the misunderstandings that surround or support them, and how to free ourselves from them.* Body traps arise from double binds caused by ignorance about our bodies on the one hand and preoccupation with them on the other. Body Traps arise from the beliefs and feelings that keep us imprisoned by anguish over how we look, anxiety over whether we are doing enough to be attractive, and feelings of shame for worrying about it. They also arise from the staggering amount of misinformation the public receives about the physiological determinants of weight.

Body traps are shared by almost every woman, even those who appear to others to have bodies that are close to ideal. The traps are as complicated and intertwined as our feelings about our bodies. They make us misunderstand the most fundamental aspects of our weight and appearance concerns. Body fixations limit other aspects of our lives. *This book will explore a major preoccupation of almost all women and now many men in America.* We are witnessing an epidemic whose victims are the millions of people who obsess about their bodies.

Do you compare yourself to every woman who walks into the room? Do you order dessert only if your dinner partner does? Do you feel ashamed of the fact that you spend time worrying about how you look? Do you feel like you are always either dieting or thinking about beginning again? All of these are signs of body traps. Most people misunderstand that the factors that influence our thoughts and feelings about how we look, and that affect our bodies and weight, are far more complicated than they have been led to believe.

Current culture conspires to promise us the allure of an easy fix. In this technology-driven society, it seems like the goal of looking good is possible for anyone if only she works hard enough, exercises long enough, and eats little enough. But the quest for the perfect body isn't easy. It is loaded with all kinds of traps, leaving most people feeling frustrated, ashamed, and defeated much of the time. Because we believe that beauty and good bodies are attainable by anyone, we spend more on beauty than on social services or education in America today.

Here are just a few examples. According to calculations of retail sales in the United States, today we buy 1,484 tubes of lipstick per *minute* at a cost of $4,566. We buy 1,324 mascaras, eyeliners, and eyeshadows a minute, costing $6,849; and 2,055 jars of skin-care products a minute, which cost $12,785. Some working women interviewed by *Glamour* magazine for its April 1991 issue each spent over $7,000 a year for their "high maintenance" look.

Many of the women my colleagues and I have studied spend as many hours on looking good as they do on their paid jobs. Susan, a successful young executive, summed it up nicely:

> It takes me an hour to get dressed in the morning, putting on creams, choosing clothes that make me look thin, worrying in front of the mirror. Then I go to work. On the bus, I try to figure out who looks better, especially thinner, than I do. If the bus crashes, I know she'll be saved first because she looks so good. I hate her. I spend all morning at work planning how not to eat the danish and what to avoid at lunch. By 3 P.M., I'm so hungry, all I can think about is dinner. But dinner is only a distant reward, after the hour of aerobics. Go out at night? Are you kidding? I have to start worrying about how to look good tomorrow.

Susan isn't a patient. She's the girl next door.

In less than one hundred years, society has changed dramatically. There are few remaining hierarchies, few social structures based simply on religion, parentage, money, or education. Society has become more egalitarian as a result, but it's intrinsic to human nature to judge, evaluate, and compare ourselves. Because we are social beings, we are uniquely, sometimes regrettably, responsive to social norms and direct social pressure. We can't help but evaluate ourselves, in part through the eyes of other people. If class and money no longer provide the yardsticks for measuring ourselves against our neighbors, what are the new social yardsticks? It is my premise that they are the more visible, tangible, observable things. For many, it is possessions—how many toys we can gather as adults—but it is also undoubtedly how we look.

Our bodies have become the new coin of the realm. Appearance, good looks, and fitness are now the measure of our social worth. Not only is how we look suddenly incredibly important, but we have come to accept homogeneous images of beauty. We have become hypnotized by a quest for an impossible, celluloid-inspired perfection.

Painting and the arts, once the primary source of imagery for bodies, style, and appearance have been replaced in modern culture by television, movies, and magazines that sell glamour. The media now expose everyone to a single "right" look and the beauty industry promises that anyone can attain it if he or she buys enough, from makeup to makeovers. Standing at a newsstand and looking at the magazines tells it all. There are any number of magazines for both men and women emphasizing looks, style, beauty, hair, fashion, and an almost equivalent number for adolescents. There are even a few now for young children. Certainly in number they rival the newsstand sections on cars, mechanics, gardening—showing that how we look has become our most important "hobby." But it certainly isn't fun, the way hobbies should be. It is a tortured pursuit for most of us.

I just went to get my mail and it is loaded with catalogs. One doesn't even have to leave home now to shop for beauty. It is another part of the new technology that was never there before, making it seem so easy to look good that we feel anyone can and should do it. But the beautiful self we want isn't real. The beautiful people—the synthetic illusions created by the media—don't look that much better than we do when they wake up in the morning. Perhaps this is the ultimate trap. We are all casualties of the technology of the fabrication of looks and the dehumanization of spirit and individualism. Our goals are unrealistic and inhuman and we are creating and recreating ourselves to embody these goals.

It has become so fashionable, so politically correct to worry about the environment. We rally to plant trees to save the earth, we worry about oil spills, but do we realize how we are defacing and dehumanizing ourselves by chemical peels, dermabrasion, hair dye, synthetic diet foods, and artificial fats and sweeteners? Where is the concern for the human part of the environment? We are losing ourselves and not worrying about it.

I'll cover several Body Traps in this book. Most of them are debilitating or limiting in some way, and they can be changed by eliminating the ignorance that many of us share about our bodies. The designations are somewhat arbitrary and as you'll see, some of the traps can and do overlap.

The Vanity Trap We are accused of being, and feel ourselves to be, vain and conceited if we're concerned about how we look. But this view overlooks the deep psychological significance of the body. Of all the ways we experience ourselves, perhaps none is so primal as the sense of our own bodies. Our body image is at the very core of our identity. Our feelings about our bodies are woven into practically every aspect of our behavior. Our bodies are also critical to our identity because they are the form and substance of our persona to the outside world. Appearance will always be important because we are social beings. How we look sends messages, whether we want it to or not, and people respond to us accordingly.

We can blame the media for creating a single look— unattainable by most—the ideal. But we can't hold them responsible for the fact that our body image profoundly influences how we feel about ourselves. Despite the importance of body image, however, we get trapped because most of us lack adequate knowledge of how our body operates and have insufficient body awareness. The difficulties some of us have in figuring out how we feel and look can diminish our sense of who we are.

The Shame Trap Shame is closely related to the vanity trap. Worrying about how we look makes us feel guilty and ashamed. It seems silly compared to the world's pressing problems. But advertisements, television, movies, and our friends are always there to remind us of how we should look, even if we try to forget. At the very heart of the feeling of shame is the feeling that we've failed to live up to some ideal that we all value. Shame affects women and men, but in different ways. New findings presented here show that women feel ashamed of their bodies; men find their body concerns shameful. Some surprising consequences arise from this difference.

The Competition Trap Physical attractiveness and weight are still the chief and most wholeheartedly sanctioned arenas in which women are encouraged to contend with each other. The ultimate contest—the beauty pageant—is still going strong. Women compete with one another for men, but their urge to be thin transcends even what they think men find attractive. Weight control, in particular, is laden with rewards for competing effectively. The challenge is sufficiently visible that it commands respect. The high chance of failure reinforces its importance. The competition trap is complicated further by the fact that concern, complaint, and worry about weight are also forms of bonding among women—a sort of friendship ritual. And women compete not only with one another, but with their own ideal self. When this drives them to become too perfectionistic, they often fall back on eating to relieve the stress.

The Food Trap Food is inextricably bound to all human activities. But with the fitness craze, *what* we eat has now taken on moral overtones—cholesterol is bad, fiber is good—and we feel correspondingly virtuous or guilty depending on what we consume. Different foods are strongly associated with feelings in other ways as well. Food is laden with symbolic meaning and is the most widely used form of self-nurturance and self-medication. For all these reasons, favorite foods are hard to give up. Yet, we are made to do so in our quest for more perfect bodies.

The Dieting-Rituals Trap Dieting has become a ritual. It means much more than losing weight. It's a spring cleaning, a new slate, a fresh beginning. It also holds the promise of rejuvenation. That's why it's so hard to give up. But restrictive dieting may be one of the worst forms of weight control. In fact, it may be one of the major causes of weight gain and disordered eating. And our genes have a much greater influence on our body shape and size than our dieting efforts, which leaves some people caught fruitlessly in the wrong battles and others attempting the impossible. Yet, society treats dieting as if it were equally easy for all, creating still another aspect of this body trap.

The Fitness Trap The benefits of exercise are real. It improves mood and helps to maintain health. But you *can* have too much of a good thing. In the case of exercise, too much may be worse than none at all. There are also other health risks, including heightened weight preoccupation and even eating disorders, which are associated with intensive athletic pursuits for many. Exercise is increasingly viewed as morally right, an attitude that ironically encourages harmful excess.

The Success Trap Success at weight control and looking good is the brass ring, the final reward for many. But, surprisingly, achieving it may lead to unhappiness for some rather than joy. Many people feel like frauds because of the enormous time and money it takes to look good. Maintaining their false self puts them under chronic and intense stress. And few develop the confidence that they can sustain the success. Another part of this trap arises for those who hoped their lives would be transformed by success. Often these very expectations set them up for failure. Success also sometimes threatens close relationships, or changes other parts of our lives in ways that are frightening.

Body concern has escalated dramatically in the last several years. While twenty years ago appearance was felt to be an issue, today, national surveys show that we have never been so preoccupied and dissatisfied with our bodies. Our solutions are not always healthful. New and more radical weight-control strategies flood the market, and more children than ever are dieting. Current studies reveal that now most "normal" women show some characteristics that are similar to women with eating disturbances. In fact, questionnaires originally designed to diagnose the eating disorders—bulimia and anorexia nervosa—can no longer be used alone to provide a clinical diagnosis, because almost all women endorse items such as, "I am terrified of gaining weight," or "I am always on a diet."

What is different about this particular moment in time that seems to be increasing both the pressures and the stakes in the beauty quest?

We live in a self-conscious society. First, the marketing of beauty has become big business—a multibillion-dollar industry. Second, this is a period in which sex roles are becoming increasingly blurred. Women have moved into traditionally male domains and men are increasingly becoming involved in the household. In many ways our bodies remain our most visible means of expressing a difference between the sexes. The right body and appearance may be a way for women in traditionally male occupations to demonstrate their feminine identity without compromising their professional persona. And a muscled, masculine look may reaffirm a man's sense of masculinity at a time when his occupational role alone no longer can do so. Third, the fitness movement has made our bodies visible testimony to our pursuit of good health. But perversely, the shape of our body is now taken as evidence of how hard we have worked at self-improvement—it tells the world how virtuous we are.

Scientists have only recently begun to study and understand the compelling psychological and social reasons for our body concern. Perhaps it seemed shameful, almost silly to serious scientists to acknowledge that the body and appearance matter as much as they do. The importance of understanding the topic, however, became clear in the 1980s when extreme body concern, coupled with difficulty in achieving society's ideal beauty standards, encouraged widespread disregulated eating patterns and more serious eating disorders such as bulimia and anorexia.

The explosion of new research, much of which has taken place at Yale, has led to some extraordinary insights. We now understand how body image is formed and the intimate relationship between body image and self-esteem. We know that men also experience body preoccupation, some quite intensely, but that it affects them differently from women. New studies show how parents unintentionally encourage disordered eating and weight preoccupation in their children, beginning as early as age one. Most important, we now understand how maladaptive many of our body-improvement efforts have been, how in our headlong urgency to do ourselves good, we may have been doing the very things that make our success more unlikely.

I will also draw on the insights we have gained from the patients we have seen at the Yale Eating Disorders Clinic who want help for their weight, compulsive eating, or body preoccupations. With my colleagues Ruth Striegel-Moore and Lisa Silberstein, I have supervised the treatment of hundreds of troubled men and women, people who finally seek help because they suffer so much from their body concerns that other aspects of their lives are compromised.

At the clinic, we also study people who are of normal weight and who eat in a healthy way, to help us understand those with more extreme behavior. From this work, I have come to realize that all people, regardless of their weight, worry about their bodies. For all the time they spend worrying, however, most people really know very little about their physical selves or the real source of their feelings. And they, like many of you who will read this book, simply have not understood that when they have tried to improve themselves, they have out of ignorance done themselves harm. As a result, they fall victim to their own body traps.

Beatrice, one of our patients, exemplifies a lifelong obsession with weight and dieting. Beatrice started her first diet at age twelve. At the time, she was normal weight, a fact she realized only much later in life, when looking at old family albums and seeing pictures of herself. Beatrice matured early, developing full breasts at age nine. She was taller and heavier than her classmates and she felt "clumsy and enormous" compared to them. Her mother and her aunt were "exquisitely beautiful." Both had short careers as fashion models before marrying into wealthy families and devoting their lives to active social calendars. Beatrice's sister, two years her senior, had inherited her mother's looks. She was small-boned and fair-skinned, with beautiful thick black hair. "She looked like a china doll," Beatrice told us, "and she always stole the show." In contrast, Beatrice took after her father's family, where everyone was "tall, square, muscular, and the women all had big chests. They have freckles and sort of bushy hair, and the women just don't look classy the way my sister, my mother, and aunt looked. Appearance was very important in our family," remembers Beatrice.

The women in Beatrice's family often discussed other women's physical features, forever drawing comparisons. Her mother's schedule revolved around hairdresser appointments, going to fashion shows, and supervising her daughters' classes in ballet, ballroom dancing, and manners and etiquette. Although Beatrice herself has not followed her mother's footsteps in terms of devoting her own life to beauty and fashion, she has internalized her mother's view that being attractive is extremely important. Because she is overweight, Beatrice feels she cannot focus on any other aspect of her appearance, however, until she has lost "the weight." Thus, she purchases cheap, baggy clothes ("It's not worth spending the money on nice clothes when you're fat").

Shame was another prominent feature in Beatrice's life story. From an early age, Beatrice felt that she could not measure up to the other women in the household. When she entered puberty, she felt that her body betrayed her. She was teased and harassed by the boys in her class. "I was *so* ashamed of my body. I would hide behind my clothes. I always insisted on buying my school uniforms a size larger than I really needed, you know, the blouses and sweaters were huge enough to cover up my breasts." Like many girls who enter puberty early, Beatrice was confronted with sexual advances beginning at an early age. She felt highly ambivalent about these advances. On the one hand, she was relieved finally to be noticed by the boys in her neighborhood or class, who would pressure her into letting them fondle her breasts. On the other hand, she was ashamed by what she had to do in order to get their attention. She did not feel entitled to say no to their advances for which she always blamed herself. She was too embarrassed to talk with anyone about her problem. "My parents were headed for a divorce at the time, so they were all caught up in their own stuff, and my sister would have only used this information to make even more fun of me."

With tears in her eyes, Beatrice continued telling us her painful experiences so typical of someone struggling with shame. "Of course, we had to take dance classes, and classes in manners. After all, my parents were part of the upper class in Boston and we had to be prepared for marriage to some wealthy man, and so on. So, anyway, I remember going to these classes and hating every minute of it. I was taller and bigger than all the girls and taller than pretty much all of the boys. None of the boys wanted to dance with me, and I would be so anxious that sweat would run down my back. I felt absolutely gross—huge, fat, vulgar." She withdrew more and more from her peers and began dieting in an effort to reduce her "grotesque body."

Thus, Beatrice experienced a devastating blend of issues characteristic of the shame trap, the vanity trap, and the dieting rituals trap. Deeply ashamed of her body and by extension, herself, yet greatly valuing attractiveness and assuming that beauty was of utmost importance in a woman's life (in her social and familial context rightly so), she devoted herself to ever more drastic dieting efforts to shape her body into a form that, as she now recognizes, was utterly unattainable for her. For about thirty years of her life, Beatrice "tried every diet under the sun, with short-lived successes and long-term failures." She learned to think of herself as unattractive and believed that others found her physical appearance repulsive.

To be effective, our treatment needed to address these several issues. The goals were to help Beatrice put appearance and weight into perspective, acknowledging that our society does in fact value thinness and beauty, yet that there is more to life than the pursuit of weight loss. Beatrice's lifelong pattern of dietary chaos needed to be broken and replaced with balanced, healthful eating habits that allowed for enjoyment of food without guilt. Finally, Beatrice needed support to find relief from the profound sense of shame that eroded her self-esteem and made it impossible for her to feel in touch with her body and to properly appreciate and take care of herself. In the chapters that follow, I'll describe how we helped Beatrice and others overcome their traps. What makes me most satisfied is that Beatrice now likes herself for the first time in her life.

The first step to breaking the body traps is to understand the problem and your own personal issues. I will present research findings and cases from many of the patients we have gotten to know over the years, and you will surely recognize yourself among some of these people. I will also give several of the tests we use to diagnose various aspects of the body traps to help you identify specific areas you might want to work on. Once you have identified your particular problems, you will learn many ways to reconnect your bodies to your inner selves in a more healthy, unconflicted way.

This is not a diet book. It is a book that will increase your self-understanding about why weight and appearance matter so much. In every chapter of this book, you are provided with specific techniques to break the body traps you are in now and to avoid becoming vulnerable to others in the future. New understanding of why you act, or fail to act, in certain ways will help you choose more effective ways of dealing with problem situations.

Issues of body image are serious. How we feel about our bodies and, in particular, our weight, is a highly charged issue and one worthy of attention because of its social and psychological consequences. *This is a book for the 1990s precisely because body concern has become more harmful to both individuals and society alike.* It's a problem that demands our immediate attention. This book is intended to help you take the first step.

—1—

Why Now?

In her review of the decade of the eighties, columnist Vida Roberts writing for the *Baltimore Evening Sun*, concluded:

> The body was the strongest fashion statement for the 80's. It was the essential element of style, with clothes mere accessories. And it was a fashion of our own design that we could stretch, pump and diet into shape. Cher promised it was so if we would "just do it." The decade allowed no excuse for droopy thighs or flabby midriffs.
>
> But being fit was not enough, you had to look good. As the workouts started to work, the healthy set bagged their sweat suits, and the run on sexy active wear was on.
>
> They preened and fluttered in the spa mirrors like iridescent tropical birds in full mating plumage. The look was tight, the colors were hot and bodies gleamed with Lycra and Spandex. There were unitards and "legotards" and bike pants and running tights. Workout clothes climbed high on the thigh, disappeared at the midriff, plunged at the bosom, rode high on the fanny.
>
> They looked so good that the stretch look went public and into the streets.

In the last ten years, body preoccupation has become a social mania. We have been driven to think, talk, strategize, and worry about our bodies. Questions like "Do I look good enough?" "Am I fit enough?" or "Am I thin enough?" are thoughts we all have, but they are obsessions for many. In this chapter, I'll explore how culture and society have set the stage for making these concerns so prevalent.

While I think that forces like the industrialization of beauty and current social trends have escalated the stakes at this moment in particular, it is clear that concern with appearance and weight is not simply an aberration of contemporary Western culture. Every period of history has had its own standards of what is beautiful and what is not. And each culture has unique, and very different notions about the proper size, shape, and decoration of the body. In the twelfth and thirteenth centuries, Chinese women bound their feet tightly to create the narrow, divided sole look that was the fashion of the day, a practice that hobbled hundreds of thousands. And in the nineteenth century, attaining the beautiful female body required wearing a corset, which led to difficulty in breathing, constipation, weakness, and a tendency to violent indigestion. Women's bodies have always and everywhere been perceived as unfinished, in want of carving, perforating, incising, refining, and realignment to make them a thing of beauty and joy to individual and society alike.

But if we moderns resemble our forebears throughout history, technology has enabled these concerns to reach staggering new heights.

Narcissus and the Boob Tube The industrial achievements of the twentieth century have had an enormous impact on how we feel about our bodies. In particular, since the rise of the mass media, including the use of photographs and motion pictures, we have become exposed to extremely uniform standards of beauty and fashion, and magazines and movies make us all more conscious of how we look. Television has brought celebrities into our homes and made them part of our daily lives. The implications of this are frankly staggering. We see beautiful people as often as we see some of our own family members, making exceptional good looks seem real and attainable. Narcissus was lucky. He only looked into a lake. Like a modern-day Narcissus, today's woman looks at television and wants to see herself. When she doesn't, she works harder and harder to match the unnatural reflection. She ignores the hours the movie stars spent with makeup and hairdressing specialists. She forgets how easily the camera lies.

Since the celluloid reality of movies and television has invaded our lives, we are also bombarded by images of exercise specialists with beautifully molded bodies, shouting at us to "move those thighs, stretch those arms, tuck in those tummies." Even if we flip the channels quickly, we can't help but feel guilty if this is a day in which we didn't "go for the burn." These beautiful people—with us in our living rooms and bedrooms as we eat breakfast or wind down from the day—are the constant reminders of what the correct look is. And "the look" is now marketed relentlessly.

Beauty has become a major growth industry, with advertising promoting body preoccupation for everyone. "With most cosmetics, you're basically selling dreams, hope in a bottle," says Martin Stevens, former creative director at Revlon. The diet industry is now a multimillion-dollar enterprise, built on the promise of a better, more beautiful self.

In 1972, Nora Ephron wrote a piece in *Esquire* magazine called "A Few Words About Breasts." It was the humorous confession of the woes of a less-than-amply-endowed woman. This piece seems so dated today. Bodies are now seen as malleable, correctable. For many years, plastic surgery was generally regarded as an indulgence of vain aging women having face-lifts and spoiled, rich high school girls having nose jobs. But in the 1980s, it became a much bigger business. According to a report issued in 1985 by the American Society of Plastic and Reconstructive Surgeons (ASPRS), its 2,700 board-certified surgeons performed 477,000 "aesthetic" surgeries in 1984, up 61 percent from 1981. These included dermabrasion (peeling the skin), abdominoplasty (tummy tuck), mentoplasty (chin implant), mastopexy (breast lift), otoplasty (ears), and hair transplantation. The percent increase for these types of surgeries ranged from 7 percent for hair transplantation to 40 percent for chin implants. But the leader by a wide margin—growing 300 percent in only four years—was surgical body contouring.

This recent phenomenal growth in plastic surgery is the by-product of a change in the role of appearance. In addition to their traditional ornamental roles, the face and the body are increasingly being pressed into service as essential business accessories, a mobile billboard, for their owner's brilliance, energy, and savvy. There are currently few occupations for which appearance is not important. To take but one example, a study of accounting firms by business school professors Jerry Ross and Kenneth Ferris showed that both salary and the likelihood of becoming a partner were more strongly related to physical attractiveness than to whether the person had a graduate degree or to the quality of the school he or she had attended.

In fact, now your body shape and wardrobe are not your only possessions that go in and out of style. Your face does too. A panel of plastic surgeons reported at a recent ASPRS meeting that facial features may be "in" one decade and "out" another. These doctors evaluated their patients' surgery requests over the last thirty years. They found that the face of the decade of the eighties was a far cry from that of the fifties. Women of the eighties wanted to see themselves as intelligent and assertive. The preferred image moved from young Elizabeth Taylor to Christie Brinkley. Women wanted a more vertical forehead, prominent cheekbones, deep-set eyes, wider eyebrows, narrower eyelids, fuller lips. "They tell me, 'I don't want to look sweet,'" says Dr. Norman J. Pastorek, a New York facial plastic surgeon. "'When I'm toe to toe with those guys on the stock exchange, I don't want to look ineffective and vulnerable.'"

Men, too, are changing their look, with wide noses and sagging eyes no longer acceptable in many circles. According to a joint survey by the American Academy of Cosmetic Surgery (AACS) and the American Society of Liposuction Surgery

(ASLS), 30 percent of all plastic surgeries were male in 1988, the most recent year for which data are available. This was up nearly 10 percent from the previous year. The top five cosmetic procedures for men, according to the AACS, are, in order: liposuction (fat removal) to diminish "love handles"; nose surgery; hair transplants; eyelid surgery; and face-lifts. The trend in men's faces now is toward fuller lips, higher cheekbones, and stronger chins. The narrow concave nose popular in the seventies has given way to a straighter nose, and shapes that are in harmony with the rest of the face, according to the AACS.

But in case this seems too extreme for you, the panel of plastic surgeons I talked about earlier ended with this reassurance. "Don't misunderstand. The face of the sixties and seventies is still acceptable, and even if you don't have the face of the eighties, you may wish to wait. The unstylish face of today may be perfect for the 1990s."

The Social Importance of Appearance The "right" look matters to us because appearance is extraordinarily important to being successful and valued in our world today. As early as preschool, attractive children are more popular with their peers, according to current studies. Researchers observed who plays with whom, which children get chosen first as work partners or for teams, and who children rate as their closest friends. These young people have apparently already absorbed the value that society places on beauty, because they like the prettiest children best. And their teachers hold the same view, rating the more attractive children as the smartest and most effective.

Among teenagers and adults, attractive people are viewed as having virtually every character trait that is socially desirable. They are seen as leading more successful and more fulfilling lives. One recent study actually measured the effect of changes in attractiveness, which were accomplished by cosmetic surgery, on how people judge one another. Research subjects saw before-and-after photographs. They rated the people in the pictures as significantly kinder, warmer, more responsive, and happier after becoming more attractive. Susan, one of our research study participants, summed up this social attitude nicely: "When you're as plain as I am on the outside, people think you're kind of ugly on the inside, too."

Many studies have also shown that physically attractive people have a distinct advantage over less attractive ones in interpersonal situations. They are more likely to receive help and to elicit cooperation. Attractive applicants appear to have a better chance of getting a job and they tend to be hired at a better starting salary. Even in the courtroom, attractive people appear to benefit from more positive outcomes, and are found guilty less often. They are seen as worthy of milder punishments and awarded more favorable judgments.

If people assume that what is beautiful is good and what is ugly is bad, how does that affect our social interactions? Do unattractive people have restricted social lives? Do they become less socially skilled as a consequence? The answer is often yes. Expectations have a way of being fulfilled. If you expect someone to be a sourpuss, then you tend to act in ways to bring out that sourpuss in them. If you expect someone to be a star, a star he or she will most likely try to be. There is a strong self-fulfilling nature to the physical attractiveness stereotype.

In a study by University of Minnesota psychologists Mark Snyder and Ellen Berscheid, and their students, men and women who were strangers were paired up in a study on the processes by which people get to know one another. To keep them from actually seeing their partners, they were asked to use the telephone to become acquainted. Before the telephone conversation began, the men were each given a Polaroid snapshot, supposedly of the woman each would be meeting, along with some biographical information. In truth, the snapshot was not of the partner. There were really only two pictures used. Half the participants saw one picture—of a very good-looking woman, and half the participants saw the second—a picture of someone quite homely.

Men were asked their initial impressions of their partner before the telephone conversation began. Participants who thought they would be talking to an attractive woman expected her to be much more sociable, poised, humorous, and socially adept. What is startling is that these expectations had a dramatic impact on their partner's behavior in the short space of the telephone call. The psychologists separately recorded the phone conversations of the men and women. The tapes were then rated by judges who knew nothing about which picture subjects had been given. Men who thought they had an attractive partner were judged as trying harder, were seen as more humorous, and more encouraging. Their partners responded accordingly. Women who had been depicted as attractive were judged to sound more animated, confident, and adept. Women depicted by the homely photo were thought to sound just the opposite.

If stereotypes held by people shape their own social reality within only ten minutes of a telephone conversation, you can imagine what happens over several years. If year after year attractive people are given more opportunities and encouragement in social interactions than unattractive people, undoubtedly attractive and unattractive people can become different social beings.

As a society obsessed with a set standard of beauty, we are especially intolerant of, and sometimes cruel to, those who do not meet it, most particularly, overweight people. We learn early in life that something is shameful about obesity. And the obese are painfully stigmatized. Studies show that children have more negative feelings about obese children than toward children with a wide range of handicaps, including those in wheelchairs, missing a hand, or having a facial disfigurement. Even children with a life-threatening chronic illness would rather be sick than fat.

Statistics show that there's discrimination against obese people in educational and work settings. In an episode of the popular television show *L.A. Law*, the issue of fat prejudice in the workplace was given a sympathetic airing. The television episode featured a storyline about an attorney who was fired from her firm for being obese. The defendants claimed that despite the fact that the woman was a good attorney, her body size was a detriment to her credibility. The woman was suing them for damages.

The managing partner of the firm testified: "For an attorney-at-law, performance and appearance are not mutually exclusive. The reality is that people look at her and say, 'Gee, if she can't take care of herself, how can she take care of me?'"

Later, the defense attorney asked her: "Isn't it true . . . for your entire life, people have readily dismissed you simply because you are fat?" "The fact that everyone does it, doesn't excuse it," she responded. "No, it doesn't," the attorney rebutted. "But if it's a reality, how can you blame my client for recognizing it? . . ."

We learn these antifat attitudes in childhood and they figure strongly into why normal weight people so greatly fear becoming overweight. Many people in our research studies state that they would kill themselves if they were fat. While we know that this is just a manner of speech, a way to emphasize how repugnant the thought is, some overweight people are so unhappy about their appearance, they do contemplate suicide and a few follow through. The test on pages 31 to 32 will give you an idea of how important society's standards are to you.

But has the situation gotten worse in the past few decades? The answer is undeniably yes.

Examining statistics about contestants in the annual Miss America contest, psychologist David Garner and his colleagues at the University of Toronto showed that body weight and measurements have decreased significantly in the last twenty years. Incredible as it may seem, since 1970, the winners have generally been the thinnest of the five finalists.

A recent study of male business school graduates, by Dr. Irene Frieze, a psychologist at the University of Pittsburgh, and her colleagues, showed a strong relationship between weight, height, and income for men. Surveying over one thousand men, they found that those who were at least 20 percent overweight made four thousand dollars less per year. Leaner men earned higher salaries over time than their overweight colleagues. Height also affected male salaries. Taller men earned

SOCIAL ATTITUDES SCALE

Please read the following statements and indicate how strongly you agree or disagree with each.

1. A man would always prefer to go out with a thin woman than with one who is heavy.

Strongly Agree	Slightly Agree	Neither Agree nor Disagree	Slightly Disagree	Strongly Disagree
_____	_____	_____	_____	_____

2. Clothes are made today so that only thin people can look good.

Strongly Agree	Slightly Agree	Neither Agree nor Disagree	Slightly Disagree	Strongly Disagree
_____	_____	_____	_____	_____

3. Fat people are often unhappy.

Strongly Agree	Slightly Agree	Neither Agree nor Disagree	Slightly Disagree	Strongly Disagree
_____	_____	_____	_____	_____

4. It is not true that attractive people are more interesting, poised, and socially outgoing than unattractive people.

Strongly Agree	Slightly Agree	Neither Agree nor Disagree	Slightly Disagree	Strongly Disagree
_____	_____	_____	_____	_____

5. A pretty face will not get you very far without a slim body.

Strongly Agree	Slightly Agree	Neither Agree nor Disagree	Slightly Disagree	Strongly Disagree
_____	_____	_____	_____	_____

6. It is more important that a woman be attractive than a man be.

Strongly Agree	Slightly Agree	Neither Agree nor Disagree	Slightly Disagree	Strongly Disagree
_____	_____	_____	_____	_____

7. Attractive people lead more fulfilling lives than unattractive people.

Strongly Agree	Slightly Agree	Neither Agree nor Disagree	Slightly Disagree	Strongly Disagree
_____	_____	_____	_____	_____

8. The thinner the woman is, the more attractive she is.

Strongly Agree	Slightly Agree	Neither Agree nor Disagree	Slightly Disagree	Strongly Disagree
_____	_____	_____	_____	_____

9. Attractiveness decreases the likelihood of professional success.

Strongly Agree	Slightly Agree	Neither Agree nor Disagree	Slightly Disagree	Strongly Disagree
_____	_____	_____	_____	_____

The above items test how much you believe that appearance matters. Score your responses as follows:

Items 1, 2, 3, 5, 7, 8: Give yourself a 0 if you said _Strongly Disagree;_ a 1 for _Disagree;_ a 2 for _Neither Agree nor Disagree;_ adding one more point up to a 4 for _Strongly Agree._

Items 4, 6, 9 are scored in reverse: Give yourself a 0 for _Strongly Agree_ and a 4 for _Strongly Disagree,_ and points 1 through 3 for remaining responses.

Add together your points for all nine questions. A score of 28 or higher means that you are vulnerable to being influenced by the great importance that current society places on appearance.

about six hundred dollars more *per inch* than shorter executives. Such differences were not evident twenty years ago.

Since findings such as these vividly reveal our changing tastes, it is not surprising that in even as short a time span as fifteen to twenty years, people seem to be more preoccupied and less satisfied with their bodies. The thinner and more beautiful the ideal becomes, the harder it is for most people to attain.

In 1987, the magazine *Psychology Today* published the results of a survey of its readers' feelings about appearance and weight. Only 12 percent indicated that they had little concern about their appearance and didn't do much to improve it. Of course, people who choose to return a survey on body image may be likely to care more than most about their appearance. But the results of this survey are similar to those that have recently been found in many studies where the participants are selected at random. People currently feel intense pressure to look good.

An earlier survey on body image was published in *Psychology Today* in 1972. The 1970s respondents were considerably more satisfied with their bodies than were the 1980s respondents. Men especially seem more concerned about how they look now than they used to. But for both sexes, *the pressure to look good has intensified in the last fifteen years.* Consider the table on page 34, comparing the two surveys. Our dissatisfaction has grown for every area of our bodies.

The survey also shows how central weight is to body image. Over 40 percent of the men and 50 percent of the women were unhappy with their weight in 1987. Men were most dissatisfied with their bellies and women with their thighs. These are the areas most often affected by weight gain for each sex. A survey I evaluated last year for the newspaper *USA Today* showed identical results. People now seem far more critical of themselves for not attaining the right weight and look.

Perhaps if this change had only occurred for adults it would not be of such concern. But adolescents and children are following suit. In the early 1970s, a survey of teenagers published in the medical journal *Pediatrics* found that only 6 percent

DR. JUDITH RODIN

UNHAPPY BODIES

People Dissatisfied with Body Areas or Dimensions

| | 1972 Survey | | | 1987 Survey | |
	Men	Women		Men	Women
Height	13%	13%	Height	20%	17%
Weight	35	48	Weight	41	55
Muscle Tone	25	30	Muscle Tone	32	45
Overall Face	8	11	Face	20	20
Chest/Breast	18	26	Upper Torso	28	32
Abdomen	36	50	Mid Torso	50	57
Hips and Upper Thighs	12	49	Lower Torso	21	50
Overall Appearance	15	25	"Looks As They Are"	34	38

worried about their weight. Now, a new survey in the *Journal of the Canadian Medical Association* showed that 31 percent of the teenagers—both boys and girls—worry that they weigh too much. And in a study of almost five hundred San Francisco schoolgirls, mostly from middle-income families, 81 percent of the ten-year-olds reported that they had already dieted at least once.

Mothers need to become aware of the new findings about dieting, as much for their children as for themselves. They should be aware that the more a mother is preoccupied with her own weight, the more her child is at risk. Our study of mothers and their ninth-through twelfth-grade daughters revealed that mothers of daughters with disordered eating have themselves had a long-standing concern with dieting. In fact, they started dieting at a younger age than women to whom we compared them—those with daughters who did not have eating disorders. Their actual weights did not differ from the comparison mothers, but they were substantially more dissatisfied with their own bodies, and shockingly, with their daughters' bodies, too. Mothers of daughters with disordered eating wanted their daughters to be thinner than other mothers did, regardless of the daughters' actual weight. They rated their daughters as less attractive even than their daughters rated themselves. In contrast, comparison mothers' ratings of their daughters' attractiveness were virtually identical to the daughters' own ratings. Mothers should be aware of the effects of dieting on their daughters and the issues surrounding body image in adolescence, both of which can affect a woman for the rest of her life. There are as yet no comparable studies regarding fathers and daughters, and this remains an important area for future research.

Susan and Wayne Wooley, psychologists who study body concern and eating disorders, argue that the risk has escalated precisely because these are the children of the "Weight Watchers generation"—the first generation to be raised by highly weight-conscious mothers. Many children reach adolescence only to feel their mothers' increasing criticism of their appearance. In addition, they learn how to diet, and develop aberrant eating patterns by watching their own mothers.

Now we know how early a mother's weight concerns can have an effect on her child. In a just-completed study, Steven Reznick, a developmental psychologist at Yale, and I found striking differences among mothers in how they feed and behave toward their one-year-old children. We videotaped mothers feeding their toddlers a typical meal. All the mothers and children we chose to study were of normal weight. Then raters who knew nothing of the mothers' body concerns evaluated the tapes. The ratings of how moms fed their youngsters were strongly related to the mothers' own weight concerns and body-image disturbances.

How did the mothers differ? Those who were highly weight preoccupied fed their babies more inconsistently, sometimes pushing them to eat and sometimes underfeeding them. They were rated as showing considerably more emotional arousal during the feeding than the less body-preoccupied mothers. They also tended to hurry most through the feeding interaction. In general then, as early as age one and probably even earlier, children are vulnerable to their mothers' concerns about their own bodies and weight.

Given people's increasing body dissatisfaction, it is not surprising that there has been a concurrent increase in highly disregulated eating behavior over the last fifteen years including the, by now, well-known disorders called bulimia—frequent and compulsive binge eating followed by purging, and anorexia—a syndrome of self-starvation. The growing prevalence of eating disorders among women has been widely documented. Indeed, *Newsweek* magazine called 1981 the year of the binge-purge syndrome, based on interviews with leading researchers and clinicians in the field. But according to *The New York Times* health columnist Jane Brody, experts now believe that in the 1990s, many more boys and men are suffering from these problems than doctors or the public realize. Social pressures on men to be slim and fit are increasing, leading to weight reduction and exercise practices that can set off the development of eating disorders in vulnerable men.

Part of this increase in eating disorders is surely due to the fact that smoking, drinking, and eating have become forbidden pleasures. For many young women, there is nothing left but diet and exercise. Moreover, society and the media teach us not only what the ideal body looks like, but also how to pursue it. This includes how to purge and starve. These rituals are nearly prescribed by the mass market weight control industry. For example, a best-selling diet book in the 1980s, *The Beverly Hills Diet*, advocated a form of bulimia in which binges are "compensated" for by eating massive quantities of raw fruit to induce diarrhea.

Moreover, disordered eating patterns once introduced are found to spread like an infectious disease. Psychologists and psychiatrists working at the University of Toronto showed that when a female college freshman was assigned *at random* to a bulimic roommate, she was five times more likely to have tried purging by the year's end than a similar freshman who, merely by the luck of the draw, did not have a bulimic roommate.

A positive feedback loop is being established: The more

women and men there are with disordered eating, the more likely there are to be even more people with disordered eating. Extreme psychopathologies found in some forms of anorexia nervosa and bulimia are not merely learned behavior. They are serious illnesses, experienced by only a few. But the public's heightened awareness of eating disorders and a young person's increased likelihood of personal exposure to them is a significant factor in the epidemic increase of disordered eating since the early 1980s.

Two other major social changes have occurred that may help us to understand "Why now?" The first of these is our attitude regarding sex roles and the status of women.

Changing Gender Roles Almost daily, we read or hear about women who have achieved enormous successes in spheres formerly thought to be exclusive to men. Ironically, the importance of adhering to whatever is prescribed as the beauty ideal of the moment may have increased precisely because women are now equal to men in most other ways. Looking like the current beauty ideal may serve an instrumental and somewhat paradoxical end of furthering a woman's success in a man's world. Women who are successful in previously male-dominated professions often need both to minimize their female status and to retain it. Several studies have documented that physically attractive women are perceived as more feminine. Looking feminine, while displaying "unfeminine" ambition and power, may serve to affirm a woman's identity to herself and others. Even the current feminist position accepts looking good as politically correct.

The same media that trumpet women's achievements in news programs and talk shows also exhibit a series of ever more glamorous actresses in commercials and movies—flawless in body, complexion, and hair. Each month, women's magazines feature the latest diet, the surest way to look beautiful and defeat aging, and the newest fitness regime. Analysis of the same magazines thirty years ago shows only one published diet every six months and little discussion of exercise.

Perhaps the media inundate women with so much beauty, diet, and health advice that they hardly notice. What's insidious, however, is that all this is now presented alongside exhortations to achieve professionally and personally. The various messages have become inextricably intertwined. The views communicated to women currently are therefore often quite confusing: Work hard at school, but be sure to be popular and pretty; be a lawyer, but be feminine. For example, according to *Working Woman* magazine, "That's really what all this looking and feeling good—your professional-image obsession—is about, effectively presenting yourself to have the best shot at getting the attention and rewards you and your ideas deserve. And that's worth wearing panty hose in the summer."

It has been suggested that professional women aspire to be thinner today because slimness is the antithesis of the ample female body. It represents an unconscious rejection of the role of woman only as mother, a "traditional" woman, the family caretaker. Studies have also shown that people now associate a full-bodied build with being less competent and intelligent than a thinner build.

The look for the nineties woman is not skinny, however, according to the magazines and movies. Thin is in but a good body tone is *de rigeur*. *American Health* magazine's account of a recent Gallup survey suggests that the model Elle Macpherson is our new ideal. She's fit and sinewy. The *American Health* report asserts, "La cream puff is finally out; strong and sensuous is in."

These changes could be reflecting the trend toward greater health consciousness or they could be a new way of competing on a masculine level. A woman's body today is weighted with new meaning. It's become symbolic of strength, independence, and achievement as well as attractiveness. A strong, lean body looks powerful, not vulnerable, and may reflect a change in how women are thinking about themselves. As always, women are using their bodies as the medium; but in the nineties the message may be that they want to appear capable of pulling their own weight.

Men's appearance concerns also seem affected by shifting gender roles and expectations. Once a man could be assured of his masculinity by virtue of his occupation, his interests, or certain personality characteristics. According to the historian Mark Gerzon in his book, *A Choice of Heroes: The Changing Faces of American Manhood,* there have been five traditional archetypes of masculinity throughout history: soldier, frontiersman, expert, breadwinner, and lord. Frontiersman and lord are no longer available roles for anyone, and expert and breadwinner are no longer exclusively male. Men may be grasping for the soldier archetype—the strong, muscle-armored body—in an exaggerated, unconscious attempt to incorporate what possible options remain of the male images they have held since youth. Male actors such as Arnold Schwarzenegger and male mannequins project the current muscle-bound, macho ideal. The newest window dummies are six feet two inches tall, have forty-two-inch chests, and need a size forty-two suit, quite different from the old industry standard size thirty-eight-regular. Mannequin designer Lowell Nesbitt calls them "Greco-Roman with a touch of Mussolini Modern."

One of our research subjects, Steve, talks about the importance of "looking like a real man." A good body makes him feel powerful, strong, and aggressive. For many men, a muscular physique has become the symbolic embodiment of desirable personal characteristics. Men experience an intimate relationship between body image and potency. As their roles become less gender specific, their bodies have become the expression of their sense of gender.

It is worth considering whether this ubiquitous interest in achieving the maleness-as-soldier ideal is a reflection of the conservative militaristic trends in current Western society. Is it a coincidence that men are opting for muscle building at a time of greater United States military intervention in foreign countries, and increased xenophobic patriotic media events such as *Rambo* and its clones, movies in which overly muscled mesomorphs avenge American pride and honor?

The Fitness Movement Our urge toward health and fitness is certainly another major social force currently increasing our body awareness. Health clubs, corporate fitness programs, video workouts, and triathalons are the hallmarks of the 1990s. Over fifty thousand businesses in the United States are implementing programs to promote physical fitness among their employees. Over a billion dollars was spent on exercise devices last year, most of it on equipment for the home. In many circles, it's considered gauche not to be on some kind of fitness regimen.

A recent Harris survey reported that approximately 15 percent of American adults participate regularly in *high* physical activity, exercise that leads to an energy expenditure of more than fifteen hundred calories a week. This translates into an hour of walking at three miles an hour every day, a daily twenty-to-thirty-minute run at six miles an hour, or one hour of swimming at one mile an hour for five days a week. About 20 percent more participate in moderate activity regularly.

Clifford Adelman, a researcher in the U.S. Department of Education, studied the "thirtysomething" generation in 1989, people who had been in the high school graduating class of 1972. He reports in *The New York Times*:

> Nearly 30 percent of the class took courses in aerobics, jogging, body-building, karate, yoga and the care of athletic injuries. Instead of studying subjects necessary to maintaining a technological economy in a world marketplace, the class of '72 maintained its physical well-being.

Women may feel they are getting more from the fitness boom than men, perhaps because they started with so much less. Denied most athletic outlets, traditionally encouraged to be weaker and slower, women have really jumped on the fitness bandwagon. They were spending a larger percentage of the fitness dollar than men by 1984, the year the Olympic Games staged its first marathon for women.

Now, in the nineties, we are entering the era of strength. As new surveys are showing, more and more people are weight training. Sales of free weights and strength machines topped three hundred million dollars in the United States in 1988–89. And all the major exercise machine manufacturers have redesigned their weight equipment so that they can be used by smaller bodies—presumably women.

— 40 —

Changing our life-styles, managing our weight and fitness, are now seen as major forms of health promotion. The modern burdens of illness, such as heart disease, are viewed as preventable by behavior change. But the body has come to symbolize the extent and effectiveness of our ability to engage in self-corrective behavior. *Looking* healthy is the external sign of the sought-after state of *being* healthy.

Undeniably, exercise is important for physical health. And feeling fit also provides personal satisfaction. It lifts depression, improves mood, and reduces anxiety. Several studies show that people who exercise regularly perform better in tasks that require thought and concentration. But making exercise and fitness a social virtue has put too much emphasis on our bodies as the reflection of how good we are. We've been misled to believe that we can control more than we actually can.

Women's bodies are genetically programmed to have a fairly high proportion of fat; and female hormones are disregulated when the percentage of body fat drops below a certain level. The no-fat ideal reflects an "unnatural" standard for many women. Yet, as a result of the fitness movement, there has been a redefinition of the ideal female body, which is now characterized not merely by thinness but by firm, shapely muscles (while avoiding too much muscularity) as well. The strong implication is that anyone who "works out" can achieve the lean, healthy-looking ideal. Such attainment is viewed as a direct consequence of personal effort and therefore worthy of pride and admiration.

But many women are set up to fail by their genes, not their lack of hard work. The inability to achieve the "aerobics instructor look" leaves many women feeling defeated, ashamed, and desperate. The pursuit of fitness represents a step beyond the pursuit of thinness. It has become another preoccupation, compulsion, even obsession for many.

Working to make our bodies more perfect is now a symbol for values that we hold important in Western society. The closer someone gets to approximating an ideal body, the more other people admire his or her control. Feelings of self-competence increase, too. Many people believe that changing one's body is the most tangible and readily accessible form of accomplishment under their control at the present time. It's certainly the most visible means of showing the world how well we have done, on a par with professional success, but presumably more available to anyone. No wonder we have become victims of body traps.

— 2 —

The Vanity Trap

For many of us, it's the sense of deviance and not the degree that matters. Because we find ourselves imperfect, we spend an enormous amount of time each day looking at ourselves, worrying about our appearance. Do we have too much hair or too little? Too big a chest or too small? Too much fat—does it ripple? When Jennifer looks at herself in the mirror, which she does at least twenty times a day, it's not with pride and self-admiration. She can't resist the impulse to check, to verify, to scrutinize. To be fully confident of herself, she needs to know at all times exactly how she looks. She's really quite attractive, but somehow doesn't feel it.

Is she vain and self-obsessed because she is preoccupied with her appearance? No. She's not drawn to the quest for thinness and good looks by vanity. It's missing the point to call it conceit when we spend so much time worrying about how we look. The concern reflects the deep psychological significance of the body. That's part of the vanity trap. Of all the ways we experience ourselves, perhaps none is so primal as the sense of our own bodies. The body is the very core of our psychological identity. It is what we come into the world with and what we leave behind. The messages of the mind must be routed through the body and often the body itself *is* the message.

Body image is fundamental to our sense of who we are, and yet, body concern traps us in a society in which body has taken on too much importance and where surface appearance has become essential. In this way, we are in a terrible double bind. Bodies do matter, they have deep psychic importance. Caring about your body is normative. But preoccupation and obsessive worrying are normal responses pushed to the extreme by a society that has placed too great an emphasis on how the body looks.

Women seem to have less body awareness than men because they are pushed to care so much about meeting an externally established ideal that they fail to develop accurate knowledge about their own bodies. They often lack a sense of comfort, a sense of what their bodies dictate they should look and feel like. Such women often lack a true sense of their own shape and size, which has a profound psychic outcome. If the body is central to the sense of self, and yet we are always pushing, reshaping, and remaking our bodies, our sense of self can fluctuate too greatly. This is not psychologically healthy. Ideally, we should have a stable sense of body. Women are struggling with their self-concept in part because the body component of their self-image has the quality of quicksand. It is little wonder that many women have problems figuring out how they look and feel—even who they are.

Kim, a participant in one of our studies, is five feet nine inches and weighs one hundred twenty pounds. She talks about being fat and gets angry when people disagree with her. She told us her legs are so fat that she can't sit in a comfortable position. Kim is not grotesquely shaped; she just has no sense of how her body really appears. Instead, she thinks she knows her body well and does not realize that her skewed view of her thighs is not only unrealistic but is contributing to a lower self-image.

Are you caught by this part of the vanity trap? The test on page 45 will help you to find out.

Even without the enormous social pressure that we are currently experiencing with regard to our looks, we are a society that is ambivalent about the body, especially about sexual-

HOW BODY IMAGE CHANGES

First make a general drawing of how you perceive yourself. Then draw each of the following:

— How do you think people with a positive influence in your life see you (e.g., a friend)?
— How do you think people with a negative influence in your life see you (e.g., a person you do not get along with)?
— How do you think women perceive you?
— How do you think men perceive you?
— How do you think your lover, significant other, or spouse perceives you?
— How do you think your mother sees you?
— How do you believe your father sees you?

These various drawings will show you your multiple, and diverse, body images. They are useful for helping to see how our sense of our bodies is influenced by other people—the nature of our relationships with them and how we think they see us. The drawings can help to clarify your own assessment of your body image. Body-image problems may be rooted in too many different views of who you are and how you look.

ity. We are constantly giving and receiving mixed messages when it comes to our bodies. As a result, we don't get to know or like our own bodies very well, further deepening the body traps.

Remember the fundamental message of this chapter: It's not vanity and conceit that make you worry about your appearance. Nor is it petty or stupid to be concerned. The body has deep psychological, social, and cultural significance. The problem is that social attitudes have conspired to make *how* you look too important. Your concern can sometimes be pushed out of proportion so that it becomes dysfunctional. A closer look at each issue will help you to understand how the vanity trap works.

DR. JUDITH RODIN

Exploring the Vanity Trap

The media and fashion industries bombard us with the ideal beauty image and instructions on how we can and must achieve it. But blaming these sources for the significance placed on the body is wrong. We *can* blame the media for making a single look—unattainable by most people—the ideal. But we can't hold them responsible for the fact that our looks influence how we feel about ourselves.

A recent film called *Gap-Toothed Women*, by Les Blank, is about women who all had slight physical imperfections that made them feel different and uncomfortable. It's a great film with an important message. One of the women was Lauren Hutton, the model. All her ads for Revlon were retouched by the photographer and the gap between her teeth was filled in, reminding her that others saw her as flawed and imperfect. She celebrates her own liberation when she finally feels confident enough to appear on the screen with the gap between her teeth exposed. The movie captured beautifully the real pain that countless women feel who are just a little different from the ideal, whether they are slightly fat, slightly short, or slightly plain. And some never free themselves as Lauren Hutton did.

Society sets the standards for the "right" look and to the extent we accept and internalize those standards, they become the measures by which we judge ourselves. But not everyone is alike. Psychologists increasingly believe that people differ in the degree to which they attend to the private or the public areas of the self. The private self—the one for you alone—consists of your own personally held feelings and attitudes, your covert thoughts, and other aspects of yourself that are not easily available to others. The public self—the one you show to others—is the socially apparent self. It consists of the kinds of things from which impressions are made: one's overt behavior, mannerisms, stylistic quirks, and expressions. And central to the public self, of course, is the body. The following test allows you to assess your own degree of public self-consciousness.

PUBLIC SELF-CONSCIOUSNESS SCALE

To determine where you stand in terms of public self-consciousness, complete the following items. Rate each on a scale from 0 (extremely uncharacteristic) to 4 (extremely characteristic).

	0	1	2	3	4
I'm concerned about my style of doing things.	—	—	—	—	—
I'm concerned about the way I present myself.	—	—	—	—	—
I'm self-conscious about the way I look.	—	—	—	—	—
I usually worry about making a good impression.	—	—	—	—	—
One of the last things I do before I leave my house is look in the mirror.	—	—	—	—	—
I'm concerned about what other people think of me.	—	—	—	—	—
I'm usually aware of my appearance.	—	—	—	—	—

Add your responses to each question to get a total score. The higher your score, the higher you are in public self-consciousness. You are quite likely to be more sensitive to the impressions you are creating on others. While this sometimes makes you more accurate in predicting the impressions you convey, it doesn't necessarily mean that you actually do better in making a good impression. And you are probably more focused on your body image than someone lower in public self-consciousness. A score of 24 or higher suggests that you may be vulnerable to the vanity trap.

The vanity trap is a problem for people high in public self-consciousness. They attach greater importance than most to those aspects of the self that contribute to their outward, social persona, especially their physical features and appearance.

Jennifer, an attractive career woman, would not accept an invitation to a social event during the week. She said, "I simply don't have enough time between coming home from work and going out, say to a movie or a party during the week. It takes me a good three hours to get ready. First, I have to exercise for an hour to feel slimmer, then I have to do my hair, and my nails, and then it takes me another hour to make up my face." When asked what would happen if she just went without her make-over routine (after all, she goes to work all made up) she replied, "I would feel like some gross slob, kind of naked, actually."

Jennifer sought our help because she felt "obsessed by how I look. I just want to get more out of my life." She was a thirty-one-year-old woman with an MBA from an excellent southwestern university. She was third in command at a branch of a major New York bank and had risen quickly through the ranks. Jennifer would look slim and attractive to you. She's five feet six inches and weighs 129 pounds, has lovely clothes, wears makeup tastefully, and is aware that she frequently catches a man's admiring glance. Jennifer is married and has a young daughter, Sophia. Jennifer was paralyzed by fears that she might do the same thing to Sophia that her mother did to her.

Jennifer recounted that she was forever being told how cute and pretty she was as a child. Her mother paraded Jennifer in front of her friends, to the point where Jennifer now labeled herself as her mother's prize possession. "I remember always being put on display," she recalls. "Can you believe that my mother's nickname for me was 'dollbaby'?" She believed even then that her looks meant more to her mother than anything else about her, recalling how her mother told her repeatedly that the pretty girls get everything—boys, popularity, and success, and therefore, she would have it all. Jennifer's mother drummed society's message into her, over and over again. Not surprisingly, Jennifer now believes this too, although she hates both the fact that she thinks it and that it's probably true to some extent. That's why she's so worried that she might do the same thing to Sophia.

Jennifer felt that her mother never helped her to develop other areas of competence; she felt allowed to achieve only in the appearance domain. She remembers begging for tennis lessons and having her mother tell her she was too delicate. When she wanted to play field hockey in high school, her mother flatly refused. They fought for days but her mother remained adamant, telling her, "If you mess up your face getting hit, you won't have anything left." Jennifer felt terribly guilty whenever she and her mother fought. She knew that she was all her mother had. Her father left her mother when Jennifer was five and they never heard from him again. Jennifer used to dream that he would come back and when he saw how pretty she was, he would want to stay at home. Her mother used to berate herself, blaming the fact that she "let herself go" for his walking out on them. "That's why it's so important to look good, dollbaby," her mother would say, "so this miserable thing won't happen to you." No wonder Jennifer can't help worrying if her husband loves her and that her career has advanced only because she is pretty. When her attractiveness was mentioned positively in her job performance reviews, it merely escalated her worries that her appearance was all that mattered in her success.

For all of us, not only people like Jennifer, the body represents our unique base of operation in the world. It isn't surprising then that some people like Jennifer can get trapped into devoting endless energy to how they present themselves. Society strongly reinforces our feelings that looks matter. But to understand the vanity trap fully, we must also confront the *inner* world of body preoccupation.

Body Image

Body image is a subjective experience. In other words, it is a psychological phenomenon. It is the picture of our own body which we form in our mind, and thus relates to all other images and attitudes we hold about ourselves. Body image plays a major role in our self-concept. Of course, self-concept is a complex structure that embraces not only our body but also social roles, material possessions, and personal relationships. But the body figures as a central element.

Body Focus Because of the centrality of body image to self-concept, focusing attention directly on the body influences our experience of other aspects of ourselves. This is vividly demonstrated by a series of experiments where people are given a mirror or are shown videotapes of themselves and asked to focus their attention on their bodies. We react to our mirror image by becoming more aware of all aspects of ourselves, even those that aren't visible. For example, people focusing on their heads as reflected in the mirror begin to think about their attitudes and opinions. Those focusing on their bodies become more aware of the their feelings and emotions. Many popular books and magazines recommend this type of intense self-focus as a prescription for becoming more attractive. For example, George Masters, the Hollywood celebrity makeup artist, wrote a best-selling beauty and makeup book in which he tells us:

> Beauty is much more than hair and make-up. It's a total look. *Crucial to your total look of beauty is body awareness* [italics added]. If you don't have it, start working on it instantly. You can begin this very second and here's how: You should start to pretend that you are naked with 40 imaginary cameras shooting from every possible angle up, down, front, back, sideways on your cheekbones, chinbone, nose, neckline, shoulderline, hips, stomach, thighs, arms and legs. All over. Anywhere and everywhere. The goal is to make you more conscious of yourself.

But psychological research shows that this kind of increased body awareness actually *lowers* self-esteem. The more people focus on their bodies, the more critical they become. Although there are some exceptions, the experience of looking at our bodies in the mirror tends to provoke negative feelings, not only toward our body but toward the self inside. Other studies show that intensified self-awareness also leads to increased conformity. The more you focus on your body, the more aware you become of its flaws, and the more you want and try to be like everyone else. Far from confirming George Master's advice, the research tells us that increased body focus hurts, not helps. The mirror feedback sets off increased body awareness, which can heighten guilt, intensify self-dissatisfaction, and affect mood.

Some people focus on their bodies not only when explicitly instructed to, as in the mirror studies, but as a general style. To assess this tendency in yourself, take out a piece of paper. List the twenty things that you are most aware of right now. Once you have finished, total the number of direct or indirect references you have made to your body. When this is done under appropriate experimental test conditions, unlike here where you know what the purpose of the task is, psychologists use the score as an index of body focus. The higher the score, the more you focus on your body relative to other aspects of yourself. A score of five or more represents high body consciousness. This degree of body consciousness can be dysfunctional if it leads to excessive self-scrutiny and dissatisfaction.

Body focus does not equal body knowledge, however, and this is central to understanding the vanity trap. Just because we attend to our bodies does not mean we know them very well. Many of us have a startling lack of knowledge—sometimes amounting almost to stupidity—about our bodies.

Body Knowledge How can we know so little about our bodies when we are continually faced with pictures and reflections of ourselves? Mirrors are everywhere. Every occasion is videotaped, every event photographed. Nonetheless, we all have problems knowing our bodies because our mirror image is not the total story. Our body concept is made up of much more than our reflection.

Dava Sobel, a writer for *The New York Times*, worries:

More than 40 years of looking at myself in the mirror have left me, like so many women I know, almost totally ignorant of what I look like. The mirror image I see is not a real reflection at all, but a composite of memories, wishes and half-truths. Photographs always surprise me. Because, of course, I never thought my nose was so long. I hadn't realized my lips were that full.

At 25, while still recovering from having been a fat teenager, I was struck one day at a shopping mall by the sight of a woman of my height, wearing jeans and a sweater just like mine, but with the body type I coveted. I looked up to her face with envy, only to realize that "she" was my reflection in a display window. I had not yet learned that I was thin. Only by looking at myself as though at another woman did I see that brief, realistic picture. Had I known I was looking at myself, I would have padded my reflection with baby fat.

"I keep looking for the real me," she confides. So, recently she went for a personal make-over with an image consultant. But she confesses that she was both attracted and repulsed by the idea:

> After all, what kind of woman would submit to a make-over? What self-respecting adult would trust someone *else* to discover, in a trice, what had eluded her own years of self-scrutiny? Who would agree to pay a premium price to a total stranger for the secret of her own self-identity?
> I would.

The aspect of our body image which we most frequently distort is our size. Many studies have documented women's consistent exaggeration of their body as a whole as well as specific body parts, typically the fat-bearing areas of waist and hips. These estimation errors appear to be specific to one's own body. The same women accurately judge the body size of other people.

In an interesting series of studies, Dr. J. Kevin Thompson,

a psychology professor at the University of South Florida, has been testing "normal" women who are free of any symptoms of eating disorders. He uses a movable calipers, which participants set at the size they judge their various body parts to be. The psychologist then compares subjects' ratings with their actual measurements. More than 95 percent of the women overestimated their body size, according to Dr. Thompson. Their estimates were typically one fourth larger than their bodies really were. Almost half the women estimated at least one of the four body parts to be 50 percent larger than it actually was.

Another provocative finding is that women's feelings about their bodies influence how oversized their image of themself is. Unlike men, women see *large* as a negative characteristic. When Dr. Thompson asked subjects to rate how they *felt* about their bodies, their estimates of size were even bigger than when they gave their objective view. In turn, the more inaccurate subjects were about their body size, the worse they felt about themselves. So, inaccurate judgments of body size and shape and feelings of low self-worth influence each other in a descending spiral of poor self-image.

If you have a hard time believing how inaccurate people can be in their body knowledge, try this test on yourself. Close your eyes. Try to visualize yourself, your whole body. Estimate the size of your various body parts, especially those you like least. Now use a measuring tape to check objectively. Most of you will find that the two sets of figures do not agree. Why is it so difficult to get to know our bodies accurately?

The Body's Boundaries A tremendous amount of sensory information from the environment floods in to all parts of the body. We simultaneously see, hear, smell, and feel. It's no small feat to organize and make sense of it. These competing demands to process a great deal of external and bodily information simultaneously may reduce the accuracy of our body knowledge.

Some people have difficulty establishing their own boundaries—between self and the outside world—because so many bodily feelings arise from outside experiences. This heightens their lack of body knowledge, leading to a more diminished sense of self. If people are able to conceive of their bodies as an enclosed place that belongs uniquely to the self, they can derive reassurance from their body. Dr. Seymour Fisher, who has written an excellent book on body image, comments that "as people confront life, they need to feel that the self resides in a chunk of space that is 'mine,' a well-defined home base." Research suggests that the ability to feel protectively enclosed in one's body is related, in part, to how intrusive one's parents were. If parents continuously assert themselves in their children's most private thoughts and feelings, boundaries between "me" and "not me" are sometimes hard for these children to develop. As adults, they lack a sense of personal space that is distinct and safe from the world outside.

People's daily rituals for caring for their bodies—the long shower or certain makeup routines—can serve to maintain a comforting sense of body security. Studies by psychologist Thomas Cash at Old Dominion University and his colleagues show that women report greater self-confidence and sociability when they use cosmetics. Some people find that clothes of a particular texture or tightness, or rubbing their skin with favorite lotions are also psychologically beneficial. Fisher asserts that techniques such as these reassure people of the security of the body's boundaries.

Emotions and Our Bodies There is a special emotional aura surrounding the body as an object, which makes body knowledge more difficult. That people so rarely have an accurate knowledge of their bodies can be traced to early childhood. According to Dr. Fisher's analysis, parents and teachers give children the message that the body is a suspicious thing. They learn they're not supposed to touch, think about, or refer to certain body parts. They discover that there's not even an adequate vocabulary to describe sensations in certain off-limits body sectors. They come to understand that there are emotionally highly charged rules to tell them which body concepts and images are permissible. The result is that for many people the experience of their own body is either quite distorted, or filled with guilt, or both.

"In my family," recalls Phillipa, "everybody was really private about their bodies. Talking about your body, especially about your 'private parts,' simply wasn't done. I was the only girl and when I had my first period, my mother hurriedly handed me some sanitary napkins and mumbled some instructions. My brothers started laughing and making fun of me because they saw the box of sanitary napkins. I went to bed that night thinking that my body was a curse." To this day, Phillipa finds it difficult to talk about her body without embarrassment.

Anthropologists have found that anxiety associated with the body is widespread. Some cultures even have social rituals which go to the extreme of destroying or cutting out certain body parts. Olivia Vlahos, the anthropologist, describes the elaborate genital-organ mutilation practices of many African tribes. In these instances and many others, where a culture gives unusual significance to certain body parts, people must develop special ways to deal with sensory information from those areas. In Western culture, for example, this is true for sexual organs and sexual feelings, which are often couched in code names and vague references.

Accurate body perception can in some instances result in exposing oneself to information that is unpleasant or threatening. Research studies show that people use numerous strategies that are designed—whether consciously or unconsciously—to shield them from potentially traumatic encounters with their body or to bolster some essential body fictions. For example, Barbara, a rather large woman, recently went on a trip to the Bahamas with her boyfriend. Barbara feels very embarrassed about her ample body size and agreed to the trip only after her boyfriend promised that he would not take any photographs of her in a bathing suit. When she returned, she described how she "coped" with her anxiety and embarrassment over her body size. "Basically, I would sit in a chair, hide my face behind a book, and pretend the whole time that my body was invisible to the other people on the beach. It took an incredible amount of concentration, but it was the only way I could dare get out of the chair and go into the water. If my concentration lapsed for even a moment and I allowed myself to see myself through the eyes of the other people, I would be unable to move, let alone go into the water."

Emotions can interfere with body knowledge because body image often changes with our emotional state. People feel smaller when they experience failure or when they are in the presence of a person in authority. And the more people pride themselves on their intellectual activities, the larger in size they estimate their head to be. This kind of association is beautifully expressed in a story told by a four-year-old to Ernst Prelinger, a Yale psychiatrist: "There was a boy . . . he thought every day and with every thought he thought up, his head got bigger and bigger."

Body organs often become identified with different emotions, as pointed out by Olivia Vlahos. Grief "breaks our heart." We can't "stomach" something offensive, and rage churns our "guts." Feeling a reckless sort of courage is "gutsy." So our inner organs give location and dimension to our feelings. Body sensations accompany and intensify these feelings.

Because we experience so many of our emotions in and through our body, sometimes it is hard to distinguish just what is the result of our transitory emotion and which is our permanent body. Our emotions can color our body image. For example, when I am in a rage, I feel ugly. All my life I have learned through language that anger is ugly. So when I experience anger, I perceive myself as ugly. In reality, I may be ugly momentarily—my face becomes distorted, my mouth a grimace—but my body has not changed. When I give a successful lecture or receive acclaim, I feel beautiful. Again, I may be, since my face is aglow, my mouth upturned, but my body has not changed. But in both cases, I feel my body changing too, in concert with my feelings. It is hard to get a permanent sense of our bodies when our body image can change from situation to situation as our emotions do.

Because mood strongly affects body image, there often appears to be little connection between how attractive people really are and how attractive they feel. For example, Dr. Thomas Cash and his colleagues found that people who are mildly depressed evaluate their bodies more negatively than nondepressed people. Each of the participants in Dr. Cash's study was videotaped and objective raters evaluated their physical attractiveness. The ratings showed that there were no objective differences—as judged by the impartial observers— between the depressed and nondepressed people in physical attractiveness.

Body Image Can Be Manipulated Some people have diminished body knowledge because they deliberately manipulate their appearance with the intent of dramatizing or concealing particular themes. Claire, an investment banker who was one of our clinic patients, was terrified of her longings for intimacy, and used her body bizarrely to express her own sexuality. In a monthly ritual, she would put on a wig and dress up in some outlandish outfit—a far cry from the tailored suits she wore all week. She drove to a place distant from where she lived and worked, stood on a street corner, and recited sexually explicit poetry.

In more normal manifestations of the same principle, all of us put on and discard different masks as we move through the various aspects of our daily lives. The very word *person* derives from *persona*, the Latin word for mask. The body can hide or project a multiplicity of personas. The potential range of facades we can put on contributes to plasticity of body image, and for some people, leads to a diminished sense of knowledge of their bodies. Furthermore, if we look to others to tell us who we are by how they respond to our appearance, we lose control of a central feature of our sense of self.

Body image is so crucial to a person's core of identity, psychologists believe, that distortions in it can have significant effects that we all should watch out for. They can be as benign as just affecting our mood or as serious as creating a susceptibility to a range of psychological problems, particularly depression.

How Body Image Develops

Up to this point, I've been describing how complex the vanity trap is. Throughout the life span, socialization practices and experiences conspire to make our bodies mysterious and unknowable, while at the same time profoundly important to our sense of self. As people grow and develop, from infancy to old age, the body is the centerpiece around which personal change and new experiences and expectations revolve. These changes and experiences differ, early on, between men and women. They also differ from individual to individual, explaining why some people are higher than others in public self-consciousness.

Infants develop a sense of reality by coordinating their inner world of body sensations with the outer world. By the second year of life, 65 percent of babies recognize their own mirror images. Children's body experiences continue for some time to be central to their world and color all their perceptions.

Beginning in early childhood, girls in particular learn to pay attention to their bodies and be concerned with how they look. They often learn from their families that one of their functions is to "pretty up" the environment, to serve as aesthetic adornment. These young girls learn that being attractive is intricately interwoven with pleasing others and will secure them love. Jennifer is a classic, although extreme instance of this.

Parents are not the only ones who reinforce body awareness and concern in their daughters. Friends, neighbors, teachers, even strangers, freely comment on little girls' appearance. While shopping with her one-and-a-half-year-old girl, one of my friends ran into her supervisor, who had not seen the daughter for a while. To my colleague's dismay, the supervisor loudly announced, "Your daughter is a bit fat, but she's cute."

Similar stories abound. A teacher at a day-care center went to the center's director to express her concern over some of the comments the day-care staff made about their three-year-old students. The staff frequently discussed the girls' body types, making predictions such as, "Jane is going to have one heck of a problem with her legs when she gets older—she'll look like an elephant." Or, "Susie's going to be in for a surprise if she keeps up eating like this—just look at her potbelly now."

Girls readily internalize these societal messages on the importance of pursuing attractiveness. By age four, a Shirley Temple look-alike was telling her mother, "I have a great time at your grown-up parties. I really like it when people tell me that I'm beautiful." Body build and self-esteem are strongly related for girls, but not for boys, as early as in the fourth grade. Already among these grade-school children, weight was found to be critical in the relationship between body image and self-concept: The closer a girl came to the cultural ideal of thinness, the more likely she was to report feeling attractive, popular, and successful academically.

Studies have found that even as children, females are more dissatisfied with their bodies than are males. Although nonobese girls have a more positive attitude than obese girls toward their bodies, they still express more worries about their appearance than obese and nonobese boys.

Whatever concerns young children have about their bodies, these feelings are modest compared to the attitudes that emerge with adolescence. The profound and extensive biological changes associated with puberty make the body the most important aspect of the adolescent's evolving sense of self. Coming to terms with the vital question, "Who am I?" involves integrating the new physical self into a revised self-concept. The adolescent is forced to reevaluate the body image which was developed as a child and to form a new body image appropriate to the maturing self. It's not surprising that teenagers are so sensitive to sociocultural norms concerning appearance. And these norms may create a particular problem for girls at puberty.

Before puberty, girls have 10 to 15 percent more fat than boys. After puberty, girls have 20 to 30 percent more fat than boys. The reason is that girls gain their weight at puberty primarily in the form of fat tissue. A boy's growth spurt is predominantly due to an increase in muscle and lean tissue. Many young women feel great despair about the addition of body fat associated with their normal sexual development.

And all too often, girls receive dire warnings about the weight gain that will come with puberty. "Time to think thin" was the advice of a well-meaning grandmother when she called her ten-year-old granddaughter to congratulate her on her birthday. When the granddaughter protested, "But I'm not fat," grandmother quipped, "But you will be if you don't watch it from now on."

Given our cultural beauty ideal of the "thin, prepubertal look" for women and the tall, muscular look for men, it is not surprising that adolescent girls express lower self-esteem than adolescent boys and greater dissatisfaction with their weight. Whereas physical maturation brings boys closer to the masculine ideal, for most girls, it means a development away from what is currently considered beautiful. When adolescent boys report dissatisfaction with their weight, their discontent is due to a desire to be heavier. Girls, on the other hand, consistently want to be thinner. Quite often, women—particularly those who were very slender before entering puberty—feel that their body has betrayed them. "I was so mad at my body for doing this to me. How could I have those weird looking hips and those gross thighs?" recalled Jeannette. "I simply felt that my body let me down. It was so depressing." Study after study of adolescents, in all Westernized countries, reveal the same attitudes.

Not surprisingly, by adolescence, substantial numbers of girls are dieting—far more than boys. In a study of 195 female high school juniors and seniors, 125 girls reported that they made conscious efforts to restrict their food intake in order to maintain or lose weight. The higher the education level and income bracket of their parents, the thinner the adolescents wanted to be. And they could all clearly express that their reason for dieting was dissatisfaction with appearance.

A health psychologist at the University of California, San Francisco, Dr. Nancy Adler, tested over five hundred local adolescents. The boys' stage of pubertal development was related to their ideal body type. Those who were more mature and larger in body size defined their ideal figure as larger. For the girls, however, perceived body size and preferred body size did not appear to develop in tandem, resulting in increased body dissatisfaction relative to the boys. Girls at more advanced pubertal levels showed a greater discrepancy between current and ideal figures than did less-developed girls. It appears that in adolescence, not only do self-perceptions change, but the definition of the ideal body changes as well. For boys, it becomes heavier, which is beneficial, since that is the direction they are going in. For girls, it becomes thinner, creating increasing pressure for weight loss and heightening body dissatisfaction.

Interestingly, girls in at least one study judged themselves more harshly than they thought their peers would. Doctors Kathleen Musa and Mary Ellen Roach at the University of Wisconsin found that significantly more adolescent girls than boys rated their own appearance lower than they rated their peers' appearance. And 62 percent of the girls who rated their appearance as less desirable than peers' were found to be in the low range of adjustment. There was no relationship between self-evaluation of personal appearance and personal adjustment for boys. A new study by Princeton psychologist Joan Girgus suggests that teenage depression in girls is related to how bad they feel about their weight. Again, no relationship between body image and depression was reported in teenage boys.

In addition to the concrete physical changes that they have to deal with, adolescents have to begin to grow up in other areas as well. The three primary tasks that both male and female adolescents have to master include achieving a new sense of self; establishing peer relationships, in particular, heterosexual relationships; and developing independence. Body image is an issue for girls in each one of these tasks.

In the first task, the self-image of adolescent girls seems to be more affected by interpersonal relationships than it is for boys. Girls seem to worry more about what other people think of them, care more about being liked, and try to avoid negative reactions from others. Virginia psychologists John Hill and Mary Ellen Lynch have argued that, in response to feeling insecure and in an effort to avoid negative evaluation by others, the adolescent girl becomes increasingly sensitive to and compliant with social demands to engage in appropriate "female" behavior. The strong message to teenage girls regarding the importance of beauty and thinness (as evidenced, for example, in the teen fashion magazines) thus comes at a time when they are most sensitive to society's standards, as well as to the opinions of others. It is not surprising, then, that a teenage girl becomes obsessively concerned with her pubertal increase in fat.

Following from this, we would expect that the second task of adolescence—forming peer relationships, and heterosexual relationships in particular—would also be more of a problem for girls than for boys. Studies support this hypothesis. For example, social psychologists Roberta Simmons and Florence Rosenberg found that girls were more likely than boys to rank popularity as more important than being independent or competent. This emphasis on popularity correlated with a less stable self-image and greater susceptibility to others' evaluations. Given that attractive (i.e., thin) females are rewarded in the interpersonal and especially the heterosexual domain, the wish to be popular and the pursuit of good looks may become synonymous in the mind of the teenage girl. Mothers often unknowingly reinforce these anxieties. Two women I know were discussing their teenage daughters who had recently begun boarding school. One told the other, "Last night Tanya called, crying hysterically, because she isn't as popular there as she was at school here. I told her to come home this weekend and we would go shopping together. All that girl needs is some new clothes and she'll stop feeling that she can't make new friends."

The third task of adolescence, establishing independence, also seems to pose a different challenge to girls than to boys. According to Carol Gilligan, a developmental psychologist at Harvard, the adolescent tasks of separation and individuation are more of a problem for women, because relationships are more important to them. However, in a world that views dependence as weak, girls often begin to feel confused, insecure, and inadequate, which challenges their sense of self. Margo told us:

I come from a very close-knit family, but when I hit sixteen, everybody started talking about me going off to college in the Northeast. It was the "in" thing to do. You know, they have all those famous colleges there. So, I began applying to all the right places and I ended up at Yale, even though I would much rather have stayed closer to home. But my parents had been educated in the Northeast and they were sort of snobs about it and always said that the Midwest was no place to get a college education. I was so scared about leaving home, but I was also proud and excited about being accepted at Yale. I figured, the adult thing to do was to go on a diet, you know, get a handle on yourself, pull yourself together, be independent.

We can speculate about ways in which the adolescent girl's increasing preoccupation with weight and dieting behavior is tied to the issue of independence. When other aspects of life seem out of control, weight may appear to be one of the few areas that, allegedly, can be self-controlled. Because our society views weight loss efforts as a sign of maturity, dieting attempts may reflect a girl's desire to show others, as well as herself, that she is growing up. Hence, dieting may be a part of, a metaphor for, or a displacement of, movements toward independence.

Because of the difficulty in arriving at a new body image in adolescence, the image we develop then stays with us well into maturity. Dava Sobel's recollections, described on page 52, make that point vividly. Her body image as a fat teenager stayed with her through her adult years. The actuality of being thin didn't shake it at all. She could only add the layers of baby fat to her true reflection, to see herself the way she *felt* she was. In a similar process, a paunchy forty-year-old male I know still sees himself as trim, despite his outer appearance. He was a star high school athlete and quite lean during adolescence and that is the image of his body he carries today.

Pregnancy, and to a lesser extent, menopause, are the next developmental stages that profoundly affect the adult woman's body. Her sense of self changes as her body feels different, confusing, unknown. Surprisingly few research studies have focused on these psychological changes, since much more attention has been given to the biological events themselves. But interviews with research subjects and clinical patients leave me persuaded that many women regard their changed bodies with fear and loathing. They report not feeling like themselves, and self-concept often plummets.

Although the weight gain surrounding pregnancy signals the growth of new life inside a woman's body, it is a source of tremendous anxiety and confusion for many women. Even though medical standards are more lenient today than they used to be—most physicians consider a weight gain of twenty-five to thirty-five pounds normal—we hear countless stories of how women continue to be taken to task about their weight gain. "I hate being weighed," complains Charlene. "The nurse always makes me feel that I have sinned when I've gained a pound too many." Other people feed into these weight concerns as well. Sales personnel at maternity stores will compliment women who are small for their respective stage in pregnancy, leaving those women who develop more ample bodies feeling as if they somehow failed.

And the pressure only intensifies after delivery. "One of my colleagues called two weeks after my baby was born," Hannah told us during a research interview. "Once the usual congratulations were over, he asked me whether I had gotten my old figure back yet. After I hung up, I cried for an hour." Many women apparently never regain their old figure, according to new evidence published in the *Archives of Internal Medicine* by investigators at the Centers for Disease Control. They studied the occurrence of weight gain over a ten-year period in thousands of American men and women. The incidence of major gain was twice as high in women, and was highest in women ages twenty-five to thirty-four.

What happens in later life? Most people get fatter in old age, even if their weight doesn't change. This is especially true for older women. Studies by Michael Ross and colleagues, psychologists at Saint Louis University and Saint Louis Medical Center, show that elderly people are very self-conscious of their body appearance, perhaps reflecting a response to anticipated negative social evaluation. These feelings are sadly correct since they are viewed as less attractive than young or middle-aged people. If being attractive figures more prominently in a woman's life than in a man's, we would expect the effects of the aging process on appearance in general, and its tendency to lead to more fat and less muscle in particular, to be a greater problem for women than for men. This area awaits further research, since little is known. But in an ongoing study of elderly people, we have found that the second greatest personal concern expressed by women in the group, following memory loss, was change in body weight and fat. Weight concerns were rarely expressed by men in the study.

Breaking the Vanity Trap

In this and comparable sections at the end of every chapter that follows, there are techniques to try on your own for breaking each trap. The tests in each chapter will help you determine if any part of that trap is an issue for you. Simply reading the chapter and seeing how it relates to your own situation should be helpful, since change begins with insight. But in addition to insight, some of you will need to learn specific strategies for breaking the traps. Try those provided in each chapter, but don't be worried if not all of them are right for you. No one falls into all aspects of each trap, so focus on those that deal specifically with your issues and concerns.

Since the first step is insight, let's begin with the insight that this chapter offers. You now know that you may have wrong or inadequate body knowledge and that your body image is often too malleable. You have also learned that your feelings about your body affect your self-esteem. When you worry about how you look, you are worrying about who you are. While body preoccupation is something we all share, I am not suggesting that it's healthy to be obsessed about our bodies, or to have happiness rise and fall each day on what the scale says. All of my work with patients is an effort to help them overcome these feelings. While the struggle is very complicated, this chapter and the rest of the book will help you to understand that there are profound reasons why you and so many other people get trapped by body preoccupations.

There are several techniques that you are now ready to try. First, examine how strongly you value appearance. If your score on the Social Attitudes Scale on page 31 was higher than 28, you need to see that your appearance is important to you in part because you value society's standards excessively. This is especially problematic if you also scored high on the Public Self-Consciousness Scale on page 47. To work on freeing yourself from this part of the vanity trap, begin by identifying your fantasies about what would happen to you if you lived in a somewhat less attractive body.

Jennifer needed to confront her fantasies, her worst-case scenarios about what would go wrong, who would treat her differently, how her life would change, if she didn't look as good. That was incredibly hard for Jennifer. It's not that she couldn't do it—in fact, she'd been doing it consistently without our intervention, but always envisioning catastrophic outcomes. What we did was help her to develop alternative story lines—no lost job, no husband walking out the door. An important first step was making her visualize these more positive scenarios on her own. They were alien to her and she did a lot of hard imagery work in an effort to make them become vivid and realistic to her. She would rehearse in her mind what it would feel like to gain five pounds, or to look a little less "put together," and picture everyone who mattered still reacting favorably toward her. Much later, when she felt she was more of a person, Jennifer also tried some real-life "letting-gos," as she called them. She went to her mother's house for Thanksgiving dinner with no makeup on and then just laughed when her mother told her pointedly that the natural look wasn't "in." She was amazed that her mother gave up rather quickly (although not entirely). Ultimately, she relinquished her role as the office fashion plate, although she always looked neat and attractive. She couldn't get over that her professional status remained intact.

What are your "worst-case scenarios"? Would no one ever love you? Would you never find a good job? Would you be unable to pursue your educational goals? The answer to each of these questions should most certainly be a wholehearted "Of course not." If you scored high on the Social Attitudes Scale, however, you are probably not convinced that your answers to these questions should be "no." Often you realize the fallacy of your thinking only when you face your most secret fears. That is the purpose of this exercise. Examine the basis for your belief in the all-encompassing importance of appearance. Are all the people gorgeous who hold good jobs, or who obtain advanced degrees, or who are in love? Identify specific people whose success in each of these domains challenges the presumption that appearance is *all* that matters.

Regardless of your views on the social value of attractiveness, you would not be suffering from the vanity trap unless you also had problems caused by your own body image. The following techniques focus on heightening your body knowledge.

It is hard to have a clear body image if people influence your sense of your own body too greatly. This is one reason why the drawings you made at the beginning of this chapter can be especially helpful in appraising and confronting how the significant people in your world influence your bodily perceptions. If your drawings are all quite similar, then a fundamental aspect of this body trap—the plasticity of body image—may not be a problem for you. The more your drawings vary, however, the more images of your body you hold. This may lead to two possible problems: First, it is harder to have a clear and accurate view of your own body; second, you are permitting others to have too great an influence on your self-perception.

Try to find the drawing that you like best of all the ones you made. Memorize it (or carry it with you). Concentrate on that image when you interact with people who make you feel bad about yourself. When possible, think in advance of what you might do, say, or even wear that can keep your most-favored body image intact. For example, if your mother makes you feel fat and unlovely, consciously put on clothes that make you feel svelte and attractive before you see her. If there is no drawing that you like at present, move on to the next exercise and come back to this one after you have finished the last chapter in this book.

We are not only trapped by how others make us feel about our bodies. Many of us become our own worst enemies by holding unrealistic or unduly negative visions of our physical selves. If this is true of you, you need to develop a realistic sense of what your body really looks like. If the body exercises you completed on page 45, How Body Image Changes, showed you that your body image is malleable and you lack body knowledge, you will find the following techniques helpful.

First, you must see your body in various positions, feel it as it moves, and come to know and integrate how your body feels with how you see it. One technique useful in developing this type of body awareness involves movement. Simply allowing your body to move freely to relaxing, rhythmic music while you focus intently on the experience, can bring you in tune with your body. Videotaping yourself in various poses and in several different types of activities can also be useful. You can use the videotapes to focus on what your body looks like, how it appears, and moves. When your lack of body awareness is great, you will need to force yourself to see the tapes objectively. This task may make you feel self-critical and self-conscious. Be prepared for that and know that it is a common response. The extent to which you must struggle to overcome it can itself be an important message. The goal is to force yourself not to make judgments, but to try to see the moving snapshots of your body realistically.

Some therapists use clay and have patients sculpt their bodies. Their experience suggests that this forces people to appraise and recognize their bodies more objectively in order to recreate themselves accurately in clay. This may not be possible for some of you to do by yourselves at home, but for others it may feel easier and less embarrassing than working with your videotaped images. In both cases the goal is the same: to help you come to know how you really look in order to develop a more stable, accurate body image.

Next, you can increase body knowledge by getting in touch with the emotions that color your body image. An important strategy is to *identify your feelings*, and how they relate to your body experience. Begin with a very concrete exercise. Here's how it starts: Close your eyes and focus on what you are feeling. First, feel the chair beneath you. How does your body feel? Relaxed or tense? Hot or cold?

When you feel comfortable with this and can explore how your body feels as it touches another object—the chair— imagine how your body feels when you are angry, sad, happy, ashamed. The best way to arouse these feelings for this exercise is to focus on an event that made you feel that way—take sad, for example—and relive it in your mind. Focus on every detail of the experience so that it provokes the full intensity of the emotion. Then switch your attention to your body. What are you feeling in each of your body parts? Is your stomach knotted? Is your chest tight? Don't evaluate any feeling negatively. Simply treat it as data, information your body wishes to provide you. Be aware of every feeling and body sensation.

Often people find it helpful to write down their feelings. Not only does this increase emotional awareness, but it makes feelings more acceptable. Being aware of your feelings—even negative ones—is a core aspect of body experience and an important way to get to know your body. Denying feelings feeds into the vanity trap because it reinforces a lack of body knowledge.

The chart on page 70 is one type of recording sheet we use in our clinic as a way to help patients come to know how their emotions relate to bodily feelings. You can use this yourself at home. Any kind of notepad will do. Any time you experience an emotion, evaluate its intensity and the sensation it arouses in your body. Getting to know the various feelings associated with your emotions demystifies them and allows you to integrate them into a more complete sense of body awareness.

Emotion	Intensity	Body Feeling
anger	high	tight throat, heart beating, knotted stomach, flushed face
giddy	medium	aching cheeks from laughing, knotted stomach
sad	high	no feeling, empty in chest

A third technique for a clear and more consistent body image is learning to view yourself less critically. When you find aspects of your body that you like, your body image is less influenced by your own shifting feelings or by other people. One exercise that works well is focusing on the part of your body that you like best, a part that you think is most attractive. For some people it's their eyes or chin, for others their hands or fingers. If you can't find anything you like right now, hold off on this exercise until you have worked through some of the other body traps. For those of you who can find at least one part you like, focus on how it looks, how it feels. How can you care for it? Will taking better care improve it? Some things really do work, for example, cream for softer-feeling hands or eyewash for fresh eyes without the myopic look.

With this exercise you can focus on your body and what it needs. By starting with the body parts you like best, you avoid the critical self-scrutiny that keeps you entrapped. After a while, you'll feel ready to move to the parts you don't like as well, but the tasks and strategies remain the same. There is no substitute for getting to know and like your own body better. It is an essential component of breaking the vanity trap.

— 3 —

The Shame Trap

According to Wendy Wasserstein, the author of *The Heidi Chronicles*:

> When I embark on a new career or romantic venture, there is always a bottom line. Namely that no matter what happens, no matter how deeply I fall in love or how successful the project, I can assume that if anything goes wrong, it is because I prefer buttered rolls to bran flakes for breakfast. In other words, the stock market almost crashed because I refuse to do aerobics . . . O.K., maybe I'm exaggerating a little. But the paranoia, the temptation to blame everything on excess tonnage, is basically true.

Many women blame their weight for every failure or disappointment. One of my favorite cartoons shows a woman being judged by some divine presence. As she is dragged off to hell by a devil she screams, "It's because I have fat thighs, isn't it!" All of her sins are summed up in her imperfect body part. The converse also occurs. When some women encounter a disappointment or failure in a non-weight-related domain, they suddenly feel fat. In other words, "feeling fat" encapsulates and organizes shameful feelings about the self.

Interestingly, the connection between shame and the body

is deeply intertwined. The word *shame* derives from the word *cover*, and in Darwin's work on emotions, he described shame as a strong desire for concealment. Psychiatrist R. D. Laing observed that shame involves "implosion" of the self; it leads to body gestures and attitudes that serve to make the person as small as possible. Many people admit that when ashamed they would like to disappear.

Our *body concerns make us feel deeply ashamed.* We're embarrassed by being preoccupied with something supposedly as trivial as how we look. Shouldn't we be worrying about acid rain, AIDS, nuclear disaster, and poverty? Of course. And we probably are, but that doesn't divert our attention from body preoccupation. We also feel ashamed because advertisements, television, movies, and our friends are always there to remind us of how we ought to look. Our weight and appearance are not private matters but a topic for public consideration. Advertisements remind us that to deserve respect, we must look good. Being overweight and/or showing signs of aging are considered prima facie evidence of our laziness and ignorance.

Sunny Griffen, advertising products for the Collagen Corporation in *Vogue* magazine, confronts us in the ad in a condescending, even rebuking manner. Age forty-seven, "a mother, building contractor, and former TV correspondent and model," Sunny is there to let us know that if we expect to get any admiration or respect as women, we'd better do *something* about how we look. The ad chides us that looking your age is simply due to lack of initiative. Women are now being asked to admit their age proudly—look at Sunny, Jane Fonda, Linda Evans, Cher—as long as they don't look it.

Our culture tells us we can fix anything. No longer do we have to be young to be slim and perfect and beautiful. With present technology we can buy products, remove fat, and surgically change offending body parts. With all those available "opportunities," if we don't look great, we deserve to feel deeply ashamed, or so we are made to feel.

Freud believed that Western society was absorbed by guilt and shame. But we have perfected it to new heights today. We have so many oughts and shoulds, in fact, that psychologists are now studying a construction called the "ought-self," which is driven by a pervasive sense of what we ought to be doing. At present, there are clearer prescriptions governing appropriate behavior and a more culturally uniform set of standards than may have existed in the past. When the prescriptions are better defined, so too are the deviations. Life is now organized so as to make us feel deeply ashamed about those deviations. Our culture has added beauty values and ideals to existing moral and religious standards. Shame now comes from our new moral transgressions: eating something we shouldn't have; feeling that we don't look good enough; or we haven't tried hard enough.

Helen Block Lewis, a psychoanalyst who wrote a major book entitled *Shame and Guilt in Neurosis*, notes that shame involves feeling bad about who you are. The entire self is the target of hostility. By contrast, guilt comprises negative feelings about what you do or have done. In shame you experience yourself, rather than merely your behavior, as faulty. Self-concept plummets and you feel worthless. Lewis notes that women are more likely to feel shame, while men more typically feel guilt. This sets women up for greater trouble. Because shame is a primitive emotion, it is difficult to deal with rationally. And it is tied in with other deep-seated emotions, especially anxiety, and a profound sense of malaise. This strong set of associated bad feelings is part of the shame trap.

Women particularly have been brought up to believe that their appearance is not strictly their own business. How daughters look is an open, active topic of conversation in most families, making them feel their bodies are fair game for public scrutiny and evaluation. Many emerge feeling exposed and ashamed.

Sandra talks about her experience at the dinner table when she was a child. All the attention of her parents and brothers focused on her: Had she gained weight? Had she plucked her eyebrows too much? Were her clothes acceptable? Now she's become a "closet" eater, dining alone and snacking in private.

Sitting at a table eating with other people still floods her with memories and feelings of being judged, of being open to everyone's critical evaluation.

The test below will give you an idea of how vulnerable you are to this part of the shame trap and what the primary sources of your shame might be.

Marci, a normal-weight Yale undergraduate, diets furiously for the week before each holiday break. She can't bear her mother giving her "the look," the disapproving, but silent once-over that so many of us have experienced.

At the very heart of the feeling of shame is a second part of the trap—the sense that we've failed to live up to some ideal that we all value. These ideals come from our families and friends, and from views we share as a society about what's beautiful. *Shame arises from a felt gap between the actual self and the ideal self.*

BODY SHAME

1. How happy are you with your body?
   _____ 1. Very happy
   _____ 2. Moderately happy
   _____ 3. Moderately unhappy
   _____ 4. Very unhappy

2. How often do you take a good look at your nude body in a full-length mirror?
   _____ 1. Never
   _____ 2. Rarely
   _____ 3. Only if I have to
   _____ 4. Often

3. Check how you feel about your body parts:

	1. Proud	2. Satisfied	3. Dissatisfied	4. Ashamed
a. Breasts/chest	____	____	____	____
b. Stomach	____	____	____	____
c. Hips	____	____	____	____

d. Thighs   ____   ____   ____   ____
e. Calves   ____   ____   ____   ____
f. Waist   ____   ____   ____   ____
g. Arms   ____   ____   ____   ____

4. How much do the following influence how ashamed you feel about your body?

	1. Not at all	2. Some	3. A lot
a. Seeing yourself in the mirror	____	____	____
b. Remarks by family	____	____	____
c. Remarks by male friend/spouse	____	____	____
d. Remarks by female friends	____	____	____
e. Remarks by strangers	____	____	____
f. Seeing beautiful women or handsome men in movies, TV, or ads	____	____	____
g. Seeing beautiful women or handsome men in person	____	____	____

If you rate yourself as unhappy with your body on question 1, and indicate, on question 2, that you rarely or never look at yourself nude, you may be experiencing the shame trap. Question 3 shows which parts of your body are shame-provoking and question 4 shows which people and circumstances make you feel ashamed.

Her weight may feel so shameful that it will cause a woman to put her life "on hold." Paula, for example, kept putting off requesting an advancement of her position in a large telephone company. "How can I ask for a promotion when I am this fat? How can I think that my boss will give me control over an entire department if I cannot even control my weight?"

There are many aspects of ourselves where self-ideal discrepancies can and do arise. But none is more central than the body. Take the test on page 76 to see where you stand.

People's feelings about their bodies have been notably overlooked in psychological research until recently. I believe that

SELF-IDEAL DISCREPANCY

Find the set of figures for your sex. Working first with the array of drawings of figures from the head to waist, choose the number below the figure which best illustrates:

A How do you think you currently look? Choose the figure that best represents your actual size.

B Choose the figure that best represents how you would like to look (your ideal figure).

C Rate how ashamed you are of this discrepancy from 0 (not at all) to 5 (extremely).

Repeat the same procedure for the figures from waist to feet.

---

shame is a major factor in this omission. First, the topic generates feelings of shame in all of us. This is demonstrated vividly by reported reactions to a Kinsey survey, in which women felt more embarrassed responding to questions about their weight than about many intimate details of their sexuality.

Furthermore, if we admit to feeling ashamed of our looks and our preoccupation with appearance, we risk focusing attention on the source of shame—the body. Not surprisingly, people often find it difficult to give the proper name to these feelings. They may describe reactions to being seen or looked at by others in vague terms such as "uncomfortable," "uneasy," or "anxious." Feelings of shame, because they cut to the core of the self, are disturbing, unsettling, and may therefore tend to be repressed from awareness.

Helen Block Lewis noted that often one is *ashamed of being ashamed*. That notion seems useful here. Feeling ashamed of one's body is evidence that it matters, and it seems shameful to admit that appearance is so important. Even researchers have been hesitant to acknowledge the significance of physical appearance in the study of human behavior.

Body concerns are often shunned in psychotherapy as well. It may seem hard to believe that talking about our appearance worries would be difficult in this very protected and private

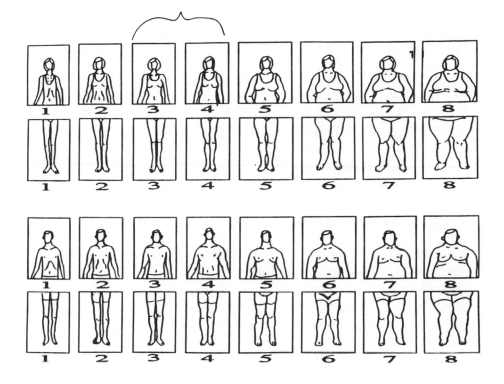

Since each figure has a number associated with it, you can calculate your body discrepancy score. The numerical difference between your view of how you think you look and how you would like to look (the answer to question A) compared with the answer to question B represents your self-ideal discrepancy. If you have a shame score of 3 or more, you should be concerned about freeing yourself from the shame trap.

relationship, but consider the situation. The discussion inevitably invites looking—by both patient and therapist. Female patients working with a female therapist may feel uncomfortable bringing up body shame because the topic invites a direct comparison of "assets" and "liabilities." In many therapeutic relationships, the patient has little access to the various aspects of the therapist's superiority or inferiority. Questions such as "Is she a better mother than I am?" "Is she better at sports?" "Does she get along well with others?" and "Is she wealthy?" are common, but remain largely unanswered for the patient. Yet, the therapist's body is available for scrutiny. Once engaged in the process, comparing one's own body with that of the therapist may be frightening regardless of how the therapist fares. Perceiving the therapist as more attractive may leave the patient even more ashamed and humiliated; an appraisal of the therapist as less attractive may result in feeling that the therapist is not "good enough."

And the therapist, too, may be wary of the comparison process. In our clinic, therapists are encouraged to discuss with one another their own body issues and how they influence doing therapy for body-image problems. When three of us were pregnant at the same time, we knew our own body changes might provide material for patients to talk about feelings regarding their own shape and size. But first we had to work through our own feelings of being looked at and exposed. As one very talented therapist admitted with embarrassment, "I almost wanted my patients to assure me that I still looked great, even though I was huge and puffy—as women, we're all part of the same collusive conspiracy of body shame."

Women working with a male therapist may be reluctant to elaborate on their body shame for fear of "sexualizing" the therapeutic relationship. Attracting attention to her body may lead the woman patient to feel as if she is flirtatious, and indeed, male therapists may misinterpret their female patients' concern with their appearance as precisely that. It is obvious that such an interpretation will leave the patient feeling even more ashamed.

We are all trapped by some aspect of shame. Some people are

ashamed of how their bodies look. Others are ashamed when their self does not match their ideal. Many are ashamed of their crazy eating practices and dieting rituals. I'm ashamed to admit to some of my academic colleagues that I am writing a book about body concern, which seems so trivial compared to some of the things they write about. These many complex aspects of the shame trap work differently for women and men in some fascinating ways. Let's consider these differences.

How the Shame Trap Works

Women's Shame

In general, women are more likely than men to feel shame, and feelings about their bodies are high on the list of causes. I've already shown that the beauty ideal for women today is fit and thin. Women have internalized this message and when they measure themselves against this standard, most feel they fall short. Women are aware of their bodies being scrutinized by others as well as by themselves. Given the likely gap between self and ideal, this intense scrutiny repeatedly provokes feelings of shame.

Anna, an overweight young woman, refused to look at herself in the mirror. Before taking a shower in the morning, she would drape a towel over the bathroom mirror to avoid "being shocked into reality." She refused to be weighed, too. When she had to have a check-up to obtain birth control pills, she insisted on being weighed by stepping on the scale backward and she made the nurse promise not to read her weight out loud.

While all of us feel scrutinized some of the time, celebrities are looked at and evaluated constantly. Articles frequently appear in magazines and newspapers commenting on some film star's latest plastic surgery, clothing style, or a weight gain or loss. A recent article on overweight celebrities in *USA Today* was headlined THE WEIGHT OF CELEBRITY with the subtitle "Fat's Heavy Toll on the Famous." How would you feel if your weight were fair game for the newspapers to discuss? Oprah Winfrey's celebrated weight loss and regain—in the cruel glare of the television camera—was endlessly talked and written about. Quoted in *People* magazine, Winfrey freely admits "It was my greatest failure."

Delta Burke, a television star in the weekly CBS sitcom *Designing Women*, told of her experience in a *USA Today* interview. Burke, a former Miss Florida, gained thirty pounds over several months while her weekly series was being taped. Reviewers in the media were quite critical in their coverage and she felt hurt and deeply ashamed. Like Winfrey, her success and her position gave her the ability to speak out, something most ordinary people don't have. In one of her programs, Burke's television character, Suzanne Sugarbaker, attends her high school reunion. She's aware of the cruel remarks being made about how much weight she's gained and to make her humiliation complete, she's named the most changed person in the class. The character then makes a heartfelt speech that was clearly how Burke felt about herself and her own weight gain. The *USA Today* article continues, "Burke got a standing ovation the night the episode was taped. Cast and crew closed ranks to offer support." The fact that she was attacked in the media and made to feel so ashamed brought her friends rallying around her. What a terrible state things are in when she needed social support to endure the shame of carrying extra pounds.

Society's view that weight is controllable (by hard work, diet, and exercise) augments the shame of being overweight and will often provoke women to engage in repeated and fruitless dieting. Often, their initial response to unsuccessful weight-loss attempts is to try even harder. For example, Sarah, a talented undergraduate student, decided that her inability to attain her "ideal" weight was the result of not giving it an all-out effort. She decided to take a semester off from college and devote herself exclusively to what she considered was her most important life task: weight loss. It was only a matter of weeks after returning to college before she regained all the weight she had lost during her self-imposed leave of absence. She felt humiliated and deeply ashamed. However, as The Dieting-Rituals Trap chapter will make clear, our weight is not entirely within our control. Numerous studies have shown that genes largely determine our body build, and to some extent, our degree of body fat.

Certainly people may feel ashamed of physical features that are not under their control—big feet, ears that stick out. But the shame is even greater when there is blame imputed as well. This is certainly the case for weight. More often than not we are made to feel bad not only because we are fat but because we have not overcome this shortcoming. For some women, this painful experience is relatively circumscribed. No matter how "crazy" they are about their weight and eating, they may be able to contain their feelings if they feel the rest of their life is relatively healthy.

Grace is a highly successful corporate executive, who skillfully juggles a demanding career and a busy family. She sees herself, however, as being in a constant battle with the scale. She has tried every diet on the market but she still heads for the cookie jar as soon as she gets home from work. "If I can beautifully manage a multimillion-dollar corporation all day," she said in an interview, "why can't I manage my waistline at night?"

For other women, failure to match the thin ideal has a profound, shame-provoking effect which colors every area of their lives. These women are driven by their body concern to question all aspects of their self-competence. The shame of feeling fat or ugly is so powerful that they avoid situations in which they will feel looked at, including potentially rewarding ones such as parties or job interviews. Sharon, a concert violinist, provides a good example in that she has kept her career from advancing because she's unable to give a solo performance. She is filled with terror, her fingers tremble, and she cannot play because she worries so that people will be evaluating her body instead of her music.

Or, if they cannot avoid social situations, some women feel extremely anxious and constricted in them. AnneMarie told us about a Super Bowl party she attended with people she had never met before. "Here I was with all these people, who were having a great time. They were all watching the game, eating chips and pretzels and drinking lots of beer, and I didn't move from my seat all night. I asked my friend John to get my drinks for me because I worried the whole time that people would see how unattractive I am."

Visits with family members or friends are anticipated with great trepidation, especially if the woman feels that she has put on weight since the last meeting. Sexual relationships may be avoided altogether because of the prospect of undressing in front of another person.

I see women across the weight spectrum who are deeply ashamed of their body size, all feeling that their bodies are gross and repulsively large regardless of reality. And I see women who, despite their good looks, feel ugly and insecure. These women typically find it very hard to assert themselves—whether at home, at work, or with friends—because they feel undeserving and disenfranchised by their own shame. For those who feel too fat, shame has made weight and the struggle to control their eating the centerpiece of their day-to-day lives. For those who feel unattractive, their efforts are directed at trying to solve the problem with every new beautifying "gimmick" that comes on the market. The consistent features of their life stories are the shame and the intolerable all-consuming effort to improve their looks, usurping time and energy from other pursuits.

Jennifer hated herself for feeling so involved with and preoccupied about her body. She felt ashamed of these concerns when her friends seemed to be worrying about more important issues. But her friends were worrying about how they looked, too. Why didn't she know it? Some women, like Jennifer, get into a situation which I call "pluralistic ignorance," where each hides from the other the extent to which she is preoccupied with her body and how ashamed it makes her feel. Then, because each woman is acting as though everything is fine, she misleads her friends into thinking that it is only they who are so weight and body preoccupied. This is not to say that women don't talk about their weight concerns; some do endlessly. But they don't often share with each other the deep and pervasive sense of shame that their body concerns engender.

Jennifer's shame about her preoccupation with weight and appearance was a private and deeply hidden feeling. Her husband repeatedly told people that she's the most "together" person he knows, so she felt like she was fooling him most of all. She was afraid of being found out but wished she could just tell someone honestly how she was feeling without getting laughed at, rejected, dismissed, or betrayed—all experiences she had in the past when she confided in friends or her mother. She remembered telling her mother some of her deepest secrets and fears as a child. "My mother would then call my grandmother to tell her what 'cute' things Jennifer had to say, and my grandmother would tease me when she saw me. It made me feel like a real dope." She would not risk seeming vain, petty, or shallow now with people she likes. She could not trust herself or them enough to try.

Layered over the shame of body preoccupation is the shame of eating. Many women experience hunger as shameful and do not think that they deserve to eat. Eating anything in public often arouses feelings of anxiety and many women avoid it. At best, they feel allowed to eat only "diet" foods such as low-calorie or tasteless foods in front of other people.

Susie, a legal secretary, never joined her colleagues for lunch. She brought a yogurt and a few crackers every day for appearances and then ate candy furtively while she worked. The thought of having her colleagues see her eat the candy was awful. Then they could blame her for the few extra pounds that she carried and her lack of self-control. Many women speak of "sinning" or eating a "forbidden" food when they eat something high in calories.

Janet, a college senior, says:

> At home, my mother, who is very weight-conscious and so tiny—about one hundred ten pounds—would always watch exactly what we ate at meals. My brother would just ignore her and eat what he wanted and he was fine.

But I would remember what she said, and feel like she was trying to deprive me of something that I should be able to have. Even when she wasn't there, I'd feel guilty that I wasn't good like she was. When I came to Yale, and she wasn't watching me closely anymore, I just kept eating and eating. I knew that I was being bad and that I would gain weight unless I got it under control, and that's when I started throwing up. I remember hearing about bulimia in high school, and thinking, "How could anyone do anything so gross?" But when I got here, I started to think, "What a cool idea, what a great way to eat all you want, and not gain weight."

Other women feel ashamed about letting people see that their eating behavior is aberrant. One patient, Melissa, confessed that several years before coming to see us for treatment, she had doubled over with acute stomach pains after a large binge. Her parents were understandably alarmed and rushed her to a hospital emergency room. Although she knew that the pains were related to her binge, she felt too embarrassed to explain this to the doctor. Instead, she agreed to have her gall bladder removed.

Shame and Compulsive Eating The many layers of shame associated with weight and eating are a powerful, painful, and often overwhelming experience for many women. We see these layers of shame at work most strongly in women who eat compulsively.

The functions of compulsive eating are diverse, but a common thread of shame weaves together many of these functions. For example, beyond a direct connection between the physiological deprivation that results from dieting and its compensation by binge eating, bingeing may represent an outgrowth of feelings of deprivation and restraint in other areas of a woman's life. For many women, dieting is a metaphor for "being good," for containing one's shameful needs and inadequacies, in obedience to an internalized prescription.

If dieting is a struggle to exert control over eating and a way of proving that one is good, then bingeing is a defiance and a rebellion against feeling constrained. In the words of one of our patients, Joan, bingeing is the "perfect little girl's solution": the woman who strives to be the perfect daughter, spouse, employee, or student and responds to everybody's demands and expectations. She uses bingeing as her secret source of need gratification. As Joan explained, the binge eater usually suppresses her own needs and "appetites." When they become too pressing to ignore, she does not make any demands on anyone else for need gratification. Rather, she attempts to resolve needs and conflicts herself by eating voraciously so as not to upset or impose on anyone.

Patty, who worked as a teacher's aide in her mother's daycare center, is a good example of this kind of bingeing. Whenever any of the other staff members stayed out sick or were late for work, Patty offered to help so that her mother would not have to feel stressed over finding a replacement. Invariably, however, Patty would come home from her long workday and binge, feeling that her sacrifice was worth a treat. But the compulsive eating made her feel deeply ashamed.

A shame-provoking experience—typically an interpersonal situation that leaves a woman feeling "embarrassed" or "stupid" or "silly"—may also prompt a binge. Or shame can be provoked by other feelings. The woman may be feeling another emotion (e.g., anger) that she feels ashamed of, and, again, eating compulsively may be her response to the shame.

Another aspect of bingeing is as an expression of despair and desperateness, a metaphor for feeling out of control over one's weight. As Janet described:

> When I'd binge, I was always in a complete panic. I'd worry about how horrible I'd look that summer in a bathing suit. I'd think about how my mother would say that I'd gained weight. I'd panic that I would bump into someone I knew while carrying a pizza or bags of cookies. "What will I say if I see someone?" I'd think, and make up these ridiculous lies about a friend in another college who was sick and had missed dinner, or say that I was having people over.

Some women try to retain a sense of control by organizing their binges in advance, planning what foods to get and under what circumstances to consume them and sometimes engaging in elaborate rituals around the binge. Even so, they are ultimately overcome by feelings of shame and disgust at their own behavior. Anne, an accountant at a large law firm, did not eat anything all day and left work feeling absolutely famished. But she had all her plans laid out. From work she would go to the supermarket, get herself a shopping cart, and load it up with all her favorite foods.

> I knew that place like the back of my own hand. I would always buy things in exactly the same order. First, I would get the bagels; then I'd stop for the doughnuts, then down the ice cream aisle, and, finally, I'd get a bag of M & M's. I would bring everything home and into my bedroom, turn on the TV, and eat everything in the same order in which I had bought it. I would feel great for a while, eating in control, until I got to the M & M's. By then, I would be so stuffed I could hardly move. Then I would begin to panic and eat the M & M's rapidly, to get rid of them. I was afraid that if I left them, I'd eat them the next day and, of course, I needed to begin my diet the next day.

Many women are compulsive eaters. Only a few are also purgers. For those who do purge, it is frequently an attempt to "undo the damage," often including trying to obliterate the shame of the binge. Like bingeing, purging may serve many functions. For some women, purging is reinforcing, while for others, it is punishing. Vomiting, for example, provides relief for some by reducing gastric discomfort and reinstating the condition of emptiness in the stomach, so bulimic women often associate purging with feeling thin and in control. "I purged after every meal," Janet recalls. "Breakfast I'd throw up. Lunch I'd throw up. Dinner I'd throw up. Afterward, I'd think, 'Great, I got rid of that bloated feeling,' and then I'd be able to refocus and do work, be productive. But a few hours later, I'd do it all over again."

On the other hand, purging may serve as punishment for the transgression of a binge, to expiate the shame. Punishment reinforces a view of the self as bad and is an attempt to rectify the problem rather than to reassert it. Laxative abuse, in particular, is a way of purging that enables the binger to feel that she has, as Fran put it, "paid up for what I did." She continued, "I would be up all night, in pain from eating a whole package of laxatives, and I would think to myself, 'Serves you right, why can't you be more in control? That will teach you.'"

The majority of women who purge do so in carefully guarded isolation. They live in fear of the shame that their secret will be discovered. An unfortunate spiral is thus set in motion. Ashamed first of her weight and then of her repugnant eating behaviors, the bulimic woman progressively withdraws into a private world. She now experiences herself as a personal failure and feels unwantable, provoking yet more shame. Many bulimic women avoid intimate relationships. They do not know how they will be able to maintain their secret behaviors, and they fear they will be rejected if they are found out or if they confess. Many bulimic women, in effect, live an isolated life, thus creating an external version of their internal isolation.

Men's Shame

Are men immune from shame? Hardly. Men also find their body preoccupation difficult to accept. But the shame has different expressions and different effects. Peter Richmond, writing in *Glamour* magazine, gave a classic example of the difference between men and women:

> Two women meet on the street, and one says, "God, my thighs are getting huge." The other says, "No, they're fine, but I can't stand my new haircut." The first one says, "Nonsense, your hair looks gorgeous." Then they move on to other matters having resolved their body anxiety for the time being. In the male equivalent, two men meet for racquetball. Each wears baggy sweatshirts and headbands

to appropriately conceal flaws. Each hopes desperately that the other won't notice how gelatinous he looks; they spend forty-five minutes talking about Madonna's lungs.

What do most men focus on when they worry about their appearance? A prime concern is weight. One survey showed that a middle torso that's too big is the source of greatest anxiety for 50 percent of men studied. Beer bellies, bulges above and below the belt, love handles, all of these are common male concerns. Since men are genetically programmed to deposit fat around the abdomen, these are fairly frequent experiences. Hair is also a major preoccupation. Men who are losing the hair on their heads—more so than those who are totally bald—agonize over the prospect of balding. Frequently, those who have too much body hair disgust themselves and often, unfortunately, others as well.

But men suppress their body concerns more than women. Perhaps they try to keep them secret because they find them so shame-provoking. It's less socially acceptable for men to think and worry about their appearance than it is for women to do so. Men experience their body concerns as unmasculine, and therefore embarrassing and shameful. This lowers their self-esteem.

Joe, a successful doctor, feels inferior to the thin athletes he treats because they are lean and he is not. Even knowing objectively how much they look up to him and envy him doesn't make him feel better about himself. When he's operating on them, he fantasizes that he's cutting out his own fat and adding it to their bodies. He is alarmed by these feelings and ashamed of his weight. But he wouldn't dare confide such thoughts to his friends.

Recently, I heard Peter Jennings report on a new trend in Japan—men using cosmetics. The film clip showed men going to the powder room between dances to freshen their makeup. Many Japanese men interviewed openly noted how important their looks were to their happiness and success. They emphasized the importance of cosmetics in influencing their attractiveness. But I was more struck by how uncomfortable the story made Peter Jennings than by the facts in the story. It seems to me that at least women get some relief from being able to openly acknowledge and talk about the agony of their body preoccupations and the tyranny of the pursuit of beauty.

Shame When Diets Fail

Most people fail at diets, which leads them to try ever more ambitious ones. Regaining weight after being visibly successful is like wearing a scarlet letter for all to see. The shame for some people is intense and saps energy and self-esteem. It can turn inward, lead to depression and deflated self-worth. But as psychologist Susan Woolcy has remarked, "If shame could cure obesity, there wouldn't be a fat person in the world."

Besides its visibility, there is another consequence of repeated weight-loss failures. Clinical work and research studies have shown that dieters who go up and down over and over again are easy targets. Everyone knows they care about their weight or they wouldn't try to lose it so often. And all know how many times they've failed. So people—passing acquaintances, family, friends—tell them how great they used to look, ask them how they could let themselves go, or make other comments, all of which exacerbates their shame.

Elaine, a doctor, painfully recalls how one of her partners commented on her eating and weight publicly, at a meeting that included all their nurses and employees. In discussing the nurses' complaints about their heavy workload, the partner suggested that the nurses felt overworked because they had to spend so much time worrying about getting food for every crazy new diet Elaine tried and then failed. The overweight doctor felt so ashamed that she couldn't speak. She felt physically struck and couldn't come to her own defense. Did she feel angry? Only a little. Her most powerful emotion was shame. She said to me, "If I didn't look like this, he [the colleague] couldn't say something that could hurt me so much. It's my own fault." In this case, she might have done well to blame her colleague for insensitivity, rather than herself.

— 89 —

DR. JUDITH RODIN

Breaking the Shame Trap

Multiple layers of shame keep us from feeling good about who we are. We feel our concerns are so petty, that we shouldn't pay attention to them, so we divert our attention in order to avoid shame rather than confront what we are feeling and deal with it directly. Breaking the shame trap requires forgiveness—forgiving yourself for not achieving all the things that current culture has been admonishing you to strive for.

To break the shame trap, *you must begin to take your current self more seriously,* rather than focusing on your ideal self and always falling short. People who feel good about themselves are likely to treat themselves better. Sounds simple. But most people caught by the body trap of shame don't like their bodies very much, so they keep delaying doing good things for themselves. They keep waiting until they have a body that they think is more deserving. Since that day often never comes, they put off treating themselves better as well.

Serena, a bank vice president, is one of the clearest examples of someone who didn't take herself seriously. I used to notice that she always wore a very inexpensive Mickey Mouse watch. Since many people like cute watches, I didn't think there was anything wrong with the watch itself. But for several weeks in a row, Serena talked about passing a beautiful and very expensive timepiece in a jeweler's window. She longed for it. Since she is quite well-off financially, she could easily afford the watch, but it was clear that she didn't think she deserved it. In fact, the Mickey Mouse watch was a sign that she didn't take herself very seriously. We worked on getting her to think that she deserved a new watch and good clothes. She came to see that she didn't need to lose weight first in order to take care of herself. In fact, the process actually happens quite in reverse. Looking and feeling good can often enable the weight loss.

Not everyone can afford expensive watches or clothes, of course, but everyone can afford small indulgences—a long, warm bath with some bath oils, a half hour time out, a new haircut. Do something nice for your body. It is an important step to breaking the shame trap. Some of you will be amazed at how hard this is, especially if the Body Shame test revealed that you are ashamed of parts of your body. When you treat your real self well, you are telling yourself, "I do deserve this. I really am a worthwhile person. I have nothing to feel ashamed about."

For Beatrice, whom I described in the Introduction, we developed specific exercises aimed at developing pride in her body. For instance, she did not think of herself as an athletic person with an impressive range of physical skills. Information about her playing various sports came out more or less incidentally during treatment, until we began to pay more careful attention to this unacknowledged part of herself. We learned, for example, that Beatrice was a formidable tennis player. She hit the ball hard, played with great precision, and was very fast, a fact that surprised many of her tennis partners. Even more interestingly, we learned that downplaying her tennis achievements was related to the shame trap: Beatrice had a hard time tolerating the attention she would get when she played at her tennis club. "Everyone would look at me and all I could think of was how these people must believe that I am a fat blob."

Because Beatrice did enjoy being physically active, sports offered an ideal opportunity to help her improve her body image and overcome her shame. Beatrice was a very good swimmer, but refused to swim when she first began treatment. She was too embarrassed to wear a bathing suit. In a couple of therapy sessions, we developed a plan to help her overcome her fear of being seen in public wearing a swimsuit. Beatrice went to a specialty store that carried sportswear for large women and selected an attractive suit. The first week, she wore the suit once a day for a practice session in her bedroom, looking at herself in the mirror, while talking to herself about how *healthy* she looked and how good it would feel to swim. The second week, she went swimming at a friend's private beach in the early morning when she felt certain that no one would be around to see her. At the same time, she continued to practice wearing the suit at home, now also thinking about other people seeing her and preparing herself for the anxiety and discomfort she might experience in a public place. We taught her to focus on positive statements such as "People will think that I am engaging in healthy behavior, that I am pursuing fitness," "People will probably wonder where I got this pretty bathing suit," and "No matter what others think, *I* think it is great that I can enjoy a swim on this beautiful day."

In breaking the shame trap, next you must work on *changing your body ideal*. The discrepancy between it and reality is a big factor in feelings of shame. The tests you took at the beginning of the chapter allow you to determine if you are ashamed of how you look and whether there is a large discrepancy between your real and ideal selves. If so, it is essential for you to closely examine your ideal. Is it really attainable? Whose ideal is it? Yours or that of your mother/friend/husband?

Start to revise your ideal by looking more critically at the magazine ads and television commercials. Remind yourself that it takes many hours a day for people to look that good and an amount of money that would probably astonish you. For models and actresses, beauty truly is a career. For the rest of us, it is not. Understand that the combined dose of self-criticism and the feeling of being observed makes us ashamed. This goes a long way to breaking the shame trap.

Working on shame means confronting squarely all the ways your ideal self-image has become established, including what you think *other* people think about you, particularly how they view your body. Practice staring back at somebody whom you sense is looking at you. Beatrice has learned that when she feels evaluated and looked at, the worst thing she can do is cringe and look away. For her and many like her, that was a clear trigger to overeat. Now she looks back. Is anyone perfect? Rarely, she finds. Suddenly, she finds little reason to feel so ashamed.

If other people make you feel bad about your appearance, you may be filled with emotions such as anger and despair which makes it harder to acknowledge and deal with the shame. Understanding the feelings that enhance your shame is a complicated but necessary process.

Jeannette, one of our clinic's patients, gained fifteen pounds after her marriage to Frank. Her husband frequently pointed out her larger size and urged her to lose weight. Jeannette began dieting and, to her distress, Frank would update his family every week about her progress. To "help her along," he also refused to have intercourse with her, telling her that he did not want her "to get comfortable being so fat." He made her feel so ashamed that she found it impossible to look at herself in the mirror. In this case Frank, the husband, set the ideal, rather than society at large, but the consequence was the same.

As a first step, we helped Jeannette identify and label all the feelings her shame provoked. Looking carefully at all the various aspects of her situation helped her uncover her feeling of shame under the layers of anger and frustration. Clearly she was (and had a right to be) furious at Frank, but it was too frightening a feeling for her, so she just blamed herself more. We tried to enable her to validate her feelings, acknowledging the pain she was experiencing. Then we tried to show how she used shame to punish herself and deny angry feelings. We guided her to try to remember when she first felt shame about her body. Who communicated to her that her body was a source of shame? Who in her life now would continue to reinforce this notion? Who would disagree? You can do the same thing by yourself. Simply by acknowledging that the shame exists and by describing its phenomenology, the shame experience becomes less threatening. As Jeannette's understanding grew, she felt an increasing sense of control over her responses. It was important for her to recognize how much other people, especially her husband, directly contributed to her feelings of shame. Then she was able to deal with her feelings and ultimately to directly confront the shame-provoking comments.

Finally, to break the shame trap, you need to identify your true needs, to ask yourself, "What do *I* want?" Not what you think your ideal self *should* want, but what you really do want. Make a list. What's fascinating is that everyone's list includes the trivial and the petty, the profound and the sensitive. Fulfilling our needs without judging them is a key to accepting ourselves as we are, which includes our bodies.

John, a medical research assistant, struggled to construct his list. All his life he worked to be what he thought everyone else wanted him to be. He wasn't really sure what he wanted. His list included:

> Tell my boss what I really think of him.
> Learn to sail.
> Be taller.
> Be less easy to push around.
> Get a more interesting job.
> Develop a sense of inner peace.
> Sleep later on weekends.
> Get to know my children better.

When you look over your own list, it will be clear that some items can only be fulfilled in fantasy, like being taller. Some might get you into trouble, like the need to tell your boss what you really think of him (or her). Others can easily be achieved if you let yourself, like learning to sail. It's amazing how rarely people vulnerable to the shame trap allow themselves to dwell on their needs, let alone fulfill them. When we stop feeling ashamed of our appearance and our body concerns, we have the time and energy—and feel we deserve—to find out what we really want and need. This is key to breaking the shame trap.

— 4 —

The Competition Trap

Women of the 1980s and 1990s have a new trademark, boasts *Working Woman* magazine: a competitive spirit. Who are they kidding? Have they missed the fact that for centuries women have competed? Beauty has always been the arena and the competition has been fierce. While competition in the working world is on the rise, physical attractiveness and weight are still the chief and most wholeheartedly sanctioned domains in which women are encouraged to contend with each other. The ultimate contest—the beauty pageant—is still going strong.

Women caught in the competition trap make comparisons between themselves and other women all the time. For some, the work is never-ending, because there are always new spas, treatments, and salons. "And just when you've had your hair colored by Princess Di's hairdresser, joined the most exclusive health club, had your paws and claws handled by the manicurist of the stars, there's always someone who's going to top you. 'Have you heard of this place where they steam the towels for herbal wraps in Evian?'"

Lori, a participant in one of our studies, sees all women in terms of how they look relative to her. When Lori comes out on top, she feels great, but when she doesn't, she feels like a loser. Each time she meets someone new, she needs to rank herself. Even lunch with her friends is a contest in which she needs to be best at restricting her eating. Every television star is a standard for her self-evaluations. These daily contests lead to emotional highs and lows that consume an inordinate amount of her attention.

Another feature of the competition trap is that weight control itself is a contest. Women most often want to do better than their friends; indeed, many caught by the trap see their relative success at weight control as a measure of how well they are doing as a woman. The trap gets even more complicated here because sharing concern, complaints, and worry about weight are also ways for women to become closer to one another. This may have developed because relationships like those with mothers and sisters are often the first place where issues of weight and appearance competition get played out.

Lisa's parents got divorced when she was nineteen years old. After a difficult period of adjusting to her new status as a divorced woman, Lisa's mother decided to "make herself over" and went on a diet that left her, according to Lisa, "weighing fifty pounds less and looking fifteen years younger." Lisa felt quite threatened by her mother's profound change in appearance and felt that she too should now go on a diet to lose some weight. "Can you imagine how embarrassing it is when your mother can wear a size seven and you wear a size ten?"

Women like Lisa who are caught by the competition trap agree with a statement such as the following: "I'm likely to evaluate how good I look by comparing myself to others." If this is true for you, is it also the case that when you compare your looks to other women's, your relative ranking affects how you feel about yourself? If so, the stakes of the competition are too high. For Lisa, losing weight is a contest with other women and gaining weight is losing the competitive edge. Think about your own views on weight and appearance. How much does competition play a role?

Most women also are competitive in their effort to secure and attract men. While attractiveness influences how both men and women interact, women's attractiveness seems to matter more. Take Dawn, for example, a single young woman who is looking for a serious relationship. She complains bitterly that in the "singles scene," appearance is the only thing that attracts men. She's constantly watching what she eats, she works out at least four times a week, and she never goes out without looking her best. "You can never tell where you're going to meet someone," she asserts, admitting that even a trip to the laundromat or trash room of her apartment building requires her to prepare herself.

Young women even learn to modify their eating behavior in order to attract men. Psychologists Shelly Chaiken and Patricia Pliner set up an experiment that resembled a dating game. College men and women met one another for the first time and as part of this first "date," they had a snack together. What the experimenters varied was how attractive the new partner was. When women were with an attractive male, they ate significantly less than when they were with an unattractive male. Women apparently feel that the amount they eat is important in making a favorable impression. Men in the study ate the same amount regardless of their date's looks.

But the competition trap has now gotten even more complex. Today's message is that women must have it all—looks, professional achievements, and a great family life. Women judge themselves and each other in a wider field of achievement and with increasingly rigorous standards. Competition is now more pervasive. It relates not only to appearance but to many aspects of their lives.

The test on page 98 will assess how competitive you are in achievement situations.

The multiple arenas in which women must now compete are causing conflicts for many. And knowing how well one is doing has become more and more difficult. That's the new part of the competition trap. Women have had a lot more experience competing with one another with regard to looks, and the nature of that competition is much more prescribed. While growing up, we learn the rules, so as adults, we understand how to try to outdo one another in the realm of appearance. There are also prescriptions that are fairly well worked out for how to compete with one another for men. We learn

ACHIEVEMENT ORIENTATION SCALE

The following statements describe reactions to conditions of work and challenging situations. For each item, indicate how much you agree or disagree with the statement, as it refers to you, by checking the answer that best applies to you.

1. I enjoy working in situations involving competition with others.

   __ Strongly __ Slightly __ Neither Agree __ Slightly __ Strongly
   Agree   Agree   nor Disagree   Disagree   Disagree

2. It is important to me to perform better than others on a task.

   __ Strongly __ Slightly __ Neither Agree __ Slightly __ Strongly
   Agree   Agree   nor Disagree   Disagree   Disagree

3. I feel that winning is important in both work and games.

   __ Strongly __ Slightly __ Neither Agree __ Slightly __ Strongly
   Agree   Agree   nor Disagree   Disagree   Disagree

4. It annoys me when other people perform better than I do.

   __ Strongly __ Slightly __ Neither Agree __ Slightly __ Strongly
   Agree   Agree   nor Disagree   Disagree   Disagree

5. I try harder when I'm in competition with other people.

   __ Strongly __ Slightly __ Neither Agree __ Slightly __ Strongly
   Agree   Agree   nor Disagree   Disagree   Disagree

Score your responses by assigning 0 to *Strongly Disagree* all the way to 4 for *Strongly Agree*. You are *competitive* if your total score is 18 or higher. Not all *highly* competitive women are vulnerable, however—just those who keep trying to compete unsuccessfully with their own unattainable ideals.

them from novels and magazines, movies and television, and through our experiences growing up.

What's much newer—and therefore, where we are on much more shaky footing—is our competition with one another and with men for professional achievement. We don't know if the same rules apply, because we haven't been doing it long enough. Male child rearing teaches men the kinds of games and rules that will later be useful in the workplace. Female child rearing teaches girls neither the skills nor the rules needed for achievement competition. This may be one reason why women who are competing in the achievement domain haven't given up the appearance domain. In other words, not only do they want or think they should have it all, but they are afraid to let go of the more traditional areas in which they've competed.

Until women are confident that they can succeed in the workplace, appearance and body competition serve as safety valves. In case things don't "work out" at work, they always have something to fall back on. And the connection between good looks and good jobs cannot go unnoticed in today's marketplace. According to Marilyn Moats Kennedy, a career strategist who advises women: "In a bad economy, you want to look good, really good. If a job hunter looks the least bit down-at-the-heels, it's a killer. Looks are more important than ever right now." As more women begin to hit the "glass ceiling," the importance of appearance may be increasing, if anything. Women may rely on their bodies as the last resort. If they can't get that raise or promotion by working harder, they can at least fix their faces or lose more weight.

Women caught by the competition trap are not only competing with others, but with their own ideal. This often leaves them feeling frustrated and inadequate. Many have excessively high standards which they feel compelled to achieve. Corinne could never take pride in her accomplishments. No matter how well she did, she always believed she should have done better. She described her life as "a leaning tower of shoulds," which she had to keep propping up. This is a graphic metaphor for the draining aspect of competing with one's own ideals. Being competitive and having unrealistic goals gets Corinne and others like her caught by the trap. The self-evaluation test on page 101 will help you determine if you are in competition with yourself.

Understanding the nature of the competition trap will help you to free yourself from it. Let's consider its many aspects.

How the Competition Trap Works

The Appearance Contest

In almost forty years, no television program in the same time slot has ever beaten the Miss America contest in the ratings. Writing about a recent Miss America pageant, Steven Stark, a reporter for *The New York Times*, commented: "With its swimsuit awards and talent competitions, the pageant might seem an anachronism in an age when women aspire to the sovereignty of the boardroom, not the Boardwalk." The psychologists he interviewed disagreed. Some argued that for women, beauty is power; others said that these contests provide one of the few opportunities for at least one woman to be a winner. The executive producer of the Miss Universe contest showed good insight. He claimed that these shows are popular because they offer a chance for women at home to "test themselves against their peers."

But even the beauty contests have been upping the ante recently. Now Miss America is not only shapely and gorgeous. She often attends a prestigious university and has serious professional aspirations. More and more, the message is that women must now prove that they do have it all.

For men, bodies are not yet a major competitive domain. But the old Spartacus movies remind us that they once were, and signs that they will be again in the future are already here. Body building is on the rise and contests are held daily in

SELF-EVALUATION SCALE

This is a scale which measures a variety of attitudes, feelings, and behavior. Some of the questions may appear to be quite similar but they tap somewhat different processes. There are no right or wrong answers, so try very hard to be completely honest in your responses. Check the answer which applies best to you.

1. Only outstanding performance is good enough in my family.

   __ *Always* __ *Usually* __ *Often* __ *Sometimes* __ *Rarely* __ *Never*

2. As a child, I tried very hard to avoid disappointing my parents and teachers.

   __ *Always* __ *Usually* __ *Often* __ *Sometimes* __ *Rarely* __ *Never*

3. I hate being less than best at things.

   __ *Always* __ *Usually* __ *Often* __ *Sometimes* __ *Rarely* __ *Never*

4. My parents have expected excellence of me.

   __ *Always* __ *Usually* *Often* __ *Sometimes* __ *Rarely* __ *Never*

5. I feel that I must do things perfectly, or not do them at all.

   __ *Always* __ *Usually* __ *Often* __ *Sometimes* __ *Rarely* __ *Never*

6. I have extremely high goals.

   __ *Always* __ *Usually* __ *Often* __ *Sometimes* __ *Rarely* __ *Never*

Score your answer to each question by assigning a 1 to *Often*, a 2 to *Usually*, a 3 to *Always*, and a 0 to *Never*, *Rarely*, or *Sometimes*. Add your scores together. If your score is 12 or higher, you may be locked in the competition trap by perfectionism.

local neighborhood health clubs. As fitness centers enter the workplace, performance at the desk may no longer be enough.

Most women admit that on entering a room, they immediately judge the other women and assess where they rank: who is thinner, who is prettier. Milly, in one of our studies, is someone who's gone further than most. She's developed a rating scheme: "*One* equals drip; not worth another nervous glance. *Two* equals O.K., but I'm probably better; no threat. *Three* equals a toss-up; let's compare us body part by body part, clothes and makeup. Watch her. *Four* equals a real looker. Stay more than fifty feet away at all times." I never asked her what she did about the number fours at small parties.

Milly's rating scheme actually reveals an interesting psychological principle. We may compete, but we typically don't do it against people who are too different from us—especially those we judge to be considerably better. It's number three who is examined closely for all the comparisons. Milly is much more clear about where she stands with one, two, and four. She wants the competitive edge against number three.

Psychologists also believe that people have fairly biased self-perceptions when comparing themselves to others. Their judgments are regulated by what are called schemas. Schemas about the self are the thoughts and feelings that organize our self-image. They determine the information we take in about ourselves and others. They guide the processing of all our experiences. They have a central role in the competition trap.

We use the test on page 103 as one way to find out if someone is schematic for body weight. Although you are now cued to think about weight by what you have been reading, try to complete the list of words here by writing in the *first* letter that comes to your mind.

People range from those intensely concerned with their body weight and everything connected with it, to those who have little feeling for or interest in this aspect of the self. Rarely are there women in this latter group! Women who are schematic for weight consistently evaluate events, people— everything with respect to their relevance to body weight. For

SCHEMA TEST

THI   ____
TRI   ____
FA   ____
DIE   ____
BI   ____
SLEE ____
SLI   ____
PLUM ____

All the words have more than one possible ending, and the words with different endings appear with equal frequency in the English language. These words were chosen to test whether someone is schematic for body weight because many of them, if completed in a certain way, relate to weight. For example, FA____ may be fan, far, or fat. So what comes to your mind first becomes a measure of your own personal issues.

-----

them, weight is the most important feature that they notice in others and consistently so.

Marlene's self-evaluations often take the form of comparative questions such as "Does she weigh more than I do?" or "Are there a lot of chubby people in this restaurant?" Her world is divided into those who weigh more, less, or the same as she does. The competition trap pushes Marlene to make comparisons. Her weight schema determines what she "chooses" to see. The existence of schemas means that we don't all see the same things when we compare ourselves to the same person. When two friends look at the same woman, for example, they are likely to rate her differently in terms of how much competition she is. What they see in her depends on their unique schemas, what's important to them about themselves. Marlene would rate a thin, but plain-faced woman as much more attractive than would her friend, who is less schematic for weight. Marlene would judge this type of woman to be much more competition than her friend would, as well.

Competition for Men

Physical attractiveness dramatically influences how men and women interact. But it's the woman's attractiveness that seems to matter most. In studies of first impressions and first dates, psychologists Elaine Hatfield at the University of Hawaii and Ellen Berscheid at the University of Minnesota found that the good-looking women were the most well liked. And men were more likely to reveal personal facts about themselves to more attractive women.

Attractiveness seems to fuel the competition trap even in young children, and more so again for girls than boys. For example, popularity with the opposite sex is more strongly linked to good looks for girls than for boys. Eleanor Maccoby and Carol Jacklin, developmental psychologists at Stanford University and the University of Southern California, have studied gender differences in children for many years, and suggest that boys with the greatest status and power, as well as reasonably good looks, interest the most attractive girls. On the other hand, only the most alluring, beautiful girls interest the highest-status boys.

Certainly the media promote and support the view that the prettiest girls get the best men. Children are exposed to the idea that appearance counts in a relationship early on, but boys and girls react differently to it. I see my nine-year-old son watching television. When the beautiful girl gets the boy and they kiss, he makes a face and turns away. He's not interested in that "stuff" yet, so the message has less impact on him. But the eight-year-old daughter of a friend watches in rapt attention. She's clearly learning what it takes to get a man. She already talks about being pretty, and which of her friends is prettier than the others.

Alexis Tan, a professor in the Department of Mass Communications at Texas Tech University, has been studying how the mass media, and television in particular, create and cultivate audience perceptions of social reality. In one study she focused on TV beauty commercials, those commercials that use sex appeal, beauty, or youth as selling points. For example, a commercial that suggests that using a certain brand of tooth-paste can enhance the user's sex appeal would be classified as a beauty commercial.

In the United States, commercials constitute a significant element in the symbolic world of television. Out of every prime-time TV hour, at least nine and a half minutes are devoted to commercials. Commercials generally can attract the attention of the "less involved" television viewer through the use of entertainment production techniques, intrusive placement in popular programs, and repetition. So it would be interesting to know if the themes in commercials affect viewers' attitudes.

Tan divided the research participants into two groups: One group saw fifteen TV beauty commercials that had been taped from network shows; the other group saw fifteen TV commercials, also taped from network shows, which did not mention or show any beauty themes. After viewing the tapes, the subjects in the study were asked a variety of questions including: "For a woman to be popular with (or liked by) men, which of the following characteristics are most important?" They were instructed: "Pick those characteristics which you think *are* important in real life, *not* those which you think *should* be important." Characteristics they had to select from were: a pretty face; intelligence; sex appeal; hard-working; a youthful appearance; articulate; a healthy slim body; a good education; glamour; competence.

Subjects exposed to the beauty commercials gave substantially higher importance ratings to the beauty characteristics for the role "to be popular with men" than subjects exposed to the neutral commercials. Certainly if such effects can be attained from a single, saturated exposure to TV commercials, it is very likely that long-term, repeated exposures (such as those occurring in the real world) must be having profound effects on viewers.

Traditional sex-role definitions specify very different sources of status for men and women. For men, easily quantifiable criteria of success are available, such as income or the value of possessions. Since women have traditionally lacked such criteria, beauty has been a central asset that has helped a woman to gain access to a man's resources. Men, conversely, gain social stature from marrying a beautiful woman.

Presenting subjects with all possible combinations of pictures of attractive and unattractive men and women as couples, two social psychologists at Boston University, Daniel Bar-Tal and Leonard Saxe, found that an unattractive male married to an attractive female received the most favorable ratings. The ratings of an unattractive female were not at all affected by the attractiveness of her mate. Marrying a beautiful woman may improve a man's status, whereas marrying an attractive man does not affect the woman's status. These differences seem to remain, despite our current, more liberated society.

Similar evidence emerges from the work of two sociologists at the University of Washington, Philip Blumstein and Pepper Schwartz, who interviewed a cross section of American couples. The heterosexual women in their sample resented it when their husbands or boyfriends were relatively more attractive than they were, while men did not at all mind the relatively greater attractiveness of their wives or girlfriends. Consistent with the Bar-Tal and Saxe study, a man viewed a relatively more attractive female mate as a positive reflection on him. Interestingly, Blumstein and Schwartz observed that although their subjects tended to assume that physical appearance would diminish in importance to the couple as the relationship progressed, women's looks continued to be critical to their partners. They found that even in long-standing relationships, attractive women experienced better sex lives and had more faithful husbands and lovers.

The following cases from their interviews reveal that the importance and appeal of a woman's beauty endures long after the courtship. These vignettes indicate that wives are keenly aware of the importance of their looks to their husbands.

Faith is a homemaker of thirty-nine, and her husband Gerry is a city manager of the same age. They have been married for fifteen years. Faith knows Gerry cares how she looks:

I don't think I am naturally attractive . . . but I take care of myself. I think he would be disappointed in me if I didn't. In fact, if I gain a few pounds, he will kid me by pinching my waist or my thigh. He's kidding, but he's also telling me to go to the gym . . . It's worth the work. I need to feel good about myself, and believe me, I wouldn't get to first base with him if he wasn't proud of my appearance.

Joe, a salesman in his late thirties, places much of the blame for his recent divorce on his wife's lack of attention to her appearance.

I think she forgot about being my lover. She got fat. She wouldn't listen to my complaints about that at all. She stopped dyeing her hair, and I got off on her being a blonde. I think she was actually relieved that I wouldn't start something . . . I put up with that horse manure for six years, if you can believe that. Not anymore!

In another study, researchers found that mothers who haven't regained their figure a year after the baby's birth pay for the extra pounds with angry husbands. The study was conducted by psychologists M. Geraldine Gage and Donna Christensen, from the University of Minnesota, St. Paul. They surveyed 454 white middle-class couples—first-time mothers and their husbands—about their marriages, life-styles, and mental states six months after delivery.

The study showed that the more weight women kept on, the less satisfied the husbands were with the marriage and the more marital conflict the men reported. Little wonder that the study found that these were the women who had lower self-esteem and felt less competent as mothers. Dr. Gage was quoted as saying that these women ". . . know how important a slim body is to men. Women feel constantly under the threat of being traded in for a later model." Women must maintain the competitive edge against other women in their appearance because female attractiveness is so clearly of basic importance in male-female relationships. One "corporate wife" we studied put it this way. "When I go to pool parties with my husband, I better look good in my bathing suit, because my body is my 'spreadsheet.'"

The scenarios of competition continue to be replayed all the way to the end of the lifespan, as well. Given that women live, on the average, eight years longer than men, there are substantial numbers of older women seeking companionship. Often, they compete for the few remaining older men. This competition is caricatured on television sitcoms such as *The Golden Girls*, but the reality is painful and hardly laughable for many.

Sally, an octogenarian, describes the women in her large retirement community who read the daily obituaries to see whose wife has died. "They descend on him like vultures," she complains, "with rolls of fat tucked in their girdles, loaded with makeup on their faces and pot roast on their platters, circling for the kill."

Author Susan Sontag has argued that women's concerns about the consequence of aging reflect a correct perception of the double standard of aging that distinguishes men from women. Whereas women are judged less worthwhile as their youth fades, men are not. This is probably partly because men are judged throughout the life cycle on the basis of their achievements rather than their looks. But in addition, the social ideal for men allows them some room to age, whereas the ideal for women seems restricted to youthfulness. Elaine Hatfield and her colleagues report that both young and old people judge old women as relatively less attractive than old men. Women appear to have a more narrowly defined template to match in terms of age, as well as appearance. Older women either give up the competition or valiantly struggle, often in frustration and despair.

Surely, there must be a happy balance that women can achieve between obsessional concern over what their spouse or other men think of them, and not caring at all about looking good. The goal is to develop a healthy personal pride in one's appearance that is neither debilitating nor motivated by another person. This is no easy feat, but many of the tasks at the end of this and other chapters are described to help you reach such a balance.

The Tournament of Weight Control

Women clearly understand that attractiveness makes them more valued by their partners and by society. But weight stands out in its importance to women and not only in order to get men. An interesting study by psychologists Paul Rozin and April Fallon supports the idea that women are not working to be *extremely* thin because they believe that's what men like.

The researchers showed men and women a series of body shapes and sizes ranging from very thin to quite heavy (which you completed in Chapter 3). Participants were asked to indicate the figure that best represented them. They also chose the figure that was their ideal and the figure they thought was most attractive to the opposite sex.

Women wished for a figure that was significantly thinner than the one they judged would be most attractive to men. In other words, women want to be even thinner than they think men want them to be! Furthermore, the figure the women thought was most attractive to men was significantly thinner than what the male participants actually said they liked. Nancy Adler and her colleagues at the University of California, San Francisco, found the same result in their study of male and female adolescents ages ten to fifteen years old. Women and even young girls don't pursue thinness merely to please men. The tournament of weight control has other rewards.

Many women caught by the competition trap are forced to diet because they understand that their bodies are more central to their attractiveness than are men's. This view was confirmed by a research study in which actual portraits of men and women in paintings, in newspapers, and in magazine articles were compared. Magazines with a more feminist orientation like *Ms.* were among those studied. Women were far more likely to be shown in full figure in these portraits and men in face only. Perhaps this different portrayal is an unconscious reflection of society's different conceptions of men and women. It suggests that the essence of men is captured by their faces, symbolizing greater importance of qualities associated with the human head. These include intelligence, character, personality, willpower and other mental-life phenomena. Women's essence is captured by showing their bodies, and the body is more closely associated with emotions, drives, and sensuality.

Not surprisingly then, when we tested a large number of people, we found that weight and body shape constituted the *central* determinants of how the overwhelming majority of women judged their own physical attractiveness. For the men, weight and body shape were important, but not central to their perceived attractiveness.

Since body weight is so important to a woman's judgment of how attractive she is, being happy with her actual weight strongly affects self-worth. Women compete in the tournament of weight control in order to feel better about themselves. Dissatisfaction with weight relates to chronic low self-esteem. It also plays a major role in more short-term and volatile fluctuations of self-esteem. In their large-scale survey of *Glamour* magazine readers, psychologists Susan and Wayne Wooley found that for 63 percent of young women in their sample, weight often affected how they felt about themselves; 33 percent reported that weight sometimes affected how they felt about themselves, and only 4 percent stated that it never did.

Despite the potential sampling problems with the *Glamour* survey (maybe only weight-preoccupied people bother to fill out questionnaires like this), thirty-three thousand people responded. This suggests the prevalence of weight-related concerns and how important they are to how we feel about ourselves. No wonder women compete to be as thin as possible.

But often women don't only want to lose weight to feel and look good. They want to do better than their friends. Many are envious when someone loses weight and they don't. One highly successful unmarried woman confessed to me recently that she was more jealous of her sister for losing fifteen pounds for her wedding than for getting married—and to a great guy!

For many, weight is a quick and concrete barometer by which to measure how well one is doing as a woman.

Dieting today is a contest among women. That may help us to understand why some have characterized boarding schools and colleges as "breeding grounds" for eating disorders. The competitive school environment fosters not only academic competition, but also competition for who is the thinnest and best-looking. Celia told us:

> I used to go on a diet together with my friend Mary. We would put together a plan and support each other. But after a few days, we would get kind of competitive. I would bring Snickers bars to school because I knew how much Mary loved them. Mary would bring in homemade chocolate chip cookies. It was a battle of wills and most of the time both of us ended up breaking the diet. But we sure tried to hold out and stick with the diet longer than the other person. Then, one time, I got really serious about the dieting, because I noticed that Mary began to lose her baby fat and I was really scared that she'd end up prettier than I was. So, I didn't even really tell her about my diet and I lost a lot of weight. I still remember how proud I was that I could wear one size smaller than Mary and I know it really bugged her.

It's not hard to understand why weight control has become a metaphor for success among women. The challenge is sufficiently difficult that it commands respect. The effects are visible and highly valued. A recent job offer, a promotion, a new love, are all highly prized, desirable spoils of our competitions. But not everyone can see how well we have won. We wear our successes in the tournament of weight control. The high chance of failure reinforces its importance.

Something that makes this particular aspect of the competition trap so complex is that shared weight complaints represent a form of bonding among women. Weight preoccupation is normative. Most women on a diet talk about it with their friends. Confessing weight concerns develops camaraderie.

Sharing the guilt of the Frusen Glädjé and the Oreo cookies has become a female friendship ritual.

The next time you have lunch with another woman, listen to the metatext, the meaning of the discourse beyond the specific words being spoken. It reveals the collusive nature of the ordering ritual. Watch the other woman when the waiter brings the dessert menu. She'll "do it" if you will. In fact, she's probably looking at you more closely than the menu. Most women—and maybe now some men too—understand this particular interchange.

Our friends are important determinants of our own weight preoccupation. Certainly our attitudes toward weight are influenced by the extent to which our friends emphasize thinness. For women, dieting often is a group activity and by participating, a woman affirms her role as a member of the group. Christian Crandall, studying sororities at the University of Michigan, Ann Arbor, found that women who reported having more friends who dieted also had more eating-disorder symptoms themselves.

Crandall's study was quite imaginative because he was able to demonstrate the importance of the norms of different friendship groups by studying women who were pledging, that is, just trying out for and then joining, a sorority. Different sororities valued weight and thinness differently, Dr. Crandall found in his interviews. And depending on which sorority a new freshman joined, she came to hold the same views on the importance of thinness as the group. And the new recruits didn't only try to do what the other group members did. They tried to outdo them! Daily the tournament of weight control was played out.

I am also struck by how easily women talk to each other about their weight preoccupation, about their latest diet, or beauty fix. It's a way of reaching out, of saying, "I'm just like you, no matter how different we may seem in other ways." In fact, our studies show this clearly. Women who wish to distance themselves from other women whom they are just getting to know (because the experimenters specifically instruct them to), talk far less about their weight concerns than women instructed to make friends quickly with one another.

There are unspoken rules in female friendships about weight and appearance. When someone breaks those rules by losing weight or changing her looks, she's disrupting the balance. Women stand to lose friendships, perhaps, by mastering some of the body traps if they stop colluding in the shared sins of weight preoccupation.

Competition in Families

The family is a major—perhaps the major—arena where attitudes and behaviors related to weight, appearance, and eating are developed. Many families place a great premium on appearance and thinness. Given sociocultural biases against overweight females, it is understandable that parents often become more concerned about their daughter's eating behavior than their son's. A leading personality/developmental psychologist at Duke University, Dr. Philip Costanzo, argues that when parents care a great deal about a particular area of their child's life, they tend to use a more restrictive parenting style to influence the child's behavior in that domain. Ironically, however, their concern and effort to control leads to a paradoxical outcome: The daughter experiences considerable anxiety and guilt over eating, and at the same time, does not develop the skills required for effective self-regulation of eating. It is important to note that parents who are highly anxious about a daughter's weight may use this parenting style regardless of her actual weight. The result is that girls of any weight are at risk for developing high anxiety and low self-discipline in regard to eating.

A mother's efforts to control her own weight may convey to her daughter the importance of thinness, as well as teach her strategies to attain it. Our studies show clearly that the most weight-and-body-preoccupied teenagers have mothers who feel that their daughters are less attractive than the daughters feel they themselves are. Some of these attitudes are undoubtedly conveyed unconsciously, but some are imparted explicitly as well. These mothers directly emphasize weight and appearance to their children by commenting on the daughter's looks and drawing invidious comparisons. Such comments have a profound and long-lasting effect on her self-esteem. One of our research participants noted, "My mother was always telling me that I should try harder if I wanted to look as good as she does. 'Looking good is the best revenge,' she would say. While I guess she didn't mean it, I used to wonder if she meant revenge against me. But I never knew what I did wrong to make her feel that way."

There are few studies about competition among sisters with regard to weight, but sibling rivalry in general has been written about at length. It hardly strains the imagination to think that sisters, in particular, would be highly competitive with one another around issues of weight and appearance. Moreover, an older sister's concern with weight and dieting efforts may accelerate her younger sister's exposure to and personal involvement with this domain. The following example is one of many in our records. Jody and her sister, who was one year younger, would size up each other's plates at dinner time. Who would take more food onto her plate? Who would eat more dessert? Who would get away with eating little despite their mother's constant nagging at them to eat more? At night, they would compete at doing jumping jacks and sit-ups.

Mother/daughter relationships frequently contribute to the competition trap beyond their interactions about weight and appearance.

Paula, the phone company executive, identifies strongly with her mother, yet rejects her weakness. But unknowingly, Paula has resolved her ambivalence about her opportunity to surpass her mother professionally by allowing her eating disorder to suppress her just as her mother was suppressed by her father. Here are excerpts from our interview.

Describe your mother:

> My mom is a quiet person. She depends on other people for most if not all decision making. She doesn't like ar-

guing or fighting of any kind, and will walk away or try to change the conversation if she is found in such a situation. She is generous when it comes to ways to help her children or grandchildren. I remember mostly that my mom would never stand up to my father when he was wrong and the one time she did was to protect me because my dad had a drinking problem. It was always understood I had to ask my dad for anything or be told by my dad what I needed to know—no questions asked. I've told my mom I understood why she didn't finish high school and needed to work to help afford the house we had. I understand or try to understand that I had to become her when I was eleven years old, because that was when she had to go to work to help out my dad.

Describe yourself:

I have strong opinions. I can be argumentative if either things don't go my way or I feel very strongly about something. I like to do jobs well—not carelessly, although I do make mistakes. At these times I'm very hard to live with and I'll bring other people misery because I'm upset. At these times I can eat like a horse as the saying goes. I also always feel that I have better solutions to problems because I will think them out more exactly, by considering all the possible endings. I'm somewhat like my mom in the peace—not fighting—area. I become upset, nervous, and anxious over these situations and usually go to any lengths to resolve what's going on, whether my input is needed or not. At this point in time, I feel so responsible for so many people and circumstances that I do not have an identity anymore. I can't seem to stop and say, I come first and I don't like myself for starting to feel this way. I think it's wrong of me to be selfish.

The challenge faced by women today is that in pursuing education and a vocation, they often are surpassing their mothers' achievements in these domains. Kim Chernin, in her book *The Hungry Self*, and Ann Kearney-Cooke, a therapist working with eating-disordered women, have argued that this dynamic produces considerable conflict for some daughters, who may feel torn between their own aspirations and their loyalty to the role model provided by their mothers. Weight preoccupation and disordered eating may represent an attempt to resolve this conflict. They allow the daughter who feels ambivalent about competing with her mother to be incompetent in one domain, and permit displaced expression of her complex feelings. Given that feeding provided the initial basis for a relationship between mother and daughter, eating and weight preoccupation may be a likely arena for later expression of mother/daughter dynamics.

The view that women compete with their mothers, to be and look better, also has been argued strongly. Rather than feeling ambivalent, many women feel challenged to do more than their moms—to "have it all" when they feel that their mothers didn't. Many of our patients express these feelings strongly.

Allison was employed by a large company started by her father. When he died suddenly, she was made president. Her mother worked in the company as an avocation, but mostly devoted herself to gardening and charities. Allison tried endlessly to outdo her mother. In fact, she was struggling to surpass both parents, being a better, more aggressive, more successful business leader than her father and a more stunning woman, more charming hostess, and more dedicated community leader than her mother. Her disordered eating was her secret solace—the one place where she could let go completely both in bingeing and purging. When her mother died, Allison realized the great price she had paid for the years of competing with her.

Or consider Fran, for whom a very different type of competitive dynamic was operating. In responding to our request to describe her mother, Fran wrote:

> My mother is in her early fifties. She is very accomplished, successful, and well respected in her field. She

has a Ph.D. in pharmacology and has tenure. She is very businesslike and conscious of her authoritative position.

My mother is very unemotional. She has a difficult time expressing her feelings. She is no longer sexually intimate with my father *at all*. However, she is my father's best friend.

My mother is proud of what she has accomplished. She struggled a lot; I believe that she turned off her emotions to survive. She had to prove herself to both my father and society.

Fran's self-description shows how she wants what her mother has, but more:

Most of all, I want to feel independent and secure without the "support" [her quotes] of a partner. However, in the future, I very much want to be close to a man.

In other words, she wants Mom's success, but without sacrificing the emotional, relational side of her life.

Competition for High Achievement

Women are feeling increasing pressures to compete their way to the top. The professional opportunities now afforded to women are long overdue, but they provide another arena where the competition trap gets played out. Cheryl, a witty, lively, and highly intelligent nineteen-year-old undergraduate, is a compelling case example.

"I cannot even imagine what it would be like to really fail," she repeatedly told us. "I think I would die," she attested. She had few close friends, which was hardly surprising since, for as long as she could remember, Cheryl wanted to be better than her friends. "I turned every cause into a challenge, and if I was less good at something than one of my friends, I would go home and practice."

Cheryl's childhood and early adolescence were notable for her achievements. Of superior intelligence, she was tracked early on with special classes for gifted students and graduated from high school at the age of sixteen. In addition, she was an accomplished ice skater and won several national competitions. She also excelled as a member of her high school's debating team, and played two musical instruments. Continually striving to be the perfect daughter, she secretly worried that her parents only loved her for her successes. Cheryl's parents' wallets bulged with news clippings of her various achievements, and she remembers endless family dinners where she was required to recount what she had accomplished that day, which teachers had praised her, and who else was doing well in her class. Cheryl's parents had both come from poor families and worked extremely hard to become successful. Her father in particular was "driven," something she admired in him tremendously. She always knew that she was his favorite of the three children, but was burdened by fears that she would lose her favored status if she were less successful. And her brother and sister always teased her about being "little goody two-shoes" or "Daddy's little girl."

Competitiveness like Cheryl's involves pursuing a standard based on the expectations or performance of others. Like Cheryl, many women appear driven to achieve both with respect to their own standards of excellence and to those established by the accomplishments of others. The stress of always trying so hard—of everything in the world being their responsibility—wears many women down. And for women, there is an intimate relationship between stress and eating. Competing creates so much pressure that they eat to salve their feelings. For such women, eating is a coping mechanism to deal with stress, but it becomes a self-defeating one.

Cheryl was frustrated to the point of despair that she couldn't control her weight. "It drives me crazy," Cheryl would lament. "I know that if I only work hard enough at it, I can be thin and gorgeous." She felt real self-hatred for her inability to stick with a program, which she took as a ridiculous failure. "After all," she exclaimed, "how hard can it be to follow a few rules about eating? If I can win national championships, why can't I follow-through with a diet?" She never saw the connection between her competitiveness and her bingeing.

Competition with Our Own Ideal

Perfectionism involves aspiring to an unreasonably high standard that you set for yourself. Sharon is a young woman we have studied since she entered Yale as a freshman. She is fiercely competitive and drives herself to perform—in the classroom and on the hockey field. While she competes intensely with other women—and men, too—her greatest adversary is herself. Her ideals for performance and appearance are so high, that she inevitably falls short. Over and over again. She is never satisfied with what she does or how she looks, because she is never as good as she thinks she should be.

Our studies show that women like Sharon—whose achievement ideals are unrealistically high and whose standards are unreasonably perfectionistic—are quite unhappy because they never feel they have done well enough. Women with perfectionistic standards and high expectations for personal performance also tend to be more dissatisfied with their own bodies and feel fatter—regardless of what they actually weigh—than less perfectionistic women. This is hardly surprising, since bodies are the central arena in which dissatisfaction with the self gets played out.

The consequences of competing against an ideal that is out of reach are evident early. A Boston psychologist, Catherine Steiner-Adair, has shown that adolescent girls whose personal goal is phrased in unattainable superlatives—famous actress, great beauty, fabulous wealth—tend to be the most eating-disordered girls in their age group. The non-eating-disordered girls had a similar picture of the ideal superwoman, but had set a more modest target for themselves. Goals are wonderful and desirable for teenagers, but too great a discrepancy between self and ideal creates problems related to eating and body issues.

Women with large discrepancies between self and ideal begin, surely by adolescence and possibly much sooner, to compete with their own ideal. In my clinical experience, I have seen women who weigh themselves before and after every meal to determine how much they can eat or whether they have eaten too much. Some women keep detailed charts of their waist, hips, and thigh measurements to monitor closely areas prone to fat. Most women emerge from this contest painfully aware of where they fall short, and are intensely self-critical of their perceived shortcomings. In many studies, researchers are unable to find even one woman who sees all of her body parts as matching her ideal.

Self-Complexity

People differ in the degree of complexity of their self-concept. Complexity is the number of different, *independent* features and feelings that we have about the self. Those who are complex have either more independent aspects in their representations or maintain greater distinctions among the various aspects. Take the test on page 121 to assess your self-complexity.

Low self-complexity fuels the competition trap. The more complex you are, that is, the more different ways you are able to think about yourself aside from your actual or wished-for weight and appearance, the more likely it is that you'll feel good about yourself. That means you're less likely to fall prey to the competition trap.

The reason is simple. With a more complex self-concept, an event that causes a change in feelings about one aspect of the self is less likely to spill over and change feelings about other aspects of yourself. So, for example, if something happens that makes you feel fatter, or less good-looking than the competition that day, you are protected from feeling devastated, if you have more areas of your self that are not closely tied to appearance. By having many different interests or roles and by maintaining clear distinctions between these various involvements, the impact of unfavorable information is localized. It is then much less likely that you will feel uniformly bad.

SELF-COMPLEXITY TEST

Consider how important each of the following dimensions is to your sense of self-worth. Give each item a rating between 1 and 10: If an item is of utmost importance to how you feel about yourself, give it a 10; if an item is of absolutely no importance to how you feel about yourself, give it a 1. Use the numbers in-between to reflect varying degrees of importance. You can use the numbers as often as you like (e.g., you can give more than one item a rating of 10).

_____ Feeling intelligent
_____ Having good friends
_____ Excelling at work or school
_____ Being at the right weight
_____ Being physically coordinated
_____ Being a good child
_____ Being altruistic
_____ Looking attractive
_____ Being creative
_____ Caring about social causes
_____ Having a romantic partner
_____ Doing well at athletic activities
_____ Being a good parent
_____ Being politically active
Others: (specify)

_____

_____

Examples of how people differ in self-complexity can be seen in the following self-descriptions, both taken from women who were asked to spend about five minutes writing about themselves:

> My mother was a compulsive eater. My father was an alcoholic. I am the product of a compulsive eater and an alcoholic.

The low degree of complexity is evident here. The patient saw herself only in the context of her parents and what they had made her. No other roles were salient, and her feelings about her appearance were bound up in this simple worldview.

The second case is also someone whose mother was a compulsive eater and dieter and father an alcoholic. Here is what she had to say about herself:

> I am twenty-four years old. I have lived for three years with my boyfriend and his brother. I work four days a week at Carvel and will be beginning an internship at a TV station next week for the summer.
>
> I've been bulimic for seven years and anorexic before that (I think). Up until I was about sixteen, I was overweight (150 pounds). I am obsessed with my weight, food, and dieting. I think about them constantly.
>
> I started and flunked out of college four times. I drank every day (night) for five years. I took my last drink September 12, 1989, after starting a day at work still drunk.
>
> I'm unhappy with myself, have one friend who doesn't like me very much, and feel like a worthless jerk a lot of the time. I stopped drinking on my own, but need help with my bulimia. I binge and purge every day (about.)

Although this is clearly the statement of someone who is highly disturbed, she has greater self-complexity than the patient in the first example. She also did not define herself in terms of her parents at all. Despite all her problems, her more differentiated sense of self provided some protective insulation and material for good work during therapy.

Studies by psychologist Patricia Linville at Duke University show that people with higher self-complexity experience less negative moods and fewer mood swings because negative feelings brought about by one aspect of the self do not tend to color feelings about other aspects. For example, a life crisis such as a divorce or failure at work will have a serious emotional impact on almost anyone. But a person high in self-complexity is more likely to be able to contain that impact, to maintain positive feelings about other aspects of his or her life. With too simple a self-structure, one does not have the buffer of other positive aspects of the self that remain intact.

Breaking the Competition Trap

The insight of this chapter is that all the striving may make the very things we are reaching for harder to attain. Being too perfectionistic, being too driven, being too competitive may not leave enough time and energy for other things. Sometimes our aspirations reflect unattainable pursuits, and being driven to achieve them is simply maladaptive. Even when success is attainable, women also need to spend their time and energy developing a fuller sense of themselves, which will give them confidence to develop their own rules and their own goals. So to free yourself from the competition trap, you have to learn to develop yourself more fully.

Define a number of aspects of yourself as important. Women who *value* a greater number of roles can more readily tolerate less than perfect achievement in any one. *The greater the number of roles in your life that you value, that seem important to you, the less any one can devastate your sense of self.*

Joe had defined himself as just a doctor and a fat boy. He now values many other aspects of himself—a skier, a parent, a friend and role model to younger men, and a car freak. He accomplished this first by identifying these areas as potentially mattering to him, and then choosing activities, experiences, and personal contacts that would make these self-aspects rewarding. For example, he developed his parent role by spending a lot more time with his children. He developed his skier role by giving himself permission to take "frivolous" ski holidays despite his busy schedule. By being more selves, he can feel good about himself. He's still trying to lose weight, but the compulsive quality is gone. It no longer has to all be off by tomorrow.

If you are like Joe, you may be using too much of your

competitive energies in the areas of thinness and appearance. Since your body isn't infinitely plastic, it may be easier to add other joys to life than to subtract pounds. Find new activities, add new roles that mean a lot. Go back over the roles listed on the Self-Complexity Test on page 121. See which ones you might try to develop more fully in yourself. It is possible to increase and nurture self-complexity in order to free yourself from the competition trap.

There's another benefit to expanding the number of roles you value. In general, multiple roles appear to be beneficial for many aspects of good health. It looks as though some "juggling" may be the best exercise of all. Of course, managing work, marriage, children, and hobbies influences the health of each woman differently, but a substantial amount of current social and biomedical research suggests that multiple roles are typically health-enhancing. It's more than just having them, however. It's how we experience our various roles. We must value and feel satisfied by the roles we occupy. They must give us some sense of control and satisfaction. Feelings of efficacy in many areas help free us from the competition trap.

But don't be too perfectionistic in trying to fulfill all these roles. Remember that studies show a very strong relationship between extreme perfectionism and weight preoccupation. In Sharon's case, perfectionism exacerbated her eating disorder, and got in the way of treatment. She found that unrealistic goals made her unduly hard on herself and resulted in turning to food for solace. She needed to learn to set realistic standards in all aspects of her life. Each morning, she made a list of what she expected to accomplish that day. You might want to try this, too. Sharon's list revealed the excessive demands she made on herself. She worked to set more reasonable goals, and found them difficult and disappointing at first. She imagined that other people would reprimand her for not achieving enough. As part of her treatment, we did some role playing. Sharon played herself and I played the others, demanding, cajoling, always asking for more. By talking back to me, defending herself from the unrealistic expectations, Sharon gradually came to demand less of herself.

Highly perfectionistic women, not just those with eating disorders, have trouble setting reasonable limits on their own expectations. If this is you, try imagining your worst-case scenario. Who will you be disappointing if you try a little less hard? If it's yourself, find other rewards besides perfect appearance and performance. If it's others, try the role-playing technique I used with Sharon, either with a close friend or by playing the several parts yourself.

Try to uncover what drives your need to achieve and to compete. By exploring the meanings of achievement and competition, Cheryl learned that she was driven by a fear of failure that left her unable to acknowledge, let alone enjoy, her achievements. For several weeks, she was asked to identify three things she accomplished each day to help her focus on her extraordinary productivity. We needed to challenge Cheryl's "scale of comparison" and make her see that she was competing with an unrealistic ideal. Like many gifted students on a campus populated with valedictorians and SAT champions, it was difficult for Cheryl to appreciate her achievements, since they appeared "ordinary." Cheryl needed to see the diversity of skills and talents that lies beneath the seemingly uniform performance of Ivy League college students. We encouraged her to share with a few close friends her fears of failure, an exercise which helped her realize that her feelings were not unusual.

Perhaps most central, though, was the exploration of Cheryl's beliefs about the importance of competition in the pursuit of excellence. While there is no denying that competitiveness may motivate us to work hard, Cheryl pushed this to an extreme. Any effort that did not leave her feeling frazzled, anxious, and "stressed to the limit" was deemed inadequate and likely to lead to failure. As a result, she never pursued a goal without experiencing intense stress, the emotional state which triggered her overeating. With our help, Cheryl worked hard to set more realistic goals for herself. An occasional B in a course became acceptable, and she aimed for a few close friends rather than widespread popularity. Cheryl also realized that allowing herself to relax and to enjoy life did not result in what she feared so much: that she would turn into a "lazy bum." Her school performance improved, in fact.

For Beatrice, the competition trap drove her to make invidious comparisons between her own appearance and that of other women. We asked her to keep a diary of her thoughts whenever she found herself doing this. In evaluating her record, she learned that her comparisons were inevitably negative to herself. She would focus her attention only on those aspects of other women's appearance that were superior to her own, never acknowledging her own physical characteristics that were attractive. Furthermore, it became clear that she was applying harsher standards when judging herself than when evaluating another person. For example, she conceded that her friend Lisa was mildly overweight and had a flabby stomach, though she quickly added that Lisa's condition was understandable, considering that she had given birth to three children. Beatrice refused to make any such allowances in her own case. Worse yet, Beatrice expected others to dislike her on the basis of her lesser attractiveness. It is not surprising that she felt tense and anxious in most social situations. Once she recognized this self-defeating pattern, she was able to challenge her previous assumptions and develop specific plans for how to deal differently with social occasions.

For example, with our help she began to question the assertion that her acquaintances and friends thought negatively of her because of her overweight. From Beatrice's accounts of her relationships, it was quite clear that people actually liked her a lot and that she was a valued source of support to many of her friends. We also helped her go into these social situations with a plan for distracting herself from making comparisons or evaluations based on physical appearance by setting herself a specific task. For example, for a party at her tennis club, Beatrice prepared a set of questions she was going to weave into her conversations with three different people. The questions were different for each of the three acquaintances and each question was tailored to the unique situation of that person. Thus, Beatrice had to concentrate on asking the questions, which forced her to divert her attention away from her obsessive thinking about appearance. This exercise was so effective that Beatrice adopted it as a regular strategy for parties. "I got so involved in my conversations with these people that I forgot to worry about my looks. What was even more amazing was that I forgot to obsess over what to eat and what foods to avoid. I had a great time!"

Many problems involve competition with your own ideal, in other words, the degree to which you feel pained by the discrepancy between what you are and what you would like to be. The strategies I have described will help you develop an ideal self-image that represents a more realistic possibility. In that case, an ideal self-image can be adaptive and a source of motivation and goal direction. Attaining an aspect of the ideal self-image may engender feelings of pride, satisfaction, and pleasure that might then serve as incentives for the pursuit of future goals.

—5—

The Food Trap

"Twenty or thirty years ago, sex was the secret subject of women. Now it's food." In fact, in the minds of many women, sex and food have become interchangeable. "I like the feel of food. I don't like knives and forks because I like to touch it all over," says one woman. Another comments, "I think it is erotic. It's safe sex. I mean, it's the safest sex you can have, eating." And for some women, food is even better than sex. According to one, "I'm still looking for a man who excites me as much as a baked potato." With the national release last year of Henry Jaglom's film *Eating* from which these quotes are taken, women's obsessive and ambivalent relationship with food may be coming out into the open at last. For women, food is emotionally evocative, profound in its impact, and full of multiple layers of meaning.

Says another woman in Jaglom's film, "Food is the only thing that I can count on for unconditional love. Food is the only thing that will comfort me and love me and be good to me. I can open the refrigerator anytime and feel good twenty-four hours a day." Food is a powerful form of self-nurturance, a way of being good to ourselves when no one and nothing else seems good enough. Many women use food to salve bad feelings, usually in secret and furtively. A woman in the Jaglom film comments, "When I wasn't eating, there was a big black hole inside of me." Food fills us up, figuratively and actually. But we hardly ever overeat in public because our eating is shameful. Don't we want to look good? How dare we eat a piece of cake without feeling guilty?

Even studying food has demanded apologetic comment. As M.F.K. Fisher, the noted food writer, says in her book *The Art of Eating*:

> People ask me: Why do you write about food, and eating and drinking? Why don't you write about the struggle for power and security, and about love, the way others do?
>
> They ask it accusingly, as if it were somehow gross, unfaithful to the honor of my craft.
>
> The easiest answer is to say that, like most other humans, I am hungry. But there is more than that. It seems to me that our three basic needs, for food and security and love, are so mixed and mingled and entwined that we cannot straightly think of one without the others. So it happens that when I write of hunger, I am really writing about love and hunger for it . . . and then the warmth and richness and fine reality of hunger satisfied . . . and it is all one.

In one of many poignant moments in the Jaglom film, the women, who are there to celebrate three birthdays, pass the same plate of cake around two or three times—no one willing or maybe daring enough to take the piece of cake. That is until the bulimics sneak upstairs to devour slice after slice. If having a good body means giving up food, then our longing for food and the many needs it fulfills are in conflict with our desire for the right look. Daily, this battle is waged for most women who berate themselves endlessly with every extra morsel. Another Jaglom woman describes: "Every time I open the refrigerator, I think *what* are you going to *eat*? You're not going to eat *again*, are you? You better be careful."

Many women's desperate, erotic, and shameful love/hate relationship with food may be the most devastating of the body traps. Who among us is fully immune? But how has the trap grown to be a monster, enveloping us, our insatiable appetites raging as we struggle to control them?

First, food is laden with meaning. Eating is associated with our earliest feelings of love and security. A casserole or cookie that has connections with our childhood, a holiday bread or pudding, a cheese discovered on our first trip abroad. All are flavored with meaning and emotions not to be found on the list of ingredients. As one respondent to a survey about the uses of food reported:

> No one is too old for comfort food. In fact, the older one gets, the more poignant becomes the memory of one's childhood securities: mother's oatmeal, mother's raisin bread pudding, mother's creamy mashed potatoes, mother's milk.

Food means comfort and caring. For Penny, like many women, gooey desserts convey those feelings best. In her family, feeding someone was a way of showing love, and her fondest childhood memories were of the smells and tastes of family dinners. It's no wonder Penny turns to food now to cheer herself up when she's down, to fill the time when she's bored, and to make her own children happy. When she's dieting, she feels like she's lost her best friend, her major source of comfort and support.

The extraordinary range of emotional functions that food serves for most women is striking. Take the test on page 131 to see how your emotions and eating are intertwined.

Food is also inextricably related to a vast array of human activities beyond feelings. Poets and painters, in their role as social commentators, have been saying this for centuries. Their works speak eloquently of the intimate relationship between person and food. Mystical rites, funerals, acts of celebration and of sacrifice always involve food as part of the ceremony. Public occasions are celebrated with banquets, business deals are forged over lavish lunches, family ties are cemented at Christmas dinner, and love is supposedly kindled by an intimate dinner à deux.

EMOTIONAL EATING TEST

	Often	Sometimes	Rarely
1. Do you have a desire to eat when you are irritated?	____	____	____
2. Do you have a desire to eat when you are depressed or discouraged?	____	____	____
3. Do you have a desire to eat when you are feeling lonely?	____	____	____
4. Do you have a desire to eat when somebody lets you down?	____	____	____
5. Do you have a desire to eat when you are angry?	____	____	____
6. Do you have a desire to eat when something unpleasant is about to happen?	____	____	____
7. Do you have a desire to eat when you are anxious, worried, or tense?	____	____	____
8. Do you have a desire to eat when things are going against you or have gone wrong?	____	____	____
9. Do you have a desire to eat when you are frightened?	____	____	____
10. Do you have a desire to eat when you are disappointed?	____	____	____
11. Do you have a desire to eat when you are emotionally upset?	____	____	____

Score a response of *Often* as a 2, *Sometimes* as 1, and *Rarely* as 0. If your score is 17 or higher, eating is related to many of your feelings and emotions.

NOTE: This test is a part of the Emotional Eating Scale which is one part of the Dutch Eating Behavior Questionnaire, along with the External Eating Scale and the Restrained Eating Scale (T. van Strien, J.E.R. Frijters, G.P.A. Bergers, and P.B. Defares, *Nederlandse vragenlijst voor eetgedrag [NVE]* [Lisse: Swets & Zeitlinger B.V., 1987]).

The renowned French writer and statesman Brillat-Savarin said, "Tell me what you eat and I will tell you who you are." He believed that the foods we like reveal something of our inner selves. The boldness of spicy, pungent foods, the mellowness of warm, steamy puddings, the moodiness of sweet-and-sour combinations—all these tell a tale about those who eat them.

Food also has mood-altering chemical properties and health-promoting effects. What was once viewed as old wives' tales and folklore about food is now turning up on the pages of leading medical journals each week. The evidence for the medicinal effects of some foods seems unassailable. In fact, food may be the most accessible, legal form of self-medication around. But here too lurks a trap.

Sally calls herself a chocolate addict. She wonders why she craves sweets so much, and often more as the day wears on or around menstruation. She's using sweets as a form of self-medication, to give her an energy boost, and to alter her mood. Her body chemistry seems to need the "fix."

Foods are not magic bullets. Biochemically, they're far more complex than drugs, and the same foods seem to have different effects in different people as a function of genetics, dietary history, and body fat. We have imbued food with too much significance in our battle against heart disease, cancer, and other major killers. Words like cholesterol, fiber, and sugar no longer just represent aspects of nutrition. They have taken on moral overtones. They are not just good or bad for us. Now they indicate how good or bad we are. We're competitive about what we cut out and what we have added. It makes good cocktail party ("Please, just a Perrier for me") conversation. Yet, the public seems more confused than ever about which foods are good for them and what they are good for. And the foods thought to be bad for us are imputed with causing not only physical diseases, but behavior problems like hyperactivity and even crime. All the conflicting information about the effects of food sets up another part of the food trap.

The final dimension of the food trap arises because the body doesn't seem to treat all foods the same way. Despite earlier medical views, we now know that all calories are not created equal. This is even true within subclasses of nutrients: For example, not all sugars affect appetite and eating the same way. Further, the taste of food is controlled by many factors, only one of which is the actual chemical property of the food itself. Time of day, your own energy needs, and what you just ate all profoundly influence how something tastes to you. So, despite what we typically believe, there may be few intrinsic properties of foods that do indeed make them "good" or "bad," tasty or neutral. Much more important is what we bring with us to the table.

Let's explore these various food traps, to see which you have fallen prey to and what you can do about it.

The Many Meanings of Food

The simple truth is that everyone needs adequate and safe nutrition. We must eat to live and we want to eat better in the hope that it will improve our health. But food means far more than mere survival. The multiple meanings and functions of food set the first part of the trap.

The connection between women and food is deep and primitive. Women are defined as nurturers and carry out this role most obviously through feeding. In addition, women themselves *are* food for their children during pregnancy and lactation, intensifying their identification with food and its relevance as a symbol. Melinda, a homemaker with three children, loved being pregnant. She felt fulfilled by providing food unambiguously for the child she was carrying. It was the only time her love of food felt unembarrassing—because she was providing nourishment to another who was unable to do without her. It was the only time she totally enjoyed being a woman.

In many cultures, as among ancient and modern Aztecs in Mexico, women are associated with the fertility of the earth and its bounty. Women are almost universally responsible for food preparation and in many cultures for production and distribution as well. It is therefore not surprising that food preparation has provided an important channel for female self-expression, although the specific messages conveyed have varied throughout history and across cultures.

According to the anthropologist Mary Douglas, modern Western women's strong concern to control their food intake is a metaphor for their efforts to control their own bodies and destinies in a culture that makes self-control a moral imperative. Many women use eating as a way to assert autonomy and control—first against their mothers and later their spouses. But it traps them into a process of reactance and self-denial at the same time. Again, the double-binding nature of body traps is apparent. The benefits of feeling in control are real—assertiveness, autonomy, and most likely, thinness, too. But the negative consequences are tangible as well, and often quite damaging—feelings of hunger, denying the need for comfort, and self-nurturance. As Susan recalled: "I could always infuriate my mother by not eating. Now it gets to Frank [her husband] in the same way. It gives me an extraordinary feeling of power. But I'd be lying if I didn't admit that I miss the Thanksgiving pig-out and the feeling of being part of the family fun and closeness."

Henry Jaglom, the writer/director of *Eating*, acknowledges that his movie isn't just about eating. "Food becomes a metaphor for how difficult it is to be a woman in this society. Women are told from childhood, by their mothers, their fathers, their men, their friends, their culture—how to feel about themselves. I don't think men understand the complexity." I don't think they do, either. My closest male friend, when I talk about the poignant, tortured women I see, sometimes seems to get it. But sometimes he says, impatiently, "I just don't understand it. If they want to lose weight, why can't they just stop eating?" Why, indeed!

Food and Feelings

The *Radcliffe College Quarterly* devoted one of its issues to "America's Romance with Food." Alumnae were asked to name their "comfort foods," with the following question: "When someone has been mean to you and everything is going wrong; when you are tired and too hot or too cold; when you are bored or overwhelmed or stuck, what foods help put things right again?" It's fascinating that it seems so reasonable to ask which foods salve feelings rather than whether foods actually are capable of doing so. The answers reflect the depth of women's emotional relationship to food. As one respondent reported:

> In our family, the first resort in times of stress, sickness, and other temporary afflictions is tapioca pudding. Nothing gladdens our hearts so much as a bowl of smooth, easy-to-swallow, snow-white tapioca with a dollop of strawberry jam in the middle of the dish.
>
> Eating tapioca has the comfort and security of the familiar—my mother made it for me, and I made it for my children; now my children make it for their children and husbands.
>
> Are you sick? Are you sad? Try a spoonful of this sweet, soothing confection, and be comforted.

Most women turn to eating in times of stress. It can be sweet and tender or tough and chewy—it's there for you to choose.

Beatrice graphically describes her choice: "When I'm stressed, I need to chew, to ravage my food; my mouth aches with longing. Only eating numbs me, like an anesthetic, it stops the pain. When I feel good, I'm rarely hungry." Binge eating for Beatrice and many other women may arise as part of a motivated attempt to escape from self-awareness in order to avoid the real causes of their stress and anxiety. Is any other form of comfort as accessible and as under our control as food? Probably not.

For women, food is a friend. "It feels like there's life in the house, like someone to come home to," says a woman in the film *Eating,* and another, one of the birthday celebrants, says defiantly, "It's my birthday and I can eat anything I choose." What greater gift could a woman give herself! It doesn't talk back, it makes no demands. "It's just there to please me," one of the my patients confides. According to still another respondent to the Radcliffe survey:

> Of the many nutritional staffs of life I have leaned upon, one of the most evocative and satisfying has been my relationship to bread. Since I can remember, breads have nurtured and sustained me, grounded and tantalized me with their variety and substance.

Eating is a way of loving yourself. The famous personality theorist at Harvard, Henry Murray, argued that people use food to provide themselves with psychological nurturance— to comfort, support, and reward. Food is the one form of self-nurturance that is accessible to everyone, except those who live in abject poverty. Few of life's pleasures are so readily available, to have when we want. Yet, fashion and society dictate that slimness is beauty, requiring us not to eat when we want to, taking away our ability to nurture ourselves freely.

Take the test on pages 137 to 138 to find out the types of self-nurturance that you are most likely to use.

Everyone uses food as a form of self-nurturance to some extent. It is part of our essence and our cultural imperative. To some degree, food is associated with our very identity. The noted psychiatrist Erik Erikson states: ". . . the newborn infant . . . lives through, and loves with his mouth, and the mother

SELF-NURTURANCE TEST

Please indicate how much the following statements are true of you.

	Not at all	*Somewhat*			*Extremely*
1. I like to celebrate when something wonderful happens to me.	1	2	3	4	5
2. I like to treat myself as special when I am hurt or sick.	1	2	3	4	5
3. I like to say things that will increase my self-confidence.	1	2	3	4	5
4. I like to have a special meal or treat when something good happens to me.	1	2	3	4	5
5. I like to be generous with myself.	1	2	3	4	5
6. I like to treat myself with kindness.	1	2	3	4	5
7. I like to cheer myself up with something to eat when something bad happens to me.	1	2	3	4	5
8. I like to forgive myself when I make a mistake.	1	2	3	4	5
9. I like to provide myself with a great deal of comfort.	1	2	3	4	5

10. I like to eat something when I feel down or unhappy.	1	2	3	4	5
11. I like to give myself my favorite foods when I am hurt or sick.	1	2	3	4	5
12. I like to give myself a great deal of encouragement in whatever I try to achieve.	1	2	3	4	5

First, add your scores on items 4, 7, 10, and 11. A score of 16 or more means you typically use food as a way to take care of yourself. Then add your scores on the remaining items (1, 2, 3, 5, 6, 8, 9, 12). Divide your score by 2, since there were twice as many questions here. A score of 16 or more means you find many ways to be good to yourself that do not involve food. Put your food self-nurturance score over your nonfood self-nurturance score. If the ratio is greater than 1, you may be trapped by using food to take care of yourself, too much more than in other ways.

---

lives through, and loves with, her breasts or whatever parts of her countenance and body convey eagerness to provide what he needs. . . . To him the mouth is the focus of a general first approach to life." But for many women, it gets perverted. Food swamps their whole identity. The *way* they eat is *who* they are. And that's a trap.

Cindy doesn't know who she is except as she relates to food. She views herself as "the chocaholic," the "food freak," the binger. When asked to describe herself in other ways, she has trouble thinking of a more accurate self-description. And while most of us can also nurture ourselves in ways not related to food, Cindy cannot. But you can get into trouble (meaning a ratio greater than 1 on the test you just took) in two ways: Either your food self-nurturance score can be unusually high relative to your other ways of self-nurturance; or your nonfood self-nurturing may be unusually low.

Our studies using these tests found that Cindy and many other bulimic women derive a far smaller proportion of their self-nurturance from activities that are not related to food than do many of their peers who do not have eating disorders. In what appears to be an impoverished self-nurturing environment, food has come to serve too central a role for the bulimic.

Caroline was different from Cindy but still had problems around food and nurturance. Unlike Cindy, she took care of herself reasonably well in nonfood ways, but she used food to excess—to comfort, reward, praise, and befriend herself. She talks about "grazing" in the kitchen when she gets home from a date if she isn't treated as well as she expected. Being good to herself means eating something she loves when other forms of love just don't seem enough.

Food often stands in for sexual feelings. In two surveys done for the Weight Watchers organization, married men were studied in 1989 and married women in 1988. Women often overate to create "physical distance" from their mates—avoiding sex because they felt their weight made them unattractive—while gorging to satisfy unmet needs for emotional nurturing. Many women feel that eating is their key to emotional survival. "Some girls have husbands and boyfriends and lovers . . . and I have rye bread and cream cheese," says a woman in Jaglom's film. Family therapists Richard Stuart and Barbara Jacobson in their book, *Weight, Sex and Marriage*, found that women use food if they don't get enough hugs and love. One of our patients described it well. "When my boyfriend leaves, I rush for the refrigerator, to fill up the empty parts he never can reach."

The Weight Watchers survey of men a year earlier found a nearly opposite pattern: About two thirds of the men said their libido was stronger than their wives', so they ate to console themselves. Nearly two-thirds reported eating to sublimate their erotic feelings—a reaction to the loss of sexual freedom that comes with marriage. Three of five ate to relieve stress caused by the financial pressures of family life. Just over half found food a way to avoid having intimate talks. Clearly, men and women differ greatly even in the sexual uses of food.

Food and Culture

Almost all social occasions involve eating. Breaking bread together is a sign of friendship and good faith. No celebration would be complete without food. In most religions and cultures, funeral ceremonies all begin or conclude with a feast, a symbolic gesture that life does go on. The sharing of food establishes communion and connection in all cultures. Groups as diverse as the hunting-gathering San of southern Africa, the Sharanahua Indians of the Peruvian Amazon, and rural Sardinians make food-sharing the very definition of who is considered a member of the family.

Food taboos help to socialize an individual as a member of his community. Every cultural system restricts consumption of certain animal and plant foods. Moslems, and Jews who keep kosher, must avoid pork, for example. Food prohibitions serve as markers of membership. Their significance lies in placing a boundary on social action beyond which members of this particular group cannot go, knowing quite well that others can. So food becomes one of the ways you define yourself as a member of a given group.

To some extent, these food restrictions and rules of cuisine are arbitrary. They have to do with the belief systems and value-structures of a particular society. For example, foods viewed as disgusting are rejected because of the idea of what they are, and not necessarily because of their sensory properties or because they are dangerous.

We find eating ants, grubs or worms disgusting, but they are readily eaten by the Chinese. Paul Rozin, a psychologist at the University of Pennsylvania, showed that American adults will not even eat a bowl of soup that's been stirred by a brand-new fly swatter, because the *idea* of flies makes the soup disgusting. Some food takes on its positive or negative properties as a function of who has come in contact with it, again showing the intimate connection between people and food. The anthropologist Anna Meigs, of MacAllister College in Minnesota, did her field work among the Hua people of New Guinea. For the Hua, the vital essence of a person, the

— 140 —

nu, extends into all the things he or she interacts with. The food one has grown, shot, killed, or cooked contains some of one's vital essence. For the Hua, food is nourishing when it contains the *nu* of those in a positive relation to the eater, whereas the food can harm if it holds the *nu* of those in a potentially hostile relation to the eater. In other societies, a chief might have to eat special foods to acquire important properties of leadership. An extreme example is the Yoruba king in Africa who has to consume the heart of his predecessor.

Perhaps more surprisingly, even modern-day American college students unknowingly hold the magical belief that you are what you eat. Paul Rozin and his colleague Carol Nemeroff made up names of imaginary tribes and described them to groups of students. For example, they told of the "Chandorans" who hunted for marine turtles and wild boar. Half the students were led to believe that the Chandorans only ate the boar; the other half thought the Chandorans only ate the turtles. They were then asked to describe the people of Chandor, using a checklist of traits provided by the investigators. To evaluate the implications of the traits selected, Rozin and Nemeroff asked a different group of students to rate the physical and personality traits of wild boar and the turtles. Almost all the traits ascribed to the animals by this group of students were also attributed to the people who ate them by the first group of participants. For example, the turtle-eating tribe was considered better swimmers, and boar eaters more aggressive. Even we who are on the threshold of the twenty-first century seem to believe that people take on the characteristics of what they eat, though we would probably laugh at this view if we were merely asked whether or not we hold it.

Foods as "Medicine"

A second part of the food trap has to do with the truths and myths about the chemical effects of foods.

Food as Drugs

There's been a clear shift in the last five years from diet books to books about nutrition, all promising good health and longer life. Whether you want to lower your cholesterol, raise your child's IQ, or protect yourself from low-level radiation, there's a book to tell you which foods can do it for you. We believe in special-purpose foods. *American Health* magazine once headlined: LOBSTER FOR ROMANCE. SALADS FOR POWER. Different types of foods are promoted for all sorts of functions—sexual prowess, intelligence, concentration, to name a few.

Thinking that certain foods have a unique function is nothing new. This has been true through the ages. Montezuma believed that chocolate was a source of strength and an aphrodisiac. According to legend, he would drink a golden goblet full of the frothing liquid before entering his harem. In the Middle Ages, rosemary was thought to have the power to prevent bad dreams. What is new is that now each of these claims is supported by scientific assertions about the biochemical effects of the food on bodily functions. For example, scientists have now found that chocolate contains small amounts of phenylthylamine, a chemical naturally produced in the brain that appears to increase when people fall in love.

Two Gallup Organization surveys conducted for *American Health* magazine support the view that people are practicing "situational nutrition." We change our habitual eating patterns to meet the needs of different situations and we know—or think we know—which foods will boost athletic performance, sharpen our wits for business meetings, or put us in the mood for romance. We eat quite differently now from the way we ate even twenty years ago. We have even greater expectations of food than our parents did and a good many different notions about what food can do for us. Indeed, foods have become a fundamental player in all our health promotion efforts. Today, food companies are increasingly developing and marketing products with "pro-active" health claims, meaning that these foods promise to enhance health, not only to prevent disease. "Pro-active health claims are the hottest

food-selling tool today," said Martin Friedman, the editor of
Gorman's *New Product News*, a trade publication. "The fantasy
is a pro-active grab-it, zap-it, gulp-it health product. The big
companies are looking at everything from folkloric food cures
to ancient Chinese botanicals."

Even our youngest children are aware that certain foods
can be "good" or "bad" for you. In a study conducted at a local
preschool, we asked three- and four-year-old children to pack
two lunches for themselves from an array of foods available
on a large table. Each child, tested individually, was given a
Mr. Happy Face lunch box and told to fill it with a lunch that
was "healthy and good for you" and a Mr. Yuk Face lunch box,
for packing a bad and unhealthful lunch.

Children as young as three years old had some very clear
ideas. Fruits and vegetables always went into the "healthy"
box. When one of the children chose an orange as healthful,
the interviewer asked why. "Because it says Sunkist on it," the
child replied. Foods with sugar were generally seen as "bad
for you," although many couldn't say why. One child thought
foods with sugar "are less bad for your health if you eat them
after dinner." Some thought cheese was good, others thought
it was bad because it had too much fat, even though according
to one child, "It doesn't look fat the way my daddy does."
Although the children clearly didn't understand all the health
aspects of food, most could identify not only the inherent
healthful or nonhealthful characteristics of the food, but also
were already aware of its supposed healthful or unhealthful
effects.

Julia Child reminisces about the good old days before we
worried about the health effects of what we ate:

> Then you pounded and whisked in masses of thick fresh
> cream—the more cream, the lighter and finer the mousse.
> Nobody gave a thought to the mounds of heavy cream
> that went into cooking, or how many eggs, or how many
> hundred grams of the best butter. Those were the halcyon
> days for gormandizing.

Now "they" are afraid of their food, especially of red

— 143 —

meat and dairy products. As a cookery writer one feels almost uneasy about suggesting . . . butter . . . or hesitant to specify more than a tablespoon or two of heavy cream.

Being afraid of one's food conjures a world of bean sprouts and tofu moistened with safflower oil. (We had a safflower-addict house-sitter one winter, and to this day I've never been able to scrape all the stuff off the stove top. If safflower oil does that to a stove, what in the world does it do to the intestinal tract?)

Now foods and food products such as oat bran and omega-three fish oils are being invoked in our efforts to prevent heart disease. Since reports in the *Journal of the American Medical Association* that oat bran can lower blood cholesterol about 20 percent—as much as most drugs—we've been bombarded with new oat bran–containing products. Even my bagels come heavily dosed with oat bran now. Although new studies challenge these earlier claims about the efficacy of oat bran in preventing heart disease, few experts doubt that it is an important component of a healthful diet.

Oat bran is one of several foods that constitute dietary fiber, which is now thought important to prevent digestive-tract cancers. Actually, there's no clear definition of dietary fiber, but in general, it's all those parts of plants that are resistant to digestion by the enzymes of humans. Physicians as early as Hippocrates observed: "To the human body it makes a great difference whether the bread be made of fine flour or coarse, whether of wheat with the bran or without the bran."

Dr. Fergus Clysdale, chairman of the Department of Nutrition at the University of Massachusetts, Amherst, worries, however, that people cannot eat the amount of fiber currently being recommended—37 grams daily—unless they consume a prodigious number of calories. In fact, he joked in his comments at a recent meeting that people would probably get more fiber by eating the boxes most of their high-in-oat-bran cereals come in than by eating the cereal inside.

While the oat-bran craze is relatively recent, knowledge about the potential importance of reducing fat in foods for heart disease has been around for a long time. The Pritikin diet, and other low-fat, semivegetarian diet plans were all aimed at using changing food habits to help fight heart disease. What's new, and quite significant, is that scientists now believe that some fats may be good for you, like olive oil and omega-three fish oils, clearing plaques from the coronary arteries. It is being suggested that with dietary changes alone, up to half of people with serious blockage may avoid bypass surgery and angioplasty. So now people need to worry about including the good fats and getting rid of the bad ones, and keeping the whole thing straight.

Charles has been following research on fats for years. His father and grandfather both died of heart attacks in their fifties and he's panicked about following in their footsteps. He's switched from safflower oil to olive oil, but with guilt and misgivings. He still can't figure out how all fat can have the same calories when some kinds are bad and others good. The labels in supermarkets and health claims of low-fat brands confuse him further, and now he worries that he'll get a heart attack from the stress of trying to stay healthy.

Our *patterns* of eating may also be important in the fight against heart disease, according to an article in the *New England Journal of Medicine* by Dr. David Jenkins from the Department of Nutritional Sciences at the University of Toronto in Canada. He gave healthy volunteers two identical diets, where they ate the same food either as three meals or as seventeen snacks given hourly. Each diet was followed for two weeks and all men received both types. They found that LDL (the bad) cholesterol was lowered by increasing meal frequency alone, with no change in the nature or amount of food eaten.

I am not advocating a nibbling diet, since many people would not be able to maintain it without increasing their overall caloric intake. In the Jenkins study, calories were tightly controlled and none of the men gained weight. But the general principle seems important: Eating more, rather than less, frequently may be beneficial in our continuing efforts to control heart disease.

Foods are now being widely used in the fight against cancer, too. An epidemiologist at the Johns Hopkins University School of Public Health, Dr. Marilyn Menkes, wrote a widely cited article in the *New England Journal of Medicine*. She studied people who developed squamous cell carcinoma—the most common lung cancer among smokers—and found that people with low levels of beta carotene were much more likely to develop this form of cancer. Beta carotene appears to be an antioxidant in the body, fighting chemicals called free radicals that attack healthy cells. She and other researchers have estimated that eating only one carrot's worth of beta carotene daily might cut the risk of developing lung cancer in half, especially among former smokers.

Cabbage consistently turns up on the list of dietary preferences of people with lower rates of certain cancers—notably stomach and colon. From epidemiologic studies, some scientists are suggesting that eating a diet high in cruciferous vegetables (cabbage, broccoli, cauliflower), deep-orange fruits and vegetables (cantaloupe, yams, carrots), and dark-green leafy vegetables (kale and spinach) may lower the risk of various types of cancer.

The trap stems from the attendant misconception that foods cure. Foods are not drugs, which are often simple compounds aimed at a particular target. And foods don't work the same way in every person. Genetic factors determine how food is metabolized and digested. It's also possible that the same foods that protect against one type of disease may increase the risk of a different type. For example, omega-three fatty acids gotten from eating fatty fish such as salmon or tuna appear to be cardioprotective because they lower triglycerides, raise HDL (the good type of cholesterol) levels, and hinder blood-clotting mechanisms. But heavy doses of oils from fish may harm diabetics, and could cause the blood of some people to run too thin.

While a glass of wine or beer a day may boost HDL (the good) cholesterol, new studies from the Framingham Heart Project, a continuing analysis of 1,968 men and 2,505 women ages seventeen to ninety living in Framingham, Massachusetts, suggest that even a drink or two a day puts middle-aged men at risk for an oversized heart. An oversized heart is linked to the development of abnormal heartbeats and forces the main pumping chamber to work harder. The greater the enlargement, the greater the risk of heart failure and death. While the effect appears smaller in women, there's increasing scientific evidence that the same amount of alcohol may increase the risk of breast cancer. So even here—where foods now seem to play an important part in preventive medicine—there's a body trap.

Try to avoid the hype. Too much of anything can be harmful, even when it appears to be a nutritious food. The ever-increasing numbers of nutrition books making magical claims are not for you, tempting as they may be.

Part of the food trap arises because these conflicting recommendations are making people hopelessly confused about what foods are good for them. Yesterday, cholesterol was bad for your heart; today, scientists are no longer sure. Some people, like Charles, change their diet with every new pronouncement by the medical and scientific community. Others have frankly given up, arguing that what's good for you today will be found to be bad for you tomorrow, so why bother. There's a kernel of truth in their argument, since scientific knowledge about nutrition and its effects on health, mind, and body, is expanding rapidly. It's hard to open a newspaper or magazine without seeing some new finding just reported at a scientific meeting or in a professional journal, which purports to dramatically change something we once thought about the foods we eat. Even something as sacred as fluoride in our drinking water is getting a second look, with new evidence on its cancer-causing potential released by the United States government in early 1990. As scientists, we worry a lot about whether this heavy media coverage is helping or merely confusing most people. Often, it merely confuses and worries the public. Take food labeling and the rise of genetically engineered foods, for example.

Scientific knowledge about nutrition began being used systematically to inform the public when the government began publishing the Recommended Dietary Allowances, or RDAs. RDAs represent the best estimate of nutrient needs arrived at by a select committee of distinguished nutritionists—the Food and Nutrition Board of the National Academy of Sciences. The newest RDAs were published in 1989. The values are designed to meet the needs of most of the population, but the establishment of definitive requirement for everyone is not possible. While they hold reasonably well for many adults, they are inaccurate for children, teenagers, and older individuals.

But what does it mean to look at a food label and see that the product provides one hundred or one thousand times the daily RDA for that particular vitamin or mineral? Should we be glad, or feel anxious? For most things, it's probably OK, although no one really knows for sure. But for some vitamins, like vitamin A, too large a dose is potentially harmful.

Food labels are now required by law in the United States for most processed products. They are intended to serve as a guide to consumers in evaluating the nutritional quality of food products. But surveys by consumer groups show that the public does not understand how to use them, and some actually find the information worrisome. With new legislation likely to increase both the types of foods that are labeled and the amount of information on the labels, many scientists and food industry employees alike are afraid that people will increasingly "turn off."

Many new products, such as fat substitutes, are now possible because scientists are using their knowledge of genetic engineering to develop new foods. Not only will they be able to make tasty foods with no calories, but they will make foods that taste better—fresher, sweeter, crunchier, whatever. The genes that actually create the various foodstuffs are beginning to be understood, making all sorts of manipulations and variations possible.

While this may sound like the ideal solution to everyone's wildest food fantasy, critics of the procedure abound. Genetic engineering, even of plants, make some people think of increased cancer risk. Some new products lead to depletion of certain essential vitamins and minerals. For example, Olestra, one of the new synthetic fats, may rob the body of its vitamin E supply. Scientists will continue this debate, but unfortunately, the public is likely to continue to get more confused and uncertain about the safety of its food supply.

Food and Mood Control

From "sugar buzz" to "sugar blues," popular lore runs the gamut in its views of how carbohydrates affect our feelings and behavior.

Diet, Crime and Hyperactivity Over the years, theories relating sugar to both antisocial behavior and hyperactivity have become widespread. Once relegated to books and articles aimed at food faddists, such theories are now widely discussed at scientific meetings and are found in books and articles aimed at personnel in the correction and criminal justice systems, and at schools and parents.

The belief that sugar has a major influence on criminal behavior has already made its way into the courtroom. The most famous example of this was the "Twinkie" defense in the Dan White murder trial. Dan White was a former San Francisco supervisor who went to the City Hall with a loaded gun, climbed through a window to avoid a metal detector, and then killed both Mayor George Moscone and Supervisor Harvey Milk.

On the surface, this appeared to be a clear case of premeditated murder. But White's attorney used a diminished capacity defense. He argued that White's ability to "maturely and meaningfully" reflect on the gravity and evil of the offense was impaired. He asserted that "White's penchant for wolfing down junk food—Twinkies, Cokes, doughnuts, and candy bars . . . exacerbated his depression and indicated a chemical imbalance in the brain." As a result, White was only convicted of manslaughter, a much lesser offense, creating a public controversy that subsequently led to the abolition of the diminished capacity defense in California.

At present, there is little convincing scientific evidence that dietary factors have any role in antisocial behavior. Although dietary intervention programs are being incorporated into correctional facilities, no data has proven their effectiveness.

Sugar has also been implicated in childhood hyperactivity. As the name implies, hyperactive children display, for their age, high levels of motor activity. In addition, they also suffer from attentional deficits and impulsive behavior. The belief that sugar causes these problems in children is widely held by the general public. This has been fueled by media reports of the "Halloween effect," when children supposedly run amok after stuffing themselves with their Halloween candies.

Several methodologically rigorous studies have now been conducted to test the effects of sugar on both hyperactive and nonhyperactive children. What makes the studies scientifically well controlled is that they were conducted in a double-blind fashion: Neither the experimenters nor the children knew when they were receiving real sugar and when they were given the sugar substitute aspartame (Nutrasweet). The hyperactive and nonhyperactive children were observed as they played and performed several tasks, each demanding different amounts of attention and levels of learning. In general, the studies have provided scant evidence for any effect of sugar on behavior.

Certainly it is still possible that individual people may show adverse behavioral responses to sugar or foods containing sugar, since there are individuals who show adverse effects to other dietary substances, for example dairy products. And sugar eaten over several days or months may have effects not observable by brief studies in the laboratory. However, the accumulated experimental evidence so far argues against sugar consumption as a general explanation of aggressive behavior or learning problems.

Mood and Fatigue But sugary foods may have mood-altering effects. No wonder so many people are hooked on them. Our special preference for sweets seems to be inborn. I have conducted studies testing newborns only minutes after birth. The results show that they suck more vigorously on the nipple when getting sweet solutions than when getting plain water. They are also capable of discriminating even at birth among different concentrations of sugar in the water—the sweeter it was, the harder they sucked. This finding generally held true whether the newborns were normal weight or chubby.

Scientists have studied sugar's effects on the body for a long time. We know that eating a lot of sugar, the amount in a candy bar for example, leads to a quick rise in the level of sugar in your bloodstream. This does provide a quick surge of energy. But this rise also signals the release of the hormone insulin, which functions to drive the blood sugar level down. The net result for some people, although certainly not all, is feeling cranky, irritable, and generally down, after the initial "high." And later, you may not think to attribute your feelings to the sweets you ate the hour before—especially because they made you feel so good at first.

Other research suggests that sugar may not have its fatiguing effects merely because of hypoglycemia, the sharp drop in blood sugar that follows after eating sugary foods. Instead, this work proposes that the effects of eating sugary food or any food high in carbohydrate (of which sugar is just one type) may be due to an increase in serotonin, one of the brain's chemical messengers.

Neuroscientists Richard Wurtman and John Fernstrom, originally working together at MIT, found that the brain is sensitive to the specific dietary constituents of what we eat, especially to the ratio of protein to carbohydrate within a single meal. They believe that diet influences the activity of brain neurons—the nerve cells that make up the brain—by affecting the synthesis of neurotransmitters, the chemical messengers that make the neurons fire. Since different neurotransmitters are now known to regulate distinct types of behaviors, dietary factors that influence the production of a variety of neurotransmitters could thereby influence behavior. It appears that the rates at which some of the neurotransmitters are synthesized and the quantity released typically vary from person to person, depending on the types of food each has eaten most recently.

Some scientists are still skeptical, and all the pieces in this regulatory puzzle are not yet in place. Nonetheless, the Wurtman data provide some tantalizing clues about how the system might work. Between the bloodstream and the brain is a semipermeable barrier called the blood-brain barrier. To affect the brain by what you eat, constituents of your diet would have to be able to pass the blood-brain barrier. Apparently, some do so more easily than others. Among those that can is tryptophan, an amino acid that is converted to serotonin and other chemicals once it enters the brain. When foods high in the amino acids found in protein are eaten along with carbohydrate, however, they compete more effectively than tryptophan to cross the blood-brain barrier. A high-protein meal therefore usually depresses serotonin synthesis. In contrast, a high-carbohydrate, protein-poor meal elevates brain tryptophan, accelerating serotonin synthesis. When carbohydrates are eaten alone, they cause the release of insulin into the bloodstream, which through the suppressive action of insulin on tryptophan's competitors, allows it to cross the blood-brain barrier more readily. Studies testing this idea have shown that meals made up only of carbohydrates do lead to more relaxed feelings and sometimes even greater fatigue than protein-rich meals, especially for women.

It may be more than a coincidence, according to Richard and Judith Wurtman, that the carbohydrates we eat and both major classes of antidepressant drugs, the monoamine-oxidase inhibitors and the tricyclic-uptake blockers, are thought to increase the quantities of serotonin present within brain synapses. Perhaps people snacking on carbohydrates are unknowingly self-medicating. Many women who come to our clinic seeking help for weight control eat about half their daily calories as carbohydrate-rich snacks. They report experiencing strong feelings of carbohydrate craving. The Wurtmans believe that they are suffering from an abnormality in the process that links carbohydrate consumption to the release of brain serotonin.

Most of these people describe themselves as feeling anxious, tense, or depressed before eating a carbohydrate meal or snack. Many characterize themselves as driven to find something high in carbohydrate. They feel more peaceful and relaxed after eating it. Sherry talks about needing a "fix" by midafternoon. She rushes home after a day of teaching and grabs sweets, crackers, chips—anything loaded with carbohydrate. She can't sit through the four P.M. teachers' meetings on Monday afternoon—where only tea and coffee are served. So she stockpiles pretzels and cookies in her desk, eating them voraciously and secretively as soon as her class is dismissed. Even the fear of being caught by a student who has forgotten something can't stop her. She believes no other activity helps her wind down as much as that midafternoon snack. She reports feeling the tension draining from her face and neck; it is a palpable sensation of relief.

There are several biological mechanisms other than levels of brain serotonin that could also be influencing the relationship between stress or depression, and overeating. Many people claim they eat more when they are stressed because they are hungrier and find food especially tasty at those moments. To test this question experimentally, we conducted a study of people who were not regular users of caffeine. We then gave half of them caffeine tablets which they thought were vitamins. The caffeine stirred them up physiologically, but they didn't attribute their arousal to the caffeine, because they didn't know whether they had received it. The other half of the participants just received placebo pills that had no active ingredients.

All subjects then were given a food they had never eaten before (mango sherbet) so that we could understand the effects of arousal on eating without the complication of their prior experience with the food. We found that the subjects who were stirred up physiologically by the caffeine actually felt hungrier and found the mango sherbet tastier than the people who just received the placebo tablets.

For many people it is just this kind of "unexplained" arousal that leads to compulsive eating. It's the feeling of agitation, being ill-at-ease, upset. These people may get "hooked" on carbohydrates, in particular, when stressed, because eating carbohydrate leads to calmness or even a welcome sense of fatigue. But the carbohydrate "blues" can set in, bringing too much fatigue and guilt over all the high calories eaten. So we're trapped by the long-term consequences of the momentary benefit we received.

One of our patients, Marcia, eats every carbohydrate in the house, including the dog food, when she feels nervous and edgy. Not being able to identify what's wrong, she keeps stuffing in food to make the feeling go away. She talks about "needing a fix" and characterizes her feeling at such moments as a "mouthful of panics." When she is almost stuporous, the bad feelings seem to drain away. For her the act of chewing is also a release. And Marcia isn't alone, although her food choices are far more extreme than most. Almost everyone who struggles with their weight eats more under stress. Why? Distress, and other forms of arousal, send chemical signals to the brain that are similar to those signals the brain gets when energy is needed during dieting. Eating alters the signals and provides relief.

Not All Calories Are Created Equal

The third part of the food trap arises because the body doesn't treat even very similar food the same way.

"A Rose Is a Rose Is a Rose"

When it comes to food, the Gertrude Stein adage could not be more incorrect. The newest scientific evidence is clear. The body simply doesn't treat all calories as equal. A small chocolate bar and a large banana may have the identical number of calories. We know that they have different nutritional value, of course, but few people are familiar with other major ways in which they differ. The banana helps to block the absorption of calories and may also speed up metabolism. The chocolate helps to add more fat.

Studies of men and women conducted by research teams at Harvard and Stanford Universities found that dietary fat may be the biggest culprit in our struggle with weight. The studies found almost no direct relationship between daily caloric intake and body weight. Instead, weight correlated only with how much fat was in people's diets. Dr. Ethan Sims, professor emeritus at the University of Vermont Department of Medicine, conducted studies on men who were prisoners in a Vermont state penitentiary. He and his colleagues paid the men to overeat and gain weight, supplying all sorts of tasty treats hardly typical of prison fare. The volunteers gained weight most efficiently when fat in the diet was increased.

If two people are eating the same number of calories but one eats a higher percentage of dietary fat than the other, he or she will hold on to more energy. There are two reasons for this. The first is that high-fat meals require fewer calories to burn in the process of digestion than high carbohydrate meals do. Second, the body converts dietary fat to stored fat relatively easily. Carbohydrate conversion to stored fat, by contrast, requires a more complicated series of metabolic steps. In studies by Dr. Eric Jecquier, at the University of Lausanne in Switzerland, 23 percent of the calories from a high carbohydrate food like a piece of bread were needed to convert those calories into fat. In comparison, only 3 percent of the calories from a high-fat food like rich ice cream were needed to convert the dietary fat into fat stores.

In a different series of studies, Dr. Claude Bouchard, a physiologist at Laval University in Canada, has recently shown that eating foods high in fat can also make you eat more calories later. In his experiments, student volunteers were given all their meals at the laboratory for several days. Unbeknownst to them, on some days the foods were high in fat content. On other days the foods looked the same but were made to be low fat. Ironically, the high-fat foods led to an increase in the number of calories the participants ate during the rest of the day. This is surprising, since the high-fat foods eaten earlier contained more calories and so should have been more satisfying. It seems your system gets revved up biochemically and you crave more, not less, food as a result.

Other studies by Dr. Bouchard add to this picture by showing that the gain in body fat associated with high fat consumption appears to be preferentially deposited around the waist and stomach areas. Epidemiologic studies show that abdominally distributed fat is associated with a far greater risk of cardiovascular disease. So cutting down on dietary fat may be one of the best things you can do for yourself.

Recently, our research has put another wrinkle into the view that not all calories are equal—this time about different types of sugar. Sugars are different in their effects on what and how much you eat next after you've eaten the sweets, despite being equal in calories. Our studies found that lemonade-flavored drinks sweetened with fructose seem to suppress hunger and food intake, while lemonade sweetened with other sugars (sucrose, glucose, or dextrose) have the opposite effect. Fructose is the sugar found in honey and fruits, whereas glucose and dextrose are found in table sugars and many candies. So watching the type of sugar you eat can be quite important.

And there's more. Fiber-rich food such as fruits, grains, and pastas may actually block absorption of some of the calories in them. Studies show that animals fed a diet rich in fiber had 25 percent less body fat than animals fed a fiber-free diet. Incredible as it may seem, the diet enriched with fiber actually contained more calories. Dr. Allen Levine, a professor of Nutrition at the Veterans Administration Medical Center in Minneapolis, thinks that this effect is due to fiber's coarseness. He has proposed that the less processed and coarser the food, the fewer calories people absorb. To test this idea, he fed participants in a research study 100 calories of fat in either peanut oil, peanut butter, or peanuts. He found they absorbed almost all of the 100 calories of fat in the oil, 94 of the fat calories in peanut butter, and only 82 calories of fat in the peanuts. A calorie is not a calorie is not a calorie.

Taste

Your sense of taste is controlled by many factors. This is an important part of the food trap. The time of day, the foods you ate previously, and the individual patterns of taste buds all affect the way something tastes. In the morning, for example, foods often taste different from the way they do at other times of day. This occurs because your taste buds have been exposed only to saliva and air while you slept. Your saliva is salty, but you generally don't notice its taste because it continually bathes your taste buds.

The taste of food is strongly influenced by what you have just been eating. If your taste buds are exposed to something sweet for a long time, a new sweet food would taste less sweet to you. Your taste buds have undergone a phenomenon known as taste adaptation. Dr. Barbara Rolls, a psychologist at the Johns Hopkins University, and Dr. Edmund Rolls at Oxford University in England have suggested that people eating a lot of one taste lose their appetite for it because of taste adaptation.

In a typical study by the Rollses, people were fed as much sweet food as they wished to eat, and were told not to stop until they felt full. If they were then offered different, but still sweet foods, they continued to decline more food, acting as if they were full. But if they were offered a different taste, for example a salty snack food such as chips, they began eating again as if they were still hungry. This phenomenon—called sensory-specific satiety—is based on the occurrence of taste adaptation. The Rollses argue that our typical pattern of several courses in the meal—all of different flavors—overrides taste adaptation and therefore encourages overeating. It also explains why there's always room for dessert.

Marla often found herself unable to stop nibbling at home. "I was so full from the bag of potato chips I had just eaten that I thought I'd explode," she once told me. "Then all of a sudden, I saw the Ben and Jerry's ice cream I'd forgotten about, and it was as if I'd never eaten."

Scientists believe that taste plays an important role in regulating eating behavior. When taste buds are not functioning properly, food intake can run amok. For example, we found that bulimic women who purged by vomiting at least three times a week or more had completely lost their ability to taste in the areas of the mouth against which they vomit when they are throwing up—the roof of the mouth and the palate. Quite

— 157 —

likely their level of bingeing is then increased by their taste loss, as they seek more and more intense taste sensations to overcome their purging-induced losses.

Many people talk about looking for a taste "hit," even if they don't have an eating disorder. Denise, for example, described her hunger as a series of cravings and taste sensations. She could eat something that was quite filling, but if it didn't have the taste sensation she was seeking, she never felt satisfied. "When I want something sour," she said, "I can actually feel my mouth puckering while waiting for it. When my mouth wants something sour, popcorn, which I usually love, tastes like sawdust."

Breaking the Food Trap

To break the food trap, you need to validate the various meanings of food. Very few of life's satisfactions are as accessible, as gratifying, or as completely under our control as food. Make a list of all the ways you use food—whether it's to give yourself pleasure or to reduce pain. As a way of getting started, go back to your answers on the Emotional Eating Test (page 131). List those negative emotions to which you often respond by eating. Then indicate how food helps these unpleasant feelings—it soothes, relaxes, makes you feel happy. Don't forget to add to your list whether you ever eat simply because you're bored, and whether you eat as a way of socializing.

After you've finished, write down other things that can also serve the same function next to each item. What's most important is that these substitutions have to be immediate, available, and under your own control. For example, going to a movie might easily replace going out to dinner as a form of socializing, but it wouldn't replace raiding the refrigerator to make you feel better after you've just had a fight with your lover or best friend.

Don't be dismayed if you find that you have very few things that can easily replace the functions of food and eating. *Proba-*

bly nothing can right now for most of us. But the strategy is to develop a list of things you might try. What could be some possible substitutes? Again, you need to do this item by item, function by function. This is not a general plan. It is a specific set of tactics to help you find substitutes for the multiple meanings and functions of food. If not, you will continue your battles with food over and over again.

Marcia, who once ate dog food, now jogs whenever she feels stressed, and practices the piano when she's bored. This was her substitution, not mine. What she learned from me was how to make the choices. She learned that she was worth the effort. She now has new forms of self-nurturance and doesn't use food as the only way to be good to herself.

You must learn that food is not a matter of good and evil. It's critical to defuse eating of its emotional dynamite. Over and over again you have to tell yourself it's OK when you eat something you believe is "wrong." Food does fulfill, so the goal is to become more conscious and analytical so that eventually you can be more in control of when and why you eat.

Part of Cheryl's treatment focused on identifying "high risk emotional situations" that were likely to result in overeating. For example, when she felt "hyperstressed," she would wander from table to table in the college dining hall, only sitting down for a few minutes at each table, eating while chatting with some people. Then she would get up, get some more food, and sit at a different table so that no one would notice how much she was eating. Often, she would continue moving from table to table until the dining hall closed. Her desperate need to feel popular and her desire for food pushed her to this pattern of behavior.

Cheryl decided to break this habit by picking out one table, and loading up her food tray with one balanced meal. Then she would sit down at the designated table and start and complete her meal there. Cheryl chose a few friends to eat with, and just focusing on developing a better relationship with them helped her break the food ritual. When feeling upset, she would phone one of them and agree to meet in the dining hall, where she would then have her meal with whoever the designated friend was, and would leave with this friend when she was finished.

To help Cheryl cope with tension, anxiety, and other negative-feeling states, we also instructed her in relaxation training. In addition, we encouraged her to develop an array of self-nurturing activities other than eating, including listening to music which she loved, and reading magazines. Cheryl had a great deal of resistance to engaging in these seemingly "frivolous" activities. "Nobody is going to give me a Nobel Prize for reading *Vogue*," she complained, even though she admitted that she thoroughly enjoyed doing so, and that she was secretly envious of her friends who were able to relax without any visible sign of guilt or remorse.

Many people have to learn to *restructure faulty or unhelpful thoughts* into ones that are more useful as a way to break the food trap. If you know about the inner thoughts and feelings that trigger eating, you can begin to learn how to use similar thought processes to work for you, rather than against you. Thought responses can be controlled and redirected just as other kinds of habitual responses can.

One kind of thought that undoubtedly leads to eating is thinking about food itself. This is an experiment that I had Marcia try. Imagine that you are walking down the street. Imagine the sign of your favorite food shop. You smell the cooking and you see people walking in and coming out with your own favorite food: steak, Chinese food, chocolate ice cream, a fresh cake. Sit back, relax, close your eyes, take a deep breath, and block out everything but the mental picture and the smell. Pay attention to what happens as you picture the scene, and remember your thoughts. Dwell on your reactions to the image.

Did it make you feel hungry? Most likely it did. This exercise will bring home to you that thoughts and fantasies about food have an arousing effect. This turn-on may be physiological as well as psychological. My research has shown that some people secrete insulin when they see or think about food. This finding is extremely important, since higher levels of insulin increase the sensation of hunger and promote fat storage. It is obvious that strategies must be learned for avoiding these mental turn-ons.

People with severe food disturbances—such as sufferers from anorexia nervosa and semistarvation—are preoccupied solely by food. As I'll describe in the next chapter, dieters often complain of an uncontrollable urge to talk about recipes, to read cookbooks, and to plan meals for other people. This kind of intense thinking about food is counterproductive. It is a direct result of the state of food deprivation, yet for dieters, it has a paradoxical effect. The more you try not to eat foods, the more you will be thinking about food.

Anne, a teacher, described how she would be preoccupied the whole day, thinking about all the things she was determined *not* to eat, only to find herself eating all evening after her day of starvation.

> I was consumed by thoughts of food. I would scrutinize the lunches my students ate and tell myself that I would not eat this or that. I would make mental lists during class of all my favorite dishes that I would *not* eat until I got thinner. I would imagine the bakery that I was determined *not* to enter on my way home. As soon as I got into my car, I headed for the nearest food store and selected my favorites. Once home, I would eat for two or three hours.

What can be done about it? Here are some strategies that we have used effectively to help people like Anne avoid their mental "turn-ons." One method, if you can't change where you are or what you are doing, is to shift your thoughts at once to something else. Since you have now seen that thinking about food may actually make you hungrier, you must try to build in some kind of distraction in the form of pleasurable thoughts about things other than food. Think about an exciting evening you had, the good book you are reading, Beethoven's Fifth Symphony, the weekend you are planning, the new curtains you would like for your living room, Shakespeare's sonnets. Jennifer tried to block out intrusive food thoughts by imagining her last great vacation or something wonderful she planned to do with her daughter Sophia. The ability to delay eating depends on the extent to which you can focus your thoughts and attention away from stimulating food cues.

Now imagine the following situation. While you are watching television, a commercial for a new munchy snack comes on: A "typical" family is shown having fun, sitting in the sunshine and enjoying the snack. Its flavor and crunchiness are described in detail, with close-ups of huge vats of swirling chocolate. What should you do when the delicious aspects of food are forced on your notice like this? Obviously, you can't turn off the television whenever the advertisements come on, or avoid stress where there are restaurants or food shops. So what you might do is try to focus on negative aspects of the food. Imagine rats in the kitchen of the restaurant; dead cockroaches in the snack bar; dwell on the way you are being overcharged, manipulated, and exploited by the manufacturer. If thinking about rats strikes you as funny or objectionable, this may be evidence that your food thoughts are in a sense sacrosanct, so that it distresses you to think of food negatively.

A third technique is to focus on aspects of the food that have nothing to do with eating. A plate of marshmallows on the table in front of you can make you think either "Mmmm—delicious, chewy, sweet, white, wonderful marshmallows," or "Those little white spheres look like clouds or bits of cottonwool." In other words, you don't have to make the image negative. Simply thinking about the object as something other than food helps to stop you wanting to eat it. This technique works well even with children, whom you would expect to be more limited in their ability to delay gratification when confronted with something appealing and tempting.

Self-arousing thoughts about food are a habit. You can even generate these thoughts when there are no external stimuli present. Equally, if you practice alternative mental responses to the same triggers—the new thoughts can become habitual, too.

There are also some very specific ways you can use the different properties of foods to your advantage. When you want to feel calm and relaxed, carbohydrates may do the trick. But go for pasta or a whole grain bread, not candy. And fiber is more filling, too. Foods rich in fiber are wholemeal bread, brown (unpolished) rice, bran, fresh vegetables, fresh fruit, potatoes, peas and beans—and try spreading out your eating throughout the day.

Boring is bad. Taste is a good cue for regulating food intake, so don't eat foods that don't taste good enough. Beatrice, for example, was convinced that all healthful foods were basically bland and boring and that she should try to avoid any palatable foods, because they would only tempt her to overeat. Hence, she needed practice eating tasty foods in small amounts to gain the experience that she could eat them without setting off a binge. Beatrice's "homework" often included a food-tasting exercise. She would purchase a small amount of one food item, for example, one brownie, take it home, and eat it in the dining room. She recorded in her diary how she felt while eating the "forbidden food," what thoughts she had about the food, eating, and herself. In the beginning, these exercises would bring up memories of the times when she would devour fattening food and then, consumed with anxiety, rush on to eat more and more food, because "I had already blown it," referring, of course, to her diet. To ensure that Beatrice would not get started on a binge as a result of her food exercises, she always planned to do something else right after she finished eating. For example, she would do the exercise right before leaving for a visit with a friend, or before going to pick up her sons from school. Gradually, Beatrice was able to enjoy the formerly "forbidden" foods and was able to eat them in moderation and without subsequent guilt or urges to binge.

The goal is to find foods that are highly satisfying but not overwhelmingly desirable. Beatrice used to think she earned a cream doughnut by suffering her way through a plate of cottage cheese. When she began to eat what she liked, focusing her attention on the taste of food as she ate it (and not eating things that she disliked, or that didn't taste good enough), she found she was actually eating fewer calories, because she was enjoying her food more. One year after she completed treatment, Beatrice told us:

> You know, I never thought I would be able to eat food and enjoy it. I thought bingeing was like being an alcoholic, that you had to fight it all the time. But the weird thing is, now I can hardly remember what it was like to be obsessed with dieting and eating and all that. Really, I just remember that I was miserable, but nothing else. It is so foreign to me now. Now, I just eat when I am hungry, and I lost some weight without really knowing it. I can tell, because all my clothes are too big. But I don't ever deprive myself of foods that I like. Basically, it's just not an issue anymore.

Oscar Wilde said, "The only way to get rid of a temptation is to yield to it. Resist it, and your soul grows sick with longing for the things it has forbidden itself." Good insight for breaking the food trap.

— 6 —

The Dieting-Rituals Trap

Television fans will remember November 1988 as the time when a slim, elegant woman in size ten jeans walked proudly onto the set of her television talk show, pulling a red wagon filled with sixty-seven pounds of fat. That was Oprah Winfrey, heralding her weight loss on a liquid diet program.

But now all the weight is back. "The reason I failed is that diets don't work," Oprah commented to reporters. "I tell people, if you're underweight, go on a diet and you'll regain everything you lost plus more. Now I'm trying to find a way to live in a world with food without being controlled by it, without being a compulsive eater. That's why I say I will never diet again."

Despite such notable resolve, for many of us, the urge to diet in the face of our own and legions of public failures is invincible. The reason why is that in the final analysis, the body is the last and perhaps the only command post of the soul. Unable to manipulate the destiny of our fellow beings, we can at least direct the destiny of our own flesh.

Part of the dieting-rituals trap is that dieting is symbolic. It has to do with a lot more than losing weight. It's a form of self-cleansing, physically and spiritually—a promise of a better life, a better self. This powerful part of the trap enhances the lure of dieting. Wendy Wasserstein, the Pulitzer

Prize–winning author, admits to feeling that "still, somewhere in me is a clean slate, a new beginning, a chance for redemption.... Liking myself means liking diet Jell-O.... Every three years or so—ever since I left school and began a grown-up, professional life—I have decided to take myself in hand." Wasserstein likens this pulling herself together to a "spring cleaning." This is part of the dieting-rituals trap. Going on a diet is painful. But it has also become a way of feeling good about ourselves, because it promises us a new chance. Even very slender women believe that their lives would be better if only they could take off a few pounds.

Industry has capitalized on our obsessions with weight control. A marketing research firm in New York calculates that Americans spent thirty-three billion dollars on diets and diet-related services in 1990, up from twenty-nine billion in 1989. If that yearly rate of growth continues, by the turn of the century we will be spending seventy-seven billion dollars to lose weight, just under the entire gross national product of Belgium. However, now in the 1990s, the dieting industry is coming under intense public scrutiny. A congressional subcommittee in the United States chaired by Oregon Representative Ron Wyden is challenging the claims, the products, and the process of weight loss offered by many of the major weight-control companies. Most experts agree that the public has been subjected to false promises of easy weight loss, with little effort to promote long-term maintenance.

Dieting wasn't always big business. In the late 1950s and early 1960s, when models and Miss Americas wore girdles, did a little exercise just for their thighs and hips, and fit into a size ten, only overweight women were on a diet. A survey of the *Ladies' Home Journal* magazines in the 1960s showed an average of only one diet article every six months. But by the mid seventies, almost every woman in the country had tried some kind of diet, and losing weight was becoming a national obsession in America. In 1978, a Nielsen survey found that 56 percent of all female respondents between ages twenty-four and fifty-four were on a diet at the time and by the late 1980s, that figure had risen to 72 percent. Some polls suggest that

that number may now be dropping in the early 1990s. On the other hand, the number of weight-loss businesses is at an all-time high, which suggests that it is too early to predict just where the trend is headed.

According to *Newsweek* magazine (September 11, 1989), the baby-boom generation is in the throes of middle-age spread. So, dieters in increasing numbers are shelling out more than ever before for weight-loss products and services. There is now a steady supply of diet books, diet aids, appetite suppressants, weight-control spas, calorie-sparing TV dinners, light beers, and even diet products for pets. With the weight-loss industry so clearly expanding, investment bankers are moving in. Says one investment banker interviewed by *Newsweek*: "We look at the business today and see a tremendous potential. Our goal is to McDonaldize weight loss."

And with all these diet-related businesses, are we controlling our weight more successfully? "No," say weight-loss experts emphatically. Most studies show that for every one hundred people who lose weight, about ninety-five will regain at least as much as they lose—and sometimes more. Psychologist Kelly Brownell, a weight-loss expert at Yale University, has pointed out that if one defines successful treatment as reaching ideal body weight and maintaining it for five years, a person is more likely to recover from almost any form of cancer than from obesity. The trap is clearly set.

Some investigators now believe that *stringent* dieting itself may be one of the major causes of weight gain. The body works hard to protect itself in times of severe caloric restriction. It actually begins to function in a way which is in competition with the dieter in you. Because basal metabolic rate is lowered by extreme dieting, fewer calories are needed for resting energy, so even eating normally after the diet is over often leads to weight gain. Thus, the self-cleansing can also be a form of self-punishment, if you eventually regain the weight. Further, biochemical changes caused by repeated cycles of gaining and losing weight—the typical scenario for most dieters—increase the percentage of calories you store as fat. Each new beginning makes the next new beginning harder. That's the problem with trying every fad diet. Each time you starve, your body gets more efficient at using the calories it gets and needs fewer to survive. Alexandra, a stewardess, has tried every diet, always restricting her food intake to the limit. She's now thirty-seven and can't understand why it's harder to lose weight than it was twenty years ago. Is it her age? she wonders. Unfortunately, it's not. It's her own diet history. Starving is the worst way to lose weight permanently.

Another aspect of the trap is that the body isn't infinitely malleable. Genes play a major role in determining body shape and size—from how much fat we can store easily to where on our bodies it's distributed. Heredity also influences weight by determining how food is metabolized. Sandra, one of our clinic patients, came from a family where everyone had solid, thick legs and big thighs. For years, she tried every diet that became popular. No matter how much she lost, no matter how thin she became, she couldn't change the size of her legs and thighs nearly as much as the rest of her body. "My greatest goal in life," she admitted, "is to have thin legs, to wear a bathing suit without hating the fat jiggling on my thighs. I know why women have liposuction. It's the ultimate solution. I used to dream about a big vacuum cleaner sucking out the fat—it was my constant childhood wish—but I just can't afford to have it done yet."

Dieting rituals also trap us because there are high emotional and psychological costs to dieting. Many women are depressed, nervous, weak, and irritable when they try to lose weight. And it has now been documented that eating disorders often begin right after a period of strenuous dieting. However, many dieters believe—and certainly the diet industry wishes to promote this belief—that the pursuit of thinness is the pursuit of better health. While this is true in some cases, new evidence is leading scientists to be more skeptical of the view that thinner is always healthier.

Society and, therefore, advertising, treats dieting as if it were easy, creating yet another part of this body trap. For all the reasons just discussed, it is extremely difficult to lose weight and keep it off. There is no medical model that says we're addicted to food so people are expected to give it up readily. As a society, we're much more sympathetic to alcoholics than to people who eat compulsively. Although food is not addictive the way heroin or alcohol are, eating and dieting habits do involve dependency problems. And even when people stop overeating, they may not lose as much weight as they'd like.

What is your dieting history? Are you caught by the dieting-rituals trap? This dieting history questionnaire on page 170 is adapted from one I developed with Doctors Kelly Brownell, a psychologist at Yale, and Jack Wilmore, Chairman of the Department of Kinesiology and Health Education at the University of Texas, Austin.

The fantasy quotient in our weight-control efforts is poignantly illustrated by the suspension of our critical faculties when it comes to dieting merchandise. On the one hand, as a nation, we are increasingly concerned about truth in advertising. Consumer groups seek legal recourse in the face of false representations. On the other hand, we are exceptionally tolerant of some obviously fatuous and occasionally dangerous dieting products that make impossible claims for success. For the dieter, this is a terrible trap, but for business, a dreamed-of opportunity: the chance to sell the same products and programs to the same people over and over again. And to make matters worse, statistics show that there are 50 percent more overweight teenagers in the United States today than there were ten years ago. A whole new—and fatter—group of customers is waiting in the wings. And the techniques some of them are using are terrifying. Grade-school girls are vomiting and using laxatives, and many youngsters are using highly addictive cocaine and crack to lose weight! According to an article in the *Los Angeles Times*, there is a new "misguided but growing perception that it is a quick, cheap and easy way to lose weight."

Drug dealers are even promoting these dangerous drugs with this in mind. A ten-year-old girl from New York reported being approached by a dealer who told her that boys only like thin girls and she should do crack to look like Lisa Bonet. An

— 169 —

YOUR DIET HISTORY

1) How often do you diet?
   a) *Never* b) *Rarely* c) *Sometimes* d) *Often* e) *Always*

2) People often have different body-weight patterns through their adult lives. Some people remain relatively constant (within five pounds), others gain weight, some lose weight, and still others find that their weight fluctuates. Please circle which general pattern best describes your weight history (excluding changes due to illness or pregnancy).
   a) *Weight Has*   b) *Steady*   c) *Weight*   d) *Lost Weight*
      Remained   *Gain in*   *Fluctuates*   *and Kept It Off*
      Stable   *Weight*

3) Are you a yo-yo dieter (do you lose weight intentionally, and then regain the weight, often)?   Yes   No

4) Currently, how often do you have to restrict your food intake to control your weight?
   a) *Never* b) *Rarely* c) *Sometimes* d) *Often* e) *Always*

5) How many times in your life would you estimate you have *lost* and *gained back* the number of pounds shown below? For example, if you have lost and gained back 30 pounds twice, you would put a "2" next to the line 21–30 lbs. Answer for each category and exclude pregnancy and monthly menstrual-cycle fluctuation.

	Sample	Your History
1–5 lbs	20 times	
6–10 lbs	10 times	
11–20 lbs	3 times	
21–30 lbs	2 times	
31–50 lbs	0 times	
51+ lbs	1 time	

If you answered *Often* or *Always* to questions 1 and 4; *Weight Fluctuates* to question 2; and *Yes* to question 3, you may be caught by the dieting-rituals trap. Question 5 assesses how likely it is that your physiology has been changed by dieting. The more times you have lost and regained eleven pounds or more, the more probable it is that the biological changes described in this chapter have taken place.

---

eleven-year-old girl reported that her friends aren't doing crack to avoid responsibility. "They do it to get all skinny," she said.

The trend cuts across all class and socioeconomic lines. Crack, which is cheaper, is used mainly by poorer users, while cocaine is the drug of choice for wealthier users. Crack and cocaine suppress hunger by stimulating the central nervous system. Users feel no need to eat or sleep, when in fact, they may not have eaten or slept in days. Some users report not eating for several weeks.

Let's see how the dieting-rituals trap works and how to break it.

Exploring the Dieting-Rituals Trap

Dieting as Self-Cleansing

There is no doubt that pressures to be thin abound. Dieting is invoked in the name of good health, good looks, good lives, and conforming to society's standards. Beyond these obvious reasons, however, lurks another answer to our obsession with dieting, one more deep-seated and psychological. Dieting is ritualistic behavior, a way of cleansing the soul. Even primitive civilizations believed that there was purity in self-denial. The rituals of the Fox, an American Indian tribe, were described in the late 1800s by the anthropologist William Jones. If a young man had ambitions for leadership, he notified the Great Spirit by fasting. If he wished to be great, he learned what was necessary by fasting. He fasted in mourning and in penitence.

Human beings appear to be the only animals who decline

— 171 —

to eat when hungry, who willingly starve the body to feed the soul. Many religions have institutionalized fasting as a way of asking for redemption—for example, Jews fast on Yom Kippur because it is the Day of Atonement, and Christians abstain from certain foods during Lent to reenact Jesus' self-denial. Certain Polynesian groups believe that denial of food brings blessing and luck. It is a wordless prayer to the divine powers, a plea to "Do for me as I do without." There is the expectation of reward after such demonstrable purity and self-deprivation.

Today, modern women perpetuate these rituals, seeking power, beauty, forgiveness, and salvation in self-denial. Did the women's movement relieve preoccupation with body weight? Hardly! In fact, today, feminist language is often used to encourage body vigilance. "Discipline is liberation," Jane Fonda tells us when promoting her body-shaping routine. "Losing weight was the single greatest achievement in my life," announced television personality Oprah Winfrey when she stood proudly before her audience in size-ten jeans. And with that statement she discounted much of the hard work and determination that it took to achieve her own hard-won fame and success.

Many women fight for the right to satisfying sex, but they censor a satisfying meal. Being "bad" means eating something you shouldn't have, not sleeping with your friend's husband. Corinne, one of our research participants, talked about temptation, sin, and guilt in discussing her weight-loss efforts. She did her fattening eating in secret, as if it were sinful behavior. And when she abstained, she talked about virtue, empowerment, and cleanliness. Her ability to diet or not was her metaphor for how good she was. According to a recent survey, 11 percent of women feel more guilty about snacking and cheating on their diets then they do about cheating on their income taxes.

Jennifer viewed dieting as a form of absolution, of atoning for any digressions from her pursuit of a good body, and as a way of reasserting her control over herself and what she wanted out of life. "When something goes wrong—at work or at home—I just go on a diet. Even though it's stupid, I can't help feeling that I'll be better, that everything will be OK."

For many women, their weight history is a way to explain the past, and weight is the lens through which they view their hoped-for future. A bad day or a bad year is one in which they felt fat; a New Year's resolution to lose weight is virtually the same as a wish for a happy year.

When asked what would make them happiest among four possible alternatives, 42 percent of the women respondents in a *Glamour* magazine survey reported that it would be losing weight. Only 22 percent endorsed success at work; 21 percent a date with a man they admired; and 15 percent hearing from an old friend. Psychologists Robert White and Marlene Boskind-White have done studies showing that women fantasize that their lives would be totally transformed if only they were thin. The ultimate dream of everyone who has been fat all her life is that she will lose weight and turn into the princess.

According to author Carol Sternhell, writing in *Ms.* magazine, "Everything in this world for women boils down to body size." In a plaintive call for respect for someone who is overweight, Sternhell admits:

> Sometimes I feel like a feminist at a Right-to-Life conference, an atheist in Puritan New England, a socialist in the Reagan White House. Sometimes I fear that fat women have become our culture's last defeated heretics, our greatest collective nightmare made all-too-solid flesh ... [But she goes on] We all know the story—the ugly duckling transformed into a swan after years of liquid protein, the virtuous but oppressed stepdaughter whose fairy godmother appears with a pumpkin and a lifetime membership in Weight Watchers. Our fantasies of transformation are desperate, thrilling; when we women imagine changing our lives, we frequently begin with our weight.

"If I'm not thin, I actually feel pretty worthless," Jennifer confessed. She was flooded with guilt if she ate ice cream or a piece of cake. Getting on the scale each morning determined how good or bad her day would be. Jennifer gained forty pounds when she was pregnant and she had trouble taking it off. The experience led her to be even more preoccupied than before with dieting and weight. Dieting rituals consumed her—the pre-summer juice diet one week before the Fourth of July; the post-Christmas four-day fast. Jennifer admitted, "I can tell you the calories of every type of food imaginable. For some foods I even know the differences from one brand to another. I definitely know more about dieting than about sex."

With lurid fascination and not a little voyeurism, we gobble up diet books by celebrity authors. They, too, feel that thinness equals happiness in their lives. How vindicated we feel when these famous people confess the same sins we commit, hiding the candy wrappers under the bed, and worrying about the same pounds and inches.

In the book *Elizabeth Takes Off*, Elizabeth Taylor admits to a five-year battle with fried chicken and fancy desserts. "I was almost 50 when for the first time in my life I lost my sense of self worth," she confesses in describing her "gluttonous rampage." She was lonely and bored; she felt that her husband didn't need her. Doesn't this sound just like the girl next door? Or perhaps it's you. A year does not go by in which some famous person, and usually several, bare their souls and promise us a new beginning if we follow their dieting road to redemption. Every day at your supermarket checkout counter you can read headlines the equivalent of DOLLY PARTON LOST 50 POUNDS AND FOUND LOVE.

Do we look the other way when they gain it back, forgiving the unfortunate lapses of our beloved celebrities? Certainly not. We secretly reveled in Oprah's regain. She was there for all to see—how the mighty have fallen. Public scrutiny of her regain has been nonstop. Winfrey fans lap up each detail, taking comfort that their large-size TV friend is back to her old self. What a relief to us, the common folk, that even fame and money can't buy a place in the heaven of eternal thinness. Our struggles, our self-denials, are made more valuable by the failures of others, particularly the failures of those whom we might have thought could have it all.

How Plastic Are Our Bodies?

People believe that their ability to shape their bodies has no limit. As I discussed in the Vanity Trap chapter, they use it as a reserve that they can call on when they want to hide defects or put themselves forward in roles for which they feel inadequate. On the other hand, the notion that the body is infinitely malleable is nowhere more problematic than in the control of weight. Part of the dieting-rituals trap comes from ignorance or misinformation about the physiological determinants of weight.

Body size and weight are highly determined by our genes. Picking the right parents is far more important than picking the right diet. Identical twins have body weights over twice as similar as those of nonidentical twins or siblings. When identical twins are raised apart, in different homes, they still are closer in weight than nonidentical twins reared in the same house. And when identical twins overeat, they gain almost identical amounts of weight and store the new fat in the same regions of the body, according to studies by Dr. Claude Bouchard and colleagues.

Genes limit our ability to shape our bodies into the bodies we would like. Assuming that body size and weight vary in the population along a continuum based on genetic determinants, only a minority of women can be expected to "naturally" match the extremely thin ideal. The great majority will have heavier bodies to varying degrees.

Heredity also influences weight by determining how food is metabolized. Metabolism determines how much fat we burn and how much we store. Consequently, the amount of overeating necessary to gain weight is far less for some people than for others. In a now-classic study, Geoffrey Rose and R. T. Williams studied people at Paddington General Hospital in London whose weights were stable over several years. The investigators put together a pair of subjects who were identical in a variety of characteristics: sex, weight, age, and activity level. The researchers then measured what each member of the pair was eating over several days. Often, one member of the pair was eating twice as many calories as the other, while both were maintaining the same body weight. Extraordinary? Perhaps. But these findings suggest that different individuals store and expend in different ways the identical type and quantity of food.

New studies published in the *New England Journal of Medicine* show that people inherit their rate of metabolism, the process by which the body transforms food into energy and then expends the energy. These studies followed the same subjects from before to after they gained weight. They showed that the people who became the fattest had the lowest metabolic rates to begin with. One of the studies, conducted by Dr. Susan Roberts of the Dunn Nutrition Unit in Cambridge, England, tracked babies born to thin or obese women. About half the babies born to the obese mothers burned nearly 21 percent fewer calories than the other babies. The babies who burned the fewest calories were overweight by the time they were one year old, while those with higher metabolic rates were not. Dr. Roberts said the babies who became obese ate no more than those who did not. Weight differences result because some people's bodies burn calories too slowly, rather than because they eat too much. The next step for researchers is to find the biochemical reasons why some people have slow metabolisms. Once the biochemistry is understood, we can try to influence it in some way.

There are also sex differences in metabolic rate. In general, females have lower basal metabolic rates than males. This is partly a function of the difference in their body size, but it is also due to differences in the ratio of lean to fat tissue. Fat tissue is more metabolically inert than lean tissue, and, females are genetically destined to have a higher proportion of fat to lean tissue than males.

Sex-linked hormones also seem to play a major role in the stimulation of fat storage and perhaps even fat-cell development. Studies have linked estrogen and progesterone, in part, to the fact that women put on their fat around the hips and thighs in particular. With increased estrogen and progesterone levels at puberty, the adolescent girl develops the biological machinery that increases her fat-making capacity at precisely the time when she is becoming most concerned with her thinness and attractiveness. These two simultaneous events can lead to the excessive dieting behavior so evident in many adolescent girls. For some reason that we do not yet understand, dieting at the time when the sex hormones are being established and regulated appears especially destructive for normal body-weight regulation. A large percentage of women who report strenuous dieting during puberty later develop problems controlling their weight.

A comparison of Carol and Penny is a good example. Right after getting her period, Carol was persuaded by her mother and sister that she was getting chubby. She recalls that she was so terrified by their admonitions that she stopped eating anything containing fat or sugar. She dropped the weight then, but she's been fighting it ever since. Since that diet, she's been riding a roller coaster of weight gains and losses. Penny, by contrast, didn't go on her first diet until she was twenty-three. Interestingly, she tried the same approach as Carol—cutting out fats and sugar—but she's had a much easier time keeping the weight off. I believe that we shouldn't encourage our daughters to diet *during adolescence*, even if they are somewhat overweight. They may lose weight naturally after puberty, and, if not, there is time then for a well-constructed, sensible diet and exercise plan. If we push our adolescents to lose weight, we may be setting them up for a lifetime of failure.

Dieting Strategies

Most people have tried at one time or another to lose weight by cutting down on calories. It takes a reduction of 3600 calories to lose a pound of fat, but if done gradually, it is effective. Weight loss of one half to one and a half pounds a week is probably getting rid of real fat, not just water or lean muscle.

But most people want a much quicker fix. In fact, it feels so good to get on the scale and see those pounds gone, who cares whether it's real fat, water, or lean muscle? You do. Water loss is ephemeral. About 60 percent of your body is water and it will eventually readjust itself to maintain that level. And lean tissue is defended, too. As soon as you stop restricting calories, you will replenish the lean tissue. This will look like weight gain on the scale and, for many, causes despair and feelings of defeat.

When diets are less than 1,000 calories a day, it is difficult to meet Recommended Dietary Allowances for several vitamins and minerals without the use of supplements. This is especially true for iron, magnesium, calcium, phosphorus, zinc, and vitamin B6. There is now evidence that inadequate nutrition during weight reduction can have serious and even fatal consequences. Some of the early low-calorie liquid protein formula diets on the market were associated with increased risk of sudden death and cardiac irregularities. While such problems have not been seen with the current version of liquid diets, even these require medical supervision.

The public's major source of information about low-calorie diets comes from the countless diet books that appear each year, and the scores of diets printed monthly in magazines and newspapers (many of which are abstracts or condensed versions of a currently popular book).

Most of these books use a standard set of techniques to capture the dieter's attention and promote adherence. Most claim a startling "new" development at science's "cutting edge," typically some effect on the biochemistry of the body that will promote weight loss. Many use the name of a well-known person or institution to give credibility to the diet. All try to stimulate adherence through the use of various gimmicks, such as an initial "crash" phase to cause rapid weight loss; fixed menus that vary with the phase of the diet, presumably linked to certain biochemical effects; establishment of various eating rituals such as a special order of eating foods or the specification of where and when to eat. Most work through a combination of novelty and rigidity. Many of the techniques encourage magical thinking, when there really is no magic; some of the most rigid methods, like month-long fasts or consumption of protein only, may be unhealthful as well.

Calorie levels on the most popular diets range from a few hundred to 1,800 calories, with the majority falling between 800 and 1,100 calories. In general, the diets that promote themselves as quick weight loss diets seem more likely to involve a high proportion of protein. Those diets promoting slower weight loss and more permanent changes in eating patterns are more likely to be high-carbohydrate regimcs.

But most of these fad diets don't stay around very long. Part of the reason is that they don't provide the quick fix people are looking for. Many of them are hard to stick to and they don't prevent regain, since they fail to focus on long-term changes in eating behavior. But even good diets often fail for another reason, this one having to do with our own dieting history.

Dieting May Cause Weight Gain

Strict dieting may be an ineffective way to achieve permanent weight loss. Many researchers now believe it may actually lead to weight gain and binge eating. In fact, stringent dieting may be the most dysfunctional response of all for those who are concerned about their bodies and appearance. How could this happen?

Each time people greatly restrict calorics for more than a few days, their metabolic rate slows. Estimates from studies suggest that such dieting can reduce the metabolic rate by an astounding 15 to 30 percent. This means that the essential functions of life—blood flow, body organs working—are carried on with less energy expenditure. A normal-weight adult would need to eat between 180 and 360 fewer calories if this type of metabolic slowdown were occurring. It is an important adaptive device, one that served us well in our early history when we had no way to protect ourselves against fluctuations in our food supply. But of course, it wreaks havoc on a dieter because it slows weight loss.

The slowing of metabolic rate induced by dieting is greatest in people whose metabolic rate is lower at the outset. Since women have lower metabolic rates than men, they are particularly likely to find that, despite their efforts, they cannot lose as much weight as they would like. And worse, a person's metabolic rate doesn't immediately bounce back to its normal level when she or he stops dieting. And the longer the diet, the longer it takes for metabolic rate to reach its original level. Clearly, someone whose metabolism remains sluggish after a diet may easily gain weight.

Suzanne is a perennial dieter. She's always trying to lose weight for this or that occasion, every vacation, every birthday. Her experience, so common to many, is that she diets strenuously up to the "big event," and then starts eating normally again. The weight seems to pile on even more quickly than the last time, and she's frustrated and unhappy with herself. She really doesn't think she's gorging, although she does seem to be going for all the things of which she deprived herself while on the diet. "I don't understand why I can't keep my weight off," Suzanne complains. "All I have to do is eat what seem like normal meals and I blow up again." Suzanne, and countless others like her, is suffering the consequences of her years of dieting.

Repeated cycles of gaining and losing weight—yo-yo dieting—escalate the stakes. Scientists have now verified that on each new diet, it actually does take longer to lose the same weight and even less time to regain. Work by Kelly Brownell and his colleagues starkly illustrates this condition. They made a group of rats obese on high-fat cuisine and then put them on a reducing diet. After the animals lost weight, the investigators returned them to the high-fat diet and they all regained. This procedure was then repeated. The first time the rats lost weight, it took them twenty-one days to reduce and forty-six days to gain it back. But in the next cycle it took them forty-five days to lose the same amount of weight and only fourteen days to regain.

Danielle Reed, a graduate student at Yale, and I asked whether food preferences would change with each period of restriction if the animals were given a choice of what to eat when allowed to "break their diet." We found that after each period of weight loss, the animals chose more fat and less protein, perhaps explaining why the rats in Brownell's study regained so rapidly. Breaking your diet with high-fat, high-calorie foods may not be a sign of your weak will after all. Your body may be driving you to replenish your fat stores the quickest and easiest way possible—by eating lots of fat.

Studies also suggest that people who have gone through repeated patterns of dieting and regain may be less biologically able to cope with overeating. The thermogenic response to food, that is the amount of energy the body spends following a meal in order to digest food, seems to be lower for some individuals who have a history of weight cycling. It may be that such people cannot expend as many calories as their equally lean peers who have not engaged in comparable bouts of dieting and regain.

Men seem to have greater success with weight-loss efforts and maintenance than women. Let's forget the moralistic or motivational explanations. The reason is mainly biological. Men have dieted less frequently and much less rigidly, so metabolic slowdown is not the same hazard for them. And they are more likely than women to use exercise as a form of weight control. But the data show that they are becoming more fashion- and weight-conscious and they too may get trapped in more intense dieting. Already diet soft drinks, light beers, and other diet products are being marketed by male movie stars and athletes. Men are finally getting hooked into feeling immoral if they eat the wrong foods. A recent "Cathy" cartoon, for example, depicts a man with Cathy and her friends, perusing a restaurant menu. "French fries?" he asks. "Why not? I'm young. I can eat anything." Then he goes on, "Who am I kidding?" and fights with himself: "One fry, no fries, what's a little french fry?" "Food guilt," Cathy notes knowingly to the other women at the table. "After all these years, men are finally learning our second language." If men get on the dieting treadmill in increasing numbers, the next ten years will see an explosion of weight problems in males.

The Emotional Costs of Dieting

Extreme dieting is a painful and exhausting process. Some experts believe it may be a source of psychological disturbance as well. More than half of dieters experience depression, nervousness, weakness, or irritability. Probably the most systematic study of the effects of semistarvation was conducted by Ancel Keys and his colleagues at the University of Minnesota. They evaluated Conscientious Objectors, men who volunteered for medical research as an alternative to military service during World War II. For six months, the men were restricted to approximately half their former food intake and lost, on the average, 25 percent of their original body weight. For most of the men, the prolonged deprivation led to irritability, anxiety, distorted body image, lethargy, fatigue, tension, insomnia, and depression. They were plagued by persistent thoughts of food and eating. In fact, food became a principal topic of conversation, reading, and daydreams. Prolonged fasting in some triggered impaired judgment and caused eventual derangement. North American Indians regularly fought while fasting. So did the Japanese Samurai. Their fasting-induced mental states may have helped to make them such formidable opponents. A state of fierce derangement may be desired in battle, but not in the throes of a busy life in modern society.

The psychological consequences of dieting and chronic body dissatisfaction may be among the causes of the high incidence of depression in women. We see many of the same effects witnessed in the Keys study in women who diet strenuously. As the diet progresses, an initial sense of elation and invigoration is replaced by irritability and depression. Katie, an insurance agent, needed to rely on her personal charm and warmth to sell insurance. But each year she began her annual presummer diet with a five-day fast, followed by two weeks of 800 calories a day. Soon, she was snapping at her children and coworkers. "Everything and everyone annoy me. I feel unappreciated and taken advantage of. I know that no one really likes me," she moaned. She couldn't understand why her sales were falling off and she felt worse and worse about her life. She never stopped to think that she might have been suffering from diet-induced depression.

Dieting and Binge Eating

An astonishingly large number of women have become compulsive eaters, as great as 20 to 40 percent nationwide according to some studies, at the same time that dieting is at an all-time high. These two trends are not contradictory; it may be the repeated dieting that has led to such high rates of bingeing.

Many women report dieting "successfully" and then suddenly, almost without warning, they binge. Whether triggered by exposure to too much food, feeling bad, feeling good, stress, or boredom, the pattern is always the same: They've been dieting, some "switch" turns off, and they have an intense desire to keep eating. Allie talks about that feeling, when she's eating as much as she wants. First, it's great—that gnawing emptiness at the pit of her stomach and in her throat is gone. But then comes the pain. She's filled with remorse and disgust. With new resolve she gets back on the wagon.

Are you a binge eater? Each of us may think so, but the test on pages 184 and 185 allows you to assess several key features of binge-eating behavior.

If you are a binger, your dieting history, not your willpower, may be at fault. The more strenuously and more often you have dieted, the more likely you are to binge. In the Conscientious Objectors study mentioned earlier, many of the men lost control and ate more or less continuously once they were allowed more food. Even after twelve weeks of rehabilitation, many felt an increase in hunger immediately following a large meal. There were weekend splurges in which intake ranged between 8,000 and 10,000 calories. Dr. Keys reported:

> Many of the men found it difficult to stop eating. Subject no. 20 stuffs himself until he is bursting at the seams, to the point of nearly being sick and still feels hungry; no. 120 reported that he had to discipline himself to keep

— 183 —

BINGE-EATING TEST

	Very Often	*Often*	*Sometimes*	*Rarely*	*Never*
1. I have times when I eat a large amount of food in a short space of time.	____	____	____	____	____
2. When eating tempting food I feel I may not be able to stop.	____	____	____	____	____
3. I eat high-calorie foods in a rushed, urgent fashion.	____	____	____	____	____
4. I eat high-calorie foods in private.	____	____	____	____	____
5. I feel stuffed and uncom-fortable after eating.	____	____	____	____	____
6. I feel an urgent physical need to eat a lot of food quickly.	____	____	____	____	____
7. I break diets by going on an eating binge.	____	____	____	____	____

	Very Often	Often	Sometimes	Rarely	Never
8. I consciously have to restrain my eating.	___	___	___	___	___
9. I just seem to crave food.	___	___	___	___	___
10. I fear being unable to stop eating voluntarily.	___	___	___	___	___
11. I feel de-pressed or think negative thoughts about myself follow-ing an eating binge.	___	___	___	___	___

Score each item by assigning a 0 to *Never*, a 1 to *Rarely*, a 2 to *Sometimes*, a 3 to *Often*, and a 4 to *Very Often*. If you score 30 or higher, binge eating and its associated feelings and consequences are clearly a problem for you.

> from eating so much as to become ill; no. 1 ate until he was uncomfortably full; and subject no. 30 had to stay away from food because he could not find a point of satiation even when he was "full to the gills."

These reports do not seem too dissimilar—except in de-gree—to what we see in many chronic dieters. And now, many clinical reports and epidemiologic surveys are suggesting that dieting may play a role in the onset of bulimia. These studies indicate that the disorder usually begins during a period of severe dietary restriction. Dr. Christopher Fairburn, an expert in the eating disorders, and his colleagues at Oxford University in England, report that 83 percent of the bulimics they studied were dieting at the time of their initial binge-and-purge episode, despite the fact that most of them were not overweight. We don't yet know how dieting is involved in causing bulimia, but present evidence suggests that it is.

Marianne dieted before every summer vacation, since she spent summers as a lifeguard at a swim club near her home. She knew she would have long days in a bathing suit and wanted to look thin and beautiful. One spring, she was having a harder time than usual taking the weight off, and she was afraid she wouldn't lose all she needed by the time the swim season started. So she cut way back, eating only 300 to 600 calories a day. After almost a month of total deprivation, she went on an all-out binge, eating a box of cookies, a bag of jelly beans, a quart of her favorite ice cream, and some frozen yogurt, too. She remembered her friend Lynne telling how she vomited to get rid of all the food she ate when she binged. Marianne decided to try it too, and before long, she was bingeing and purging several times a week. There is no simple cause for bulimia, and Marianne had many other significant risk factors, as well. She came from an extremely weight-preoccupied family, and many of her friends had highly disordered eating behavior. She was extremely perfectionistic and demanded nothing less than the ideal body. She considered even normal eating too much. But what is clear is that, in her case, with all these risk factors present, the immediate trigger for developing bulimia was her rigid and restrictive dieting.

Dieting, Fatness, and Health

Another part of the dieting-rituals trap is that weight loss has been promoted by most doctors and scientists as a health-enhancing activity. But for whom and for what? The noted physiologist Ancel Keys, who did the Conscientious Objectors study, reviewed thirteen studies on obesity and mortality and concluded that risk of early death increased only at the extremes of both under- and overweight. Risk of coronary heart disease appears to increase with increasing weight in both men and women, but Dr. Brownell and colleagues have published a recent paper showing that a history of weight cycling also contributes to risk of heart disease. In fact, weight cycling appeared to be an even greater risk for the thinner weight cyclers than for those who were more obese. For many, the unrelenting quest for the thin ideal may be the real health risk.

What may be more important to health than what a person weighs is where the fat is located. Stomach fat appears to be more dangerous than hip and thigh fat. Studies conducted by Dr. Jules Hirsch and Dr. Rudolph Licbcl, physicians at Rockefeller University, have shown that fat cells in the abdomen are metabolically different from those in the hips and thighs, and react uniquely to hormones in the body. For example, they appear to be more resistant to insulin, requiring the body to produce more of this hormone. Perhaps this is the reason that epidemiological studies show a relationship between amount of abdominal fat and risk for both diabetes and heart disease in the general population.

For once, genetics may be on the side of women. Unless you haven't looked in the mirror lately, you probably know that women are more likely to have their fat on their thighs and hips and men around their stomachs. Scientists currently believe that this difference helps to explain, at least in part, why men are at greater risk for heart disease than women. On the other hand, we have recently shown that women who are yo-yo dieters put on more abdominal fat. So again, dieting seems to be setting a trap.

You can calculate the ratio of fat around your waist to fat around your hips and thighs easily at home. Take a flexible tape measure and stand undressed in front of a mirror. Measure the circumference of your waist (about two inches above your belly button). Then measure your circumference at the widest place in the hip/thigh region. (This is tricky and may often, but not always, be near where the buttocks protrude the most.) Divide the waist measurement by the hips measurement. Statistically speaking, men with a waist-to-hip ratio of 1.0 or more, and women with a ratio of 0.8 or more, are at greater risk. If your ratio is below these numbers, and you've been dieting for your health, it's probably not necessary. If your ratio is over, dieting may not be a useful solution to your concerns, and in fact, may worsen the problem.

Breaking the Dieting-Rituals Trap

The major purpose of this chapter is to help you confront what dieting means to you. If it is a self-cleansing, a promissory note for a better future, and a contract with yourself for redemption, you need to find new ways to feel good about yourself. The exercises in the Vanity, Shame, and Competition Traps chapters are all intended to help you achieve that goal.

But suppose you really do want to lose weight? What are you to do? Many of you have dieted and regained weight countless times. For some of you, the metabolic slowdown has set in. And you may be storing more and more of your fat around your abdomen. In addition, you're likely to be finding dieting more difficult and frustrating. Then what is the best way to take off weight and minimize the dieting-rituals trap?

Our work has shown that the best weight-control strategy for people who have dieted often is one that's easy to follow, forestalls feelings of deprivation, and can be maintained over the long haul. Many diet foods are unhealthful and several so-called health foods are high in calories. Good weight-loss regimens keep fats down and add fiber to the diet in the form of fruits, vegetables, and whole-grain breads. All the evidence shows that moderate caloric restriction, with a diet that emphasizes natural, unprocessed foods, helps take weight off and keep it off the longest. The best strategy in the long run then is to give up the quest for the quick fix and resolve to eat more thoughtfully. Thoughtful eating requires a commitment to the long term. We advise patients to include at least some of the following strategies.

Assess your dieting readiness. Don't try to lose weight again until you're really ready. "I'm always ready," you think. But psychologist Kelly Brownell believes this is untrue. He has found that true readiness involves the right state of mind and life circumstances; it is not only a matter of desire. For long-term success, you must be sure that *now* is a good time. How can you tell?

First, in your mind you must develop a picture of how you will try to lose and maintain weight over the long term. Imagine six months or a year from now, not only tomorrow. For example, Jennifer had to learn to picture herself eating more, not less. She had to envision eating more frequently, with small meals spread throughout the day. She began to look forward to this in her future, making it into something special and self-indulgent, which it was for someone who had expended so much energy in self-denial.

Next, you must critically evaluate your life circumstances. Don't try to lose weight in the middle of a divorce or when you just lost your job. It's hard at any time, but since most women eat under stress, don't set yourself up for failure before you even begin. But if you are in a life transition where your habitual behaviors need to change, for example a new job with different hours, that may be a good time to institute changes in eating and exercise patterns as well.

Finally, you must assess your true motivation. Do you really feel ready now? Losing weight is hard work. If you don't truly feel motivated at present, put off your attempts to a better time.

Abandon the diet mentality—being "off" or "on," "good" or "bad," is part of the dieting-rituals trap. It's this all-or-nothing dichotomy that may set you up for the next failure. Here's how the scenario is usually played out.

It may start before you even begin your diet. Lucy, for example, has gained twenty pounds during the past three months, a fact that is astounding to her husband, because she has stated repeatedly during the same time period that she "is on a diet."

Lucy's dieting efforts typically begin with a plan. "Next Monday," she promises herself and those around her, "I'll start a new diet." Excitedly, she describes the newest miracle regimen, while finishing off a box of Valentine candy. "I can't have those around for the next month," she explains as she brushes off the crumbs from the table, the last trace of her husband's birthday cake, which she has just eaten. By Monday, Lucy notices in despair that she weighs another two pounds more than when she last had weighed herself.

After a week of finally limiting herself to nothing but fruit and water, Lucy attends a baby shower. She has offered to bring a dessert. She is determined not to have even a taste of the delicious cheesecake she makes. She announces to everyone at the party that she is on a diet and she sticks to eating fruit. At the end of the party, she helps clean up. Only a tiny piece of her cheesecake is left, not enough to save. Lucy eats it hastily, recognizing only after the fact that she has "broken" her diet. Disgusted with herself, she promises herself that she will try the diet again, starting next Monday. On her way home, she stops at a doughnut shop and eats a half a dozen in the car while driving. And until Monday, she eats "as though I am on death row—you know, it's the last time I get to eat all that good stuff and I do not want to have it around the house after Sunday."

For many women, dieting holds the promise of being the "ultimate coping strategy" to find relief from body dissatisfaction. I have found that breaking bad eating habits and beliefs and substituting healthy, more knowledgeable ones is an integral part of treating most body-preoccupation problems. The seemingly simple task of recording in great detail what you eat and under what circumstances is a consistently helpful technique which leads to some surprising insights. The record might reveal, for example, dysfunctional beliefs about food (Beatrice was convinced that healthful food was boring, a belief we uncovered when discussing her food diary), or harmful links between emotions and eating (Jennifer felt "flooded with guilt" after eating a favorite food), or maladaptive eating patterns (as in the case of Cheryl, who ate meals so small that anyone would have been left unsatisfied). Regardless of what started the bad eating habits, these behaviors become established and are difficult to change without detailed self-observation.

Some of our most troublesome problems come from our own internal dialogues—the mental running commentary we all engage in, usually about ourselves, and often in the form of a conversation. Lucy's comments to herself are a perfect example. By anticipating and vividly imagining the pain of abstinence, she allows herself to overeat before each new diet begins. Or in another instance, suppose a party hostess offers you a large piece of cake. You take it and eat it. But you had promised yourself that morning that this would be the first day of your diet. You feel awful, and your internal dialogue goes something like this: "What's wrong with me? I am such a pig! I will definitely start a new diet tomorrow." So, having eaten the cake, you overeat for the rest of the evening. Of course, when you get home that night, you are in despair.

At least two kinds of unhelpful thoughts, leading to overeating, are easily identified in this scenario. First, you blamed one small lapse (eating the cake) on personal shortcomings and appalling character defects. This made you feel useless and demoralized. Second, you decided to start dieting tomorrow: You pictured the next day as being one of such stringent deprivation that you felt you should eat everything in sight tonight.

You must identify your own unuseful thoughts and internal dialogues. These are usually negative and self-deprecatory. Replace them with more appropriate and helpful ones. Useful statements must include a plan for change. Instead of saying, "I am a pig," which is unhelpful, negative, and doesn't get you anywhere, you should identify the circumstances that made you overeat, and then say, for example, "I overeat when I drink," which pinpoints a circumstance that is possible to change.

Getting over the tendency to divide foods into "good" or "bad" isn't easy. It's promoted by the food industry, the diet business, and our own psyches. Often, we believe that *healthful* and *delicious* are mutually exclusive—a "good" (i.e. healthful) cereal tastes boring, bland, whereas a "bad" (i.e. unhealthful) cereal tastes sweet and gooey. Although there certainly are foods that are "nutritional nightmares," high in fat and salt or high in fat and refined sugar, there are many healthful foods that taste delicious. Unfortunately, however, we have brainwashed ourselves that a good diet must be boring and tasteless, leading us to believe that eating healthful foods is a burden. According to most studies, adults now express the same confusion and lack of control over their weight and food choices as adolescents do.

Believing in willpower and feeling guilty go together—you feel guilty because you think you haven't enough willpower. Both are unuseful states of mind that can undermine you. *Believing that you are in control, however, is a beneficial way of using your thoughts. This is quite different from believing in willpower.* As Delta Burke, the television star whom I discussed in the Shame Trap chapter wisely commented, "Taking control was the turning point for me. I've taken charge of my life now so I'm not in a race with myself anymore." She continued, "The body is a miraculous thing. It knows more than we think it does. So I've decided to listen to it more."

The concept of "willpower" involves continuous denial, ignoring the wisdom of the body. The concept of self-control implies that you have the skills for conscious decision-making, and the awareness of what your body needs. Uncontrolled eating is eating without decision-making and without awareness. People using self-control do not always decide "No." Sometimes, they decide "Yes, I will eat that!" Decision-making implies active and intelligent problem-solving. This counteracts feelings of helplessness and hopelessness. It's a vital part of breaking all the body traps.

Try spreading your calories out over the day. To help her break the dieting-rituals trap, we first asked Beatrice to write down carefully what she ate and the circumstances that surrounded her eating, including where, when, with whom she ate, and how she felt at the time. Her early food diaries revealed that Beatrice's eating pattern was rather chaotic. Some days she ate nothing until bedtime, and then would gorge on sweets for an hour before going to sleep. Other days, she attempted to eat "regular meals" which were actually very small meals, consisting of foods that Beatrice labeled "healthy," most of which she hated. She needed concrete advice about what constitutes a healthy, balanced meal and an adequate portion size. Like many chronic dieters, Beatrice no longer had any conception of what it feels like to be comfortably satiated and how much food she needed to eat to reach such a state.

Eating one large meal at night and nothing throughout the day is the worst strategy. The body needs some metabolic kick off in the morning after slowing down while sleeping. Eating something in the morning—a piece of toast, a half of grapefruit, almost anything—is sufficient to rev up metabolism.

A new study suggests that if the anything at breakfast contains fiber, you get an added benefit besides a boost to your metabolism. Dr. Allen Levine, a professor of Nutrition at the VA Medical Center in Minneapolis, showed that the people who ate the fewest calories at lunch were those with the highest fiber content in their breakfast meal. For example, they averaged 933 lunchtime calories after having a breakfast of Post Toasties (no fiber), 921 calories after breakfasting on Bran Chex (18 percent), and 888 calories after Fiber One (39 percent) for breakfast. Fiber slows transit time through the intestine, so a high-fiber breakfast could leave you still feeling fuller at lunch.

Studies have shown that skipping meals can lower basal metabolic rate. Dr. Wayne Callaway, an endocrinologist and director of the Center for Clinical Nutrition at the George Washington University Medical Center, has found in his studies that a one-hundred-fifty pound woman who skips meals burns 150 calories fewer than a woman of the same weight who eats three meals each day, with calories evenly spread throughout the three meals. This is due in part to the fact that each meal produces a rise in the rate calories are burned, caused by the body working to digest the food.

Many chronic dieters are night eaters. They skip breakfast, eat a light lunch, and a heavy dinner. This turns out to be a very maladaptive weight-loss strategy. What makes so many dieters determined to skip breakfast? Brenda's explanation is typical of what many other dieters have told us. "To me, being on a diet and watching my weight means not eating breakfast. I only eat breakfast when I'm off my diet. If I eat something for breakfast while I'm on my diet, I'm afraid I will not have enough calories left to eat for dinner. Since I *know* it's hard for me to eat a small amount at night, I save most of my calories for the evening meal."

Caffeine stimulates in a negative way, because it provokes insulin release and may in fact enhance the storage of what is eaten as fat. Claims that it revs up metabolism are overstated. Try to stay away from too many caffeinated beverages. Countless women drink caffeinated diet sodas to help them through their days of fasting or eating very little. This practice may lead them to feel even more hungry, and it prepares their bodies for maximally storing whatever food they eat.

Natural and unprocessed foods are more satiating. They help to influence a metabolism slowed by repeated cycles of dieting and regain. Try to eat as many fresh and unprocessed foods as possible. We've been focusing on the health-promoting virtues of complex carbohydrates, such as fruits and vegetables and whole-grain breads. Probably their most important quality, often overlooked, is that they are extremely satiating. They stay with you for a long time.

As you learned in the last chapter, not all calories are created equal. Calories from fat cause greater weight gain than calories from carbohydrates or protein. And you can eat more calories worth of protein and complex carbohydrate and still lose weight. Stay away from high-fat foods as much as possible. Cutting down on fat is a relatively easy change to make, since you can add other types of calories and not feel deprived.

Don't trust your memory. Recent research by Dr. Albert F. Smith, a cognitive psychologist who studies memory at the State University of New York at Binghamton, says everyone has trouble remembering how much and what they've eaten. Smith tested how well people would recall what they had eaten, even after they actually recorded their foods in a diary when they ate them. Recall was quite poor—only 55 percent correct at the end of the week for which the recording was done; and only 35 percent correct at the end of three weeks. We have shown that the ability to recall correctly is even worse if people don't write it down. We observed Yale freshmen in the dining halls at lunchtime and then they actually recorded everything they ate. When we asked them the next day to recall what they had for lunch the previous day, only 23 percent were completely correct. Most erred by more than 300 calories.

Part of the error comes at the input side, not in remembering. Smith's research shows, for example, that people are amazingly poor at judging portion size. The best most people can do is recall whether or not they ate a particular food. Since the size of a portion will determine its calories, people may misjudge at recall, because they were incorrect in estimating how large or small a serving they had.

So writing it down helps, but only if you know the real size of the portion you had. Otherwise, you may think you know how many calories you had, but be far from right. Focusing on correctly learning the calories in the serving size you typically eat is essential. Be realistic. Learn the calories in the serving size you are used to eating and cut or substitute as necessary.

Exercise can help. Aerobic exercise increases metabolic rate, so it can fool the body into not slowing down. Developing a moderate, positive exercise routine is a healthy way of using calories. For many people, it also reinforces healthier eating habits, and exercise may help to regulate appetite. Undoubtedly, physical activity is also symbolic of the hoped-for positive changes that are taking place. In this way, exercise can make you feel good and boost self-confidence.

All of these strategies can help you to lose weight and keep it off. But they require moderation and thoughtful commitment, not frenzied desire and religious zeal. Find other channels besides dieting and self-denial for making yourself better.

— 7 —

The Fitness Trap

Is it true that you can have too much of a good thing? In fact, in the case of the fitness trap, too much may be worse than none at all. We've all heard about exercise addicts—people who abuse exercise the way others abuse alcohol, cigarettes, or drugs. But even the nonaddicts may be headed for trouble. For some exercise-dependent people, workouts cease to be a means of improving life. They become an escape from it. Exercise makes them feel better about themselves when nothing else does anymore. Robert Lipsyte, writing in *The New York Times*, woefully reports:

> A man says to me in the health-club locker room in Chicago's Ritz-Carlton Hotel: "At least I did one good thing today."
>
> What else can he do? Work harder? The company doesn't love him. If the way the railroad mistreated his father didn't teach him, then the last 20 years of reorganizations and closings and layoffs and mergers have. What else can he do? Buy another machine? How many BMWs, VCRs, and PCs does one person need? Get into his family? His wife's out jogging too, clearing her mind for briefs, and the kids are available only for quality time.
>
> So he "works out." He wraps himself into himself and

no matter how much pain and/or injury he self-inflicts, even if he recapitulates the Type A overdrive, the paranoia, the reflexive competition of his professional life, he believes he is doing himself good; chasing the dreads, frying off fat, getting stronger, looking younger, becoming better!

For Jennifer, whom I described in detail as suffering also from the vanity trap, working out was a status symbol. Not only did it make her feel good physically, it also made her feel good about herself. Her husband bragged about her discipline and control to their friends, making her efforts seem even more worthwhile.

The fitness trap exists because exercise is both good and bad—it's entirely a matter of degree. Some exercise is good for us, although good for what is an issue I will review in this chapter. But fitness pursued to the extreme in search of good health can have precisely the opposite effect.

Fitness is a crucial health goal and, in large part, exercise makes it happen. But by the late 1960s, with the formation of the President's Council on Physical Fitness, exercise became not only good for your health, but morally righteous. The fitness boom, according to Robert Lipsyte, is:

> . . . a cyclical phenomenon, predominantly middle class, layered by money, sex, religion, charismatic entrepreneurs and fear of an early death. . . . Even if we also hope to be firm, to be hip, it is the prospect of prolonging life that justifies the money, the time and hard work by those swept up in the fitness craze.

And exercise has become big business, fueled by our adulation of athletes. Many believe that the adoration is unhealthful for both the athlete and his or her fans. Athletes are always in the public eye and many are unable to stand up either to the pressure or the public scrutiny. Star athletes are paid outrageous sums of money because television (more precisely TV commercials) has brought millions of dollars and millions

— 197 —

of spectators to sports most people never even heard of twenty years ago. Well-muscled fitness experts now have their own airtime as well. The message all of this conveys is strongly felt today: Look good and be famous; exercise hard and win. You too can escape your boring, routine lives by working on your bodies. Forget your brains. After all, how much do school-teachers and judges earn? Prestige, admiration, and money now come via a different route.

The pros and cons of exercise are hotly debated—the stakes are high for both sides. The fitness promoters want everyone out there moving. Some skeptics aren't so sure, and others are adamantly against exercise. There's evidence to support each argument. On one hand, there is indisputable proof that moderate exercise benefits most people. Certainly, it is better for physical health to exercise than not to exercise, and exercise also appears to improve mood. But doing more and more exercise may in fact lead to diminishing returns. Dr. David Costill, who is the director of the Ball State University Human Performance Laboratory, has studied swimmers in training. He found that they could reduce their exercise regimen by as much as 30 percent—that is, they could cut down their weekly mileage by one third—and still remain at the same level of conditioning.

In fact, among intense exercisers, metabolic rate may actually go down the more they exercise as their bodies struggle to conserve energy, thus compromising their energy balance. Lisa began jogging about seven years ago, first to control her weight after a twenty pound weight loss, and then to improve her aerobic fitness. Her friends admired her persistence and she felt great about herself. She kept increasing her distance, since she worried that she was getting less benefit from each run. Now she's afraid to stop. "Talk about a treadmill," she said, laughing weakly at her own cruel joke. "I really can't get off and sometimes I feel like a caged rat chasing her own tail." She panics when she's sick for a few days and started running much earlier than the doctor recommended when she sprained her ankle last year. And now—as silly as it sounds— she feels she has to eat less and exercise more in order to maintain her weight. In fact, she may be right. Lisa's caught in the fitness trap. Are you? Take the test on page 200 to see. This is a modified version of one that Doctors Kelly Brownell, Jack Wilmore, and I developed for *Runner's World* magazine.

What Is Fitness?

An inspection of human anatomy and physiology makes it obvious that the human being was designed for exercise. For example, as much as 45 percent of our body mass is skeletal muscle and the anatomical arrangement of this muscle allows for a diverse pattern of movements. Humans have muscle cells with two different kinds of contraction called fast and slow twitch. Fast twitch fibers are those that are activated during anaerobic exercise, such as sprinting or lifting. Slow twitch fibers are those called upon for endurance activities, such as distance running. Most people have about equal numbers of each.

Individuals differ greatly in their exercise capacity. This is due to variations in their genetic endowment, gender, age, and in their exercise training, nutritional, and health status. There are large hereditary differences, for example in the capacity of the cardiovascular system to transport oxygen, and in skeletal muscle mass and composition. The "trainability" of a person, for a particular sport or for fitness in general, also appears to have a substantial genetic component. Your innate capacity for athletic performance usually is evident by the time you have reached puberty or shortly thereafter. This is an attribute you cannot do much to change.

Exercise has been widely promoted as the pathway to fitness. But fitness has largely been defined by the condition of the cardiovascular system, which in fact is influenced only (or at least primarily) by aerobic forms of exercise. The easiest technique for assessing your cardiovascular fitness is to measure the time it takes for your pulse to return to its normal or "resting" rate after aerobic exercise raises it to a "target rate." That target is generally figured by the formula: 154 minus your age. For example, if you are twenty-five, your target rate

EXERCISE HISTORY

1. How many hours per week do you train or work out?
   On the average _____ *hours; at peak training* _____ *hours*

2. How many years have you been exercising at least four times a
   week?
   _____ *years*

3. Have you changed your exercise regimen over the last five years?
   Increased number or duration of workouts   _____
   Decreased number or duration of workouts   _____
   No change   _____

4. Do you feel worried, anxious, or nervous when you stop exercising
   for more than a few days?

1	2	3	4	5
Never	*Rarely*	*Sometimes*	*Often*	*Always*

5. How important would you rate exercise compared with other
   activities in your life?

1	2	3	4	5
Extremely important	*Important*	*About average*	*Low*	*Unimportant*

6. How often do you diet during periods of peak exercise or training?

1	2	3	4	5
Never	*Rarely*	*Sometimes*	*Often*	*Always*

7. How would your weight be different if you were not exercising as
   much as you do?

1	2	3	4	5
I would weigh much less	*I would weigh somewhat less*	*I would weigh the same*	*I would weigh somewhat more*	*I would weigh much more*

8. If you exercise vigorously, how many calories do you think you average each day to maintain your weight?

During peak training _____ *calories*

When you stop or reduce training _____ *calories*

9. If you exercise vigorously, do you have to eat more or less now than in the past to be at your optimal weight?

1	2	3	4	5
Much less than before	*Somewhat less than before*	*No change*	*Somewhat more than before*	*Much more than before*

People who work out four or more times a week for an hour or longer are thought to be more vulnerable to the fitness trap. This is especially true for those people exercising at this pace for three years or more, or for those who have been increasing their workouts over the last five years. If your response to question 4 shows that you often or always experience negative moods when you stop, you are more likely to be caught by the fitness trap, especially if you rated exercise as an extremely important activity in your life (question 5). People who diet intensively when exercising heavily may be developing a slowdown of metabolic rate. If you answer question 7 by saying you would weigh much more if not following your current exercise regimen, ask yourself when was the last time you actually tested that belief. One good way to test question 8 accurately is by counting calories for a few days. Finally, if you think you have to eat less now than you used to, the fitness trap may be your problem.

---

is $154 - 25 = 129$; if you are fifty-five, it's $154 - 55 = 99$. The more aerobically fit you are, the quicker your pulse returns to normal. A faster recovery suggests, although not unequivocally, that your heart is stronger, but as I will show you later, it is no guarantee that you are healthier.

The Plus Side of Exercise

Exercise can enhance your physical and mental state. The body adapts to an increase in exercise as it does to any other stress; it responds by attempting to increase its capacity to better accommodate the biological or physical alterations produced by the stress. For example, during endurance type (aerobic) exercise, a sustained stress or demand is placed on a variety of tissues and biochemical processes. They respond by increasing their ability to support a higher intensity of activity for the same time or the same intensity of activity for a longer period.

Exercise and Health Exercise has been glorified as a major health-promoting behavior. It has been suggested that exercise has potential preventive or therapeutic benefits for major chronic disorders including ischemic heart disease, stroke, hypertension, adult-onset diabetes, and osteoporosis. Recently, an exercise-cancer link has been drawn for the first time, possibly because long-term athletic training establishes a more health-promoting life-style.

Much of the evidence for the health benefits of exercise comes from studies that relate the effects of exercise to biological changes that are thought to be important in reducing the likelihood of developing these diseases: For example, altered lipid profiles (heart disease); increased insulin sensitivity (diabetes); or the effects of exercise to other healthy behaviors, for example, eating better. Scientists warn, however, that we cannot yet assume that an apparent change in any of these *causes* an improvement in health status. Furthermore, at present, the criterion used most frequently to evaluate the likelihood that a specific exercise training program will improve health status is whether or not it produces an increase in aerobic power. An increase in aerobic power provides strengthening of the heart, an improved blood flow, as well as possible benefits in rates of energy expenditure. But many other beneficial biologic changes may occur with exercise that are unrelated to aerobic power.

Strength training (with weights) stimulates retention of bone mineral content, and increases muscle and connective tissue strength. Building and retaining muscles becomes especially important as people age. It is now thought that bone loss, in older women in particular, may be due in part to

— 202 —

muscle loss, and therefore, building muscles may be essential in preventing injury to bones as we age.

Even younger adults appear to benefit from more muscled bodies. More muscles burn more calories—estimates are somewhere around one quarter to one third more calories are burned by muscle than by fat. Losing muscle means your metabolism slows down; gaining muscle speeds it up leading to increased caloric expenditure. Muscle strength prevents injuries, particularly to vulnerable areas like the knees and lower back.

Many forms of moderate exercise can improve the health of bones by increasing their mineral content. The amount of minerals in spinal bones, for example, usually decreases as one gets older, but regular exercise has been shown to help slow this loss. A few studies suggest that older women who have osteoporosis (very low bone mineral content leading to increased risk for fractures) can partially reverse this problem by adopting a regular exercise program. Flexibility exercises contribute to better maintenance of the muscles and skeletal system with increasing age.

Betty is a sixty-five-year-old woman who plays tennis twice a week and walks most mornings with a friend for about one half hour. She always delights in commenting that she doesn't feel or look her age and compares herself to her "crotchety" friends who sit around inactive, and look ten years older. Betty had a bad fall on the ice last year, but didn't break her leg, although she certainly could have, according to her doctor. Is it good luck or her exercise regimen? Betty would bet her bank account on the exercise!

Exercise has also been promoted as a life extender. GET OFF YOUR DUFF AND LIVE LONGER suggests a front-page article in *USA Today* reporting on a study published in the *Journal of the American Medical Association* by epidemiologist Steven Blair, of the Institute for Aerobic Research in Dallas. Death rates for the least fit (determined by treadmill tests which measure aerobic power) compared with the most fit were 3.4 times higher for men and 4.6 times higher for women, in Blair's study. Other studies conducted at Harvard, tracking

Harvard alumni, have found up to a two-year increase in life expectancy in men who expended at least 3,500 calories a week in some form of exercise.

If active people can be expected to live two or more years longer than their inactive peers, it must be due to the effects of exercise on risk for the diseases that cause death. Perhaps even more important than increased life expectancy is improved quality of life. Active elderly individuals can possess the exercise capacity of a person twenty to forty years younger, improving the quality of life greatly in their remaining years.

Exercise for weight control No promise makes exercise more appealing than the lure of weight loss. Witness a headline in *New Woman* magazine to introduce yet another exercise article: THERE'S ONLY ONE THING YOU NEED TO DO TO AVOID DIETING. THAT'S TO EXERCISE. SO WHICH WOULD YOU RATHER DO? GET FAT? OR GET MOVING?

Every diet program includes some kind of aerobic exercise, and those people who can stick to it do shed more pounds. The real benefit doesn't seem to come merely from the calories used while exercising. Rather, moderate exercise increases resting metabolic rate, which can be slowed by restriction of calories while dieting. When metabolism increases, so does the loss of body fat. Dieting combined with exercise stimulates energy expenditure and the burning of fat, so long as neither the exercise nor the dieting is too intense. In the latter case, as I'll explore later in the chapter, the body may try to protect itself further, thus slowing metabolic rate even more.

Whatever the role of exercise in weight loss—and there is still controversy in the scientific community—there is clear agreement that exercise helps to keep the weight off. Almost all successful maintainers have added exercise to their lifestyle in some way. Interestingly, it isn't clear how the addition of an exercise program works in maintaining weight. Some think the benefit comes from the calories you spend in doing the exercise. Thirty minutes of aerobic exercise, which elevates heart rate to about 140 to 150 beats per minute, requires an expenditure of about 150 to 200 calories. A lot of popular advice about the benefits of exercise for weight control relies on that formula. For example, *Ms.* magazine suggested that "once fit, millions sweat for the perks, among them: the freedom to gorge yourself with impunity." The article suggests "how much you can eat for free, once you've put in your time." For example, one hour of biking at thirteen miles per hour gives you a "nosh" of one free hot fudge sundae, according to *Ms*. How many of us have been done in by such easy-sounding promises?

Rather than allowing us free indulgences, exercising regularly may provide benefits, because it reduces the likelihood of giving in to the urge to "nosh." Gaby told us, "If I exercise regularly, I feel really good about myself and I don't really want to overeat. I am proud of what my body can accomplish and I feel that I really want to take good care of my body. When I don't exercise, I'm much more likely to have a 'who cares?' attitude. I'll say to myself, 'I'm a fat slob anyway, so why not eat this cream puff?' "

Some scientists think the benefits of exercise for weight maintenance go beyond calorie-burning effects. Dr. Judith Stern's research team at the University of California at Davis, for example, has recently completed a large study of several hundred people in California who were trying to maintain their weight after a period of weight loss. They found that all the successful maintainers exercised, but it didn't much matter what kind of exercise they did. It didn't even seem to matter how often they exercised or how long, so long as they had a fixed routine that they stuck to. So the woman who did ten minutes of jumping jacks three times a week was as likely to keep her weight off as the woman who jogged every day for thirty minutes. Clearly, we cannot attribute effects to increased metabolic rate or physical expenditure alone when the type and amount of exercise is so different.

To explain this surprising finding, the researchers argued that people who are able to stick to an exercise routine, no matter what it is, may be able to follow other changes—for example, in what or how much they eat. Someone who keeps up efforts in exercise may simply be a better bet to keep up an effort in all areas.

Finally, some scientists think exercise works for weight control because it makes you feel so much better psychologically. Investigators trying to understand the beneficial effects of exercise study two separate things: what happens to mood and well-being immediately after an exercise workout, and what the longer-term benefits of maintaining an exercise regimen are.

The evidence clearly shows that people feel better right after they do some form of strenuous physical activity. Exercise seems to temporarily decrease feelings of anxiety, depression, and stress. But are there also long-term gains? The highly acclaimed Perrier Survey of Fitness in America, conducted by Louis Harris and Associates, found that people who exercise certainly think so. Those who had a deep commitment to exercise reported feeling more relaxed, less tired, and more disciplined. They also reported having greater self-confidence, a sense of looking better, greater productivity in work and, in general, a stronger sense of being at one with themselves. Evidence from numerous research studies supports these people's beliefs.

Recently, Dr. Tom Stephens of Canada directed the evaluation of data from four national surveys in the United States and Canada. "The inescapable conclusion," says Stephens, "is that physical activity is positively associated with good mental health, especially positive mood, general well-being, and less anxiety and depression." This relationship was found to be stronger for the older age group (forty-plus years of age) than for the younger, and for women even more than for men.

Karen is a vibrant fifty-year-old woman we tested in a research study. She had a real zest for life that was evident even in a "get-acquainted" interview. She told us how she used to be a real couch potato, watching television while lying on the sofa all evening. But when she turned forty, she decided to take herself in hand, and she began exercising regularly, but moderately. Some weeks she swims once or twice, but usually she takes brisk walks in the evenings with a few of her friends. She claims she has none of those middle-age blues other women her age have. She feels and looks better than she did at forty. When depressed, she says, "I reach for my sneakers instead of a donut."

To some degree, the meaning of being an exerciser may be as important as the physical benefits of exercise. In other words, positive results may occur because of the psychological gains experienced from trying to get and stay fit, rather than from physical fitness, per se. Engaging in exercise may lead to an increased sense of personal efficacy and self-worth. Evidence suggests that young children and adolescents who are physically adept and participate in sports have higher self-esteem and perceived competence than children who do not participate in athletic activities. Some studies suggest that the demands and rigors of athletic competition may provide a structure that makes coping with the demands of adolescence easier. In addition, they may feel greater self-worth at a time when body concerns are usually high, because they have a body that is capable of performing athletic feats.

There are almost as many theories about why exercise is good for mental health as there are types of exercise. Our beliefs are fueled by a pervasive sense that exercise is a good thing. Some believe that exercise is a form of meditation that triggers an altered and more relaxed state of consciousness. Another theory suggests that exercise provides needed distraction, diversion, or simply time-out from unpleasant thoughts and feelings. Some argue that exercisers feel good because people who exercise are rewarded and admired by others. So far, none of these theories has been confirmed with sufficient scientific evidence.

Other theories focus on various hormones and other body chemicals as possible reasons why exercise improves psychological well-being. The body has a recently discovered hormonal system of morphinelike chemicals called endogenous opioids, whose receptors are found in the area of the brain associated with emotion, pleasure, pain, and behavior. During exercise, the pituitary increases its production of B-endorphin, one of the endogenous opioids, increasing its concentration in the blood.

Although it is widely accepted by the exercising public that endorphins are responsible for exercise-induced euphoria, convincing scientific evidence is largely absent. Surveys of habitual runners show conflicting estimates, with as few as 10 percent and as many as 78 percent reporting experiences of "euphoria" during a run. Twenty-seven different adjectives or phrases have appeared in the literature describing the runner's high, and this attests to its highly subjective nature. Most researchers have found that the increase in B-endorphin is unrelated to the improvement in mood following exercise. Most researchers have been unable to demonstrate that after the pituitary secretes endorphins into the blood, the substances are able to cross the barrier and gain entry into the brain.

Dr. James Wiese of Alberta Hospital and a research team at Arizona State University have both discovered that during exercise, there is an increase in brain emission of alpha waves. These brain waves, which are associated with a relaxed meditationlike state, appear twenty minutes into a thirty-minute jog, and are still measurable after the exercise is over. Researchers speculate that the increased alpha wave power could contribute to the psychological benefits of exercise, including reductions in anxiety and depression. Other researchers suggest that exercise decreases muscle electrical tension. Some advance the idea that exercise increases oxygen transport to the brain.

If exercise does have a positive psychological impact for some people, it undoubtedly is due to some change it produces in the brain. But despite all these theories, we simply don't really know at present why, or even if, people who exercise always feel good.

The Down Side of Exercise

Fitness and health are not synonymous. After all, as we are often reminded, the elite runner Jim Fixx dropped dead while exercising. Fixx's autopsy revealed advanced atherosclerosis —the progressive circulatory disease in which plaque attached to the inside of the arteries eventually closes the blood vessels. A moment comes when the body needs a rush of oxygen-bearing blood that cannot be delivered. Fixx was fit when he died, but he was not healthy. Exercise is just one part of the puzzle. In his case, bad genes were insurmountable. Maybe one of the reasons he was driven to run was to delay the tides of a family history loaded with heart disease. Exercise advocates argued that he probably would have died much sooner if he had never run. But in some circles it's become as fashionable to warn against exercise as it has been to promote it in others. Fitness skeptics wonder if it wasn't the intensity of exercise that overtaxed Fixx's flawed system. If he had never run, if he had missed that particular stressor, perhaps he would have lived longer.

Exercise and Health Risks First let's look at health and disease to see what the risks of exercise might be. For people who have a high risk of heart disease, for example those who have a lot of heart disease in the family or who themselves are overweight or smoke, *vigorous* aerobic exercise has been found to promote sudden death from heart attack during the exercise period. The Loyola Marymount basketball star Hank Gathers, knowing that he had heart disease, played basketball and died from a heart attack during a game.

Less serious risks are far more prevalent. For example, heavy people are much more likely to injure muscles and tendons because of their weight, and one of the chief risks of excessive exercise for everyone is damage to the joints, ligaments, tendons, and muscles of the feet and legs. Most studies show that activities that require jumping and running, such as aerobic dancing and jogging, promote the most injury.

Less well known is research showing that excessive exercise, like marathon running, may depress the immune system, thereby lowering the body's defense for fighting off infections, colds, and flus. Sara, a competitive runner, talked about the lore of the marathon. People who finished a race feeling that they had exceeded their usual performance would frequently joke that they were sure to get sick in the next few days. No one knew why but everyone "knew" that it happened. In a study conducted on twenty-three hundred Los Angeles Marathon runners, flus and colds increased 600 percent in the runners who ran the marathon as opposed to those who decided at the very end not to run.

Distance running frequently has other negative consequences. One potential hazard is overheating. (This is true of all endurance events, not just marathon running.) In hot climates, endurance sports put a great strain on the person's circulatory and temperature regulation systems. Regardless of climate, anyone who suddenly undertakes excessive, prolonged physical activity is at risk of heat injury. Older people may be affected more than their younger counterparts, since they possess significantly less heat tolerance. Heavily built and fatter individuals have a greater problem dissipating heat. Fatigue and lack of sleep also predispose one to heat illness.

Another health risk of intense exercise is what has been called "runner's anemia." Studies have shown that many competitive runners have lower than normal total iron stores, and a smaller percentage have overt anemia. Many competitive runners actually have gastrointestinal blood loss while running, a loss which appears to be higher in those who run faster.

A common problem that affects women athletes is menstrual dysfunction. There is strong evidence that intense exercise disrupts normal menstrual function and can cause amenorrhea, which is no menstruation at all. Scientists still don't fully understand this phenomenon and several possible factors have been suggested, including excessive body weight loss, low body fatness, stress, and hormonal changes. There is also a great deal of evidence that young athletes have delayed onset of menstruation, especially those who train heavily. Delayed menarche also appears related to the age of initiating training. Elite college swimmers and runners were recruited to take part in a study conducted by a team of investigators at Harvard's School of Public Health. Those athletes who began training before puberty had an average age of reaching menarche of 15.1 years. Those who began training after puberty reached menarche at 12.8 years, on the average.

The study shows that each year of training before menarche delayed puberty by five months.

Concern about disruption in menses or delayed menarche has grown recently following reports that women with this complication have a decreased bone mineral density, making them more vulnerable to fractures and other musculoskeletal injuries. But menstrual dysfunction may not be the only culprit when it comes to weak bones. Recently, Grace Wyshak, of Harvard's School of Public Health, and a team of researchers asked 2,398 women of all ages a series of questions about lifestyle, diet, participation in college athletics, and bone fractures. They found that among former college athletes, soda drinkers were about twice as likely as nonsoda drinkers to suffer a first bone fracture after forty. That's the age when women begin to lose bone, and the earliest that fractures due to brittleness would occur.

"It was a surprising result," says study coauthor Rose Frisch of Harvard's Center for Population Studies, "and troubling, because many athletes drink huge amounts of soda." She adds that soda drinking had no perceptible effect on the bones of nonathletes—perhaps because they drank fewer soft drinks than the athletes. Just one type of soft drink produces this apparent effect—those colas which contain phosphoric acid. Animal studies, along with scattered case reports from humans, suggest that phosphorous interferes with the absorption of calcium, which the body uses to build bone.

Exercise and Weight Control For many, the health risk of intense exercise is worth it, since exercise helps burn those calories. Nothing is too great a price to pay for weight control! But evidence is beginning to mount that challenges the benefits of exercise even in this area.

First, there are problems caused by cyclic exercise. Many sedentary people begin exercise programs they don't stick to. For the occasional exerciser, it may be worse to have started and stopped than never to have begun at all. Mary is an example of someone who was always starting some new exercise program or other. She was really committed and would buy all the equipment and bore all her friends with her talk of little else. But she never stayed on any program very long. Occasionally, she pushed herself too hard and burned out; sometimes she got bored; other times, things just seemed to get in the way. It is highly likely that she was putting herself at risk by these behaviors.

Dr. Judith Stern at The University of California, Davis, put some groups of animals on an exercise program while others led a more sedentary life. When the exercised rats were taken off their regime, they overate and gained weight and soon looked just like the sedentary animals. But when Dr. Stern and her colleagues measured their blood pressure, insulin levels, and metabolism, they were even worse off than the sedentaries. And they had a higher percentage of body fat. Bad news for those of us who gear up after a New Year's resolution of fitness, only to have given it up by spring. Some weight gain may be the least of our problems.

Even the many athletes who train during their season and then slow down or stop off-season may be at risk. The well-trained athlete who goes through cycles of training may also be doing herself some harm if the cycles are too extreme. Cycles of stopping and starting exercise may build up body fat, especially in the risk regions around the abdominal organs. Sudden weight shifts may also be common among athletes because they diet for a competitive edge, or to meet a specific weight limit. The extreme is wrestlers, who repeatedly lose weight in order to compete in a certain weight classification— called "cutting weight"—and then regain it after the match.

Athletic Performance and Disordered Eating Although extra pounds—especially in the form of fat—will slow you down, an obsession with thinness can help defeat you, too. Exercise-induced problems appear to be increasing for athletes, in particular. Many report an urgency to minimize body fat for performance, leading to excessive weight reduction and a pathologic degree of food and fat aversion. Athletes and coaches recognize the importance of having maximum strength, endurance, and quickness for each pound of body weight taken into competition. The presumed, as well as real, advantages of a minimal level of fatness in athletic performance, plus the strong negative and moral connotations of being too heavy in our society, combine to create strong pressures on many young athletes to abhor excess weight. The idea that fitness improves performance gets distorted, and many succumb to a blind mentality of thin equals win.

Fat aversion is commonly reinforced by coaches who think nothing of telling girls they're too fat. A successful Southwestern swimming coach who sends many athletes to the Olympics is well known for giving packages of beef fat to his team members who may have gained a few pounds. He also encourages team members to make oinking sounds when a transgressor enters the room.

Cheryl's eating problems had begun when she turned fifteen years old, and her skating coach recommended that she lose five pounds for an upcoming skating competition. "I never thought about what I ate until that day," Cheryl said. "I was naturally skinny, and of course, was on the ice anywhere from three to six hours a day. When my coach told me to lose five pounds, I thought, No sweat, anybody can lose five pounds. Besides, I really wanted to win and the thought of Celina [her chief competition] having a competitive edge just because I weighed a bit too much—well, that killed me."

What seemed to be an easy task turned out to be impossible. Cheryl's body was still growing and she never managed to get down from ninety-five to ninety pounds. She tried to starve herself, but soon realized that food was a great source of comfort to her, the only pleasure she ever allowed herself. When she tried to diet, she found that she was calmed by food, and needed her periods of overeating. By the time she reached college, Cheryl "resolved" this dilemma by making herself throw up whenever she overate. Although she never became truly bulimic, she liked thinking that she could "control the damage by vomiting."

When not training, the athletes who have been the most restrictive often gain the most weight. Those reporting the most severe weight swings also have the highest incidence of eating disorders and are least satisfied with their bodies. The high fluctuators also maintain their weight on the fewest calories, possibly because the weight fluctuations have gradually forced their bodies to adapt to low calorie levels.

Greg came to our clinic after finishing his third successful wrestling season. Despite his many medals and honors, he found himself agitated and depressed. His profile perfectly matched Marnie's, the captain of a major Southwestern swimming team. Neither could eat very much anymore, even when they were in training, or they would gain weight. And both were obsessed by thoughts of food. Both had been through numerous cycles of gaining and losing weight.

Recently, Doctors Jack Wilmore, Kelly Brownell, and I evaluated findings from a survey answered by 4,542 readers of *Runner's World* magazine. The respondents were long-term athletes, averaging seven and a half years of training, and running an average of eight hours a week.

Most of us, when looking at these athletes, think they are lucky, that they can eat as much as they want and never gain weight. The truth is, however, that many runners only *wish* this were true. If only they *could* eat and never gain an ounce. As the results of our National Runner's Survey on Dieting and Eating indicate, a surprisingly large number of runners worry not only about their weight, but also about what they eat and how they look. Contrary to what we may think, many runners are unhappy with their bodies, and some resort to abnormal eating patterns in their quest for physical perfection.

Alice is one such runner. Following a relatively common pattern, she developed an eating disorder while in pursuit of athletic success. Four days before a race, she'd starve herself, denying her ravenous body all but 1,000 calories. As soon as she finished a race, she'd go to the cafeteria and quickly wolf down as many as 6,000 calories. She usually followed that binge with two days of "normal eating," but then the cycle would repeat. Instead of building a foundation for a healthy future and improving her performance, Alice was running slower and developing an eating disorder.

In many athletes, daily losses of a pound or more are not uncommon. These athletes experience and tolerate hunger pangs and, like Alice, often go on eating binges at the end of a tournament or season. Such gorging can be hazardous because of salt-induced water retention and cardiovascular overload.

Being too thin is unhealthy, and the steps many people take to achieve thinness often result in long-term metabolic (and psychological) problems. But just how many runners become too focused on thinness? And why do some runners succumb to the obsession, while others remain unaffected? The answers are not simple, but the statistics from the *Runner's World* survey suggest some explanations.

According to the study's findings, dieting and weight concerns were greatest among runners at the highest levels of performance. Nearly three fourths of the women and two thirds of the men said they dieted even during peak periods of running. Many found it difficult to control their weight and claimed that the difficulty increased with the length of their training. Fully 60 percent of women and 75 percent of men said they eat less now than in the past in order to control their weight. How can this be so, when one of the benefits of regular exercise is that it boosts metabolism making weight control easier? But excessive exercise, like severe dieting, may do just the opposite.

For most of us, a good run will push up our metabolic rate for an hour or two or more. That's a plus when you're trying to burn off last night's mocha fudge. But intense exercisers may experience the exact opposite—their metabolic rates may actually go down the more they exercise, new studies suggest. Since their bodies conserve energy, they may need far fewer calories to maintain their weight and their workouts than most people do.

For "workout-aholics," exercise is like dieting, which can slow down metabolism as a defense against starvation. Ultra-athletes burn off so many calories in their workouts, some researchers speculate, that their bodies respond by conserving calories. In three studies of female runners, women who averaged running thirty-three to sixty-five miles a week reported being able to eat only about 1,400 to 2,000 calories a day, although they should have been able to eat at least 3,000.

This paradoxical negative effect of overexercising is most likely to take its toll on athletes for whom leanness and appearance count most—long-distance runners, gymnasts, figure skaters, and ballet dancers. When a gymnast's or runner's metabolism becomes more efficient as fitness improves and he or she burns fewer calories to perform the same amount of work, balancing intake and expenditure becomes more difficult. Think of your body as an automobile engine: When your engine is fuel efficient, you get more mileage on less gas. The same is true for a food-efficient body.

Women may be most at risk for a metabolic turndown. The reason: Reproductive function is more readily threatened when fat stores change. If body weight or body fat gets so low as to threaten such a vital function, the body "fights back" by becoming more efficient at conserving calories. In the studies that showed surprisingly low caloric needs in female runners, the women who had stopped menstruating were maintaining their weight on even fewer calories than those who still had their menstrual periods.

For many athletes, concern with dieting, weight, and their bodies turns to obsession. There is still controversy about the extent and severity of eating disorders among athletes, but all experts agree there is cause for concern. Our survey showed that 38 percent of female and 23 percent of male runners say they eat excessively and out of control at least once a month. When asked, "Have you ever purged (used self-induced vomiting, laxatives, or diuretics) to control your weight?" 26 percent of the women and 4 percent of the men said yes. If we had tested wrestlers, the percentages for men would be even higher. The most serious athlete is not immune from disturbed eating; in fact, she may be the most profound example. While the presence of eating disorders in athletes does not *prove* a causal link with sports participation, many studies show it is the better athletes who are most likely to show both physical and psychological symptoms of eating disorders.

A whole new category of research now deals with "sports-induced eating disturbances." These studies have focused especially on gymnasts, figure skaters, and dancers, where the requirements for thinness sometimes go beyond what is necessary for the performance of a certain athletic endeavor, thereby becoming an aesthetic preference. The most obvious example is the ballet dancer who, unless she is very thin, may not be accepted in a national company, regardless of talent. A study by Dr. Jeanne Brooks-Gunn showed, further, that the level at which ballet dancers compete is related to their incidence of anorexia nervosa. In her survey, most instances of anorexia were in national (the most competitive) rather than regional companies.

Exercise Addicts The concept of being addicted to exercise has gained widespread acceptance among athletes and the general public alike. Addiction, in general terms, is based on the experience a person derives from a particular substance or activity. The experience usually has a physiological and psychological component, and the person comes to need that experience—to be unable to do without it. Indeed, the perception of being addicted to exercise has become part of the athlete's self-concept. It is almost expected among those who are supposed to value athletics the most.

Why do people overexercise? Though the public calls it "exercise addiction," researchers are more comfortable with terms like "exercise dependency." But both terms imply that this is something akin to drug or alcohol addiction. In fact, that's true. Like other addicts, people dependent on exercise appear to suffer from the effects of withdrawal. Reports on the nature of these effects vary, but generally include some feelings of anxiety, guilt, tension, and irritability. In one study of highly competitive runners and swimmers—those competing at the international, national, or regional levels—the researchers studied the effects of one- to five-day layoffs. While virtually all of the athletes reported being "addicted" to exercise, the findings showed the most pronounced negative effects among males and athletes competing at a high level. Relief, rather than withdrawal, was typically experienced by females and athletes competing at a lower level. So the effects of exercise addiction may be evident only among those athletes who train at the most intense levels.

William P. Morgan of the University of Wisconsin-Madison Sports Psychology Laboratory has done many studies arguing in favor of the benefits of exercise. Yet, his own recent work supports the view that *over*training can *cause* depression. Dr. Morgan assessed the mood states of Wisconsin varsity male and female swimmers during intentional "overtraining"—a technique that requires swimmers to push their bodies to the limits of endurance early in the season, then taper off before competition. Overtraining is thought to leave the athletes faster and stronger in competition.

Morgan found, however, that the physical drain experienced by some of the swimmers caused significant emotional and psychological problems. Mood disturbances increased as training became more intense, and were always greatest when the swimmers exercised the most. This wasn't simply a mild case of the blues; many of the swimmers were referred to outpatient psychiatric services, and 80 percent had clinically significant depression. Nor was the stress of college life to blame; a control group of swimmers who were not over-training had none of these problems.

Morgan acknowledges the paradox of his latest findings. While moderate amounts of vigorous exercise can reduce depression, "depression also seems to be a product of over-training," he says. The athletes' symptoms were "remarkably similar" to many of those seen in serious depression, often including chronic fatigue, insomnia, increased emotional tension, and decreased libido. As if all these reasons aren't enough, Morgan adds that overtraining may also lead to significant metabolic, hormonal and cardiovascular changes. In fact, one twenty-year-old swimmer in Morgan's study had a heart attack while overtraining.

If you look at the benefits of moderate exercise—reduced tension, increased energy, improved sleep, and perhaps a better sex life—there seems to be little reason for overtraining, unless you are a competitive athlete. Most of us simply don't have the time to overtrain anyway. The more usual complaint is that we don't have enough time to fit exercise in.

But for exercise addicts, cutting back is akin to failure. Worried that more moderate exercise will erase the performance gains they've made, they continue to work out compulsively, despite their discomfort. The old jock mentality, "No pain, no gain," prevails. Those who overexercise start with a reasonable idea, but keep raising the standard. They're not exercising for the sake of fitness; they're pursuing an unreachable goal. The desire for ever-increasing performance has become an obsession for such people. The need for always doing more has become an end in itself.

Suya Colorado, aerobics director at the San Francisco Bay Club, has noticed that overexercisers "often have family or other social problems. They think, 'I don't want to go home, so I'll go running instead.'" For others, exercise simply replaces another addiction. Colorado discovered for herself the dangers of overtraining after being treated for cocaine abuse. "I saw the possibility of using exercise as a way of getting back into my life," she explains, "but I realized I could be just as compulsive about that." She headed off a dependency problem by working out with a trainer for the first two months after she stopped using drugs. For many exercise addicts, the hardest part is learning to take exercise less seriously.

Anabolic Steroid Use by Athletes For more than three thousand years, athletes have used substances to enhance their performance. The desire for greater athletic achievement has resulted in a startling increase in drug use. Recent pharmaceutical advances offer contemporary athletes easy access to a great variety of potentially harmful drugs. As athletics have become a prosperous international business and source of entertainment, use of anabolic steroids to potentially aid athletic performance has increased. Anabolic steroids are synthetic hormones that have the same muscle- and tissue-building effects as testosterone and other naturally occurring male sex hormones. They are consumed not only by power athletes, that is, football players and weight lifters, but also by endurance athletes, for example, swimmers and distance runners. Some estimates suggest as many as one million Americans are spending one hundred million dollars on black market anabolic steroids, including an estimated quarter million high school seniors.

New surveys suggest that even non-athlete teenagers are now jumping on the steroid bandwagon. Particularly disturbing is that two thirds claim they started before age sixteen, when many are still growing, says Dr. Conrad Andringa, a sports medicine expert at Dean Medical Center in Madison, Wisconsin. Girls are doing it to cut their body fat and increase lean muscle; boys, to build muscle size and strength.

Concern over steroid use centers around its side effects. Minor side effects—very common in users—include sleep disturbance, mood and personality changes, acne and, in women, masculinization. More serious effects include liver tumors and hepatitis, rises in cholesterol and blood pressure, and stunted growth.

According to a new report in the *Journal of the American Medical Association* by two professors of psychiatry at Yale, Kenneth Kashkin and Herbert Kleber, use of anabolic steroids may also be addictive. Doctors Kashkin and Kleber note distinct similarities between the effects, withdrawal symptoms, and complications exhibited by heavy steroid users with those of cocaine, alcohol, or other opiate users. For example, anabolic steroid users describe increased self esteem, libido, and energy, with a decreased need for sleep.

Some studies suggest that long-term steroid abusers continue to use the substance, even when the victims' lives begin to deteriorate from steroid abuse. Abstinence leads to severe depression and strong withdrawal reactions, including panic and paranoid delusions.

The Kookier Risks I have friends who joke that they are allergic to exercise, but some people really may be. Exercise-induced anaphylaxis is a potentially deadly allergy that can cause hives, itching, coughing, hoarseness, difficulty breathing, and sometimes a dangerous drop in blood pressure. If this sounds familiar to you, see an allergist, because it really can be quite serious.

Male bike riders who train at high intensity often suffer from sexual impotence. It used to be attributed to too much exercise, but it now seems that the bikers' impotence is due to repeatedly thrusting down on the pedals. Banging the groin on the seat damages critical arteries and nerves. The first warnings are numbness in the seat-of-the-pants area and difficulty getting an erection for a day or two. Unfortunately, many riders react to the stress of impotence by biking more. An aggressive riding style can worsen the damage.

Breaking the Fitness Trap

The advice here can be captured in a single word: *moderation*. The research results speak quite loudly: *More* is not always *better*. The greatest gains in fitness and health are evident in people who go from being totally sedentary to doing some type of exercise. According to Dr. Ralph Paffenbarger, an expert on exercise at the Stanford University School of Medicine, "Each stair climbed and each leaf raked contributes to health," especially among the inactive. Evidence is much weaker for real health benefits of increasing amounts of exercise in people who are already exercising heavily. Furthermore, metabolism may actually slow down in the face of excessive demands on the body by too much exercise. For people who enjoy eating, this can be undeserved torture borne of virtue.

Not only does the biological research show that moderation works best, but the behavioral and psychological studies resoundingly support this idea. People stay with a moderate exercise program longer and more willingly than a regimen of intense grueling workouts.

A good exercise program is one that lets you feel in control of it, rather than vice versa. It is one in which you feel positive about yourself when following the exercise guidelines you have set. It is not good if you feel driven, compelled to exercise, and guilty when you don't. If your exercise plan is right for you, you should *not* be giving too much conscious thought and attention to it. It should be enjoyable, and not feel like

— 221 —

"doing chores" or "taking medicine." Exercise can and should be fun.

Pushing ourselves to exercise to the limit is just one more example of how our society's emphasis on being in overdrive hurts us. Philosophically, a good healthy emphasis on moderation in all things, including exercise, can increase our physical and psychological health.

Jennifer had reached the point of diminishing returns in her exercise workouts, but she was afraid to cut down. To work through the fitness trap, Jennifer had to learn to exercise without guilt—giving up the fear that, no matter how hard she worked, it was never enough. We encouraged her first to test several different regimens until she found one that yielded a high overall benefit. For her, that was running four days a week instead of seven. She figured this out by running one day less a week for several weeks and keeping a notebook of how she felt and any fluctuations in her weight and eating. She gave herself days off when she was hurt. But most important, she tried to relax and exercise with less pressure and more pleasure. She began to love the freedom of her runs, reframing them in her thinking as time out from her anxieties, rather than the embodiment of them.

One question that Jennifer and others often asked was: "What type of exercise should I do?" The answer is that there is no single right form of exercise. One interesting finding from exercise studies is that consistency seems more important than the type of exercise.

This is one area where my advice might run contrary to what you have heard elsewhere. Many people believe there is only one "right" type of exercise, but the *right* exercise depends totally on what you hope to accomplish. Therefore, aerobics or strength training is not necessarily better than some other type of activity, if we accept the proposition that consistency is the key. Focusing on consistency raises a whole new set of questions such as "How much do I enjoy a certain type of exercise?" and "How hard is it for me to do this exercise regularly?" These questions are as important as questions about heart rate, coronary efficiency, and so forth.

Decide what type and amount of exercise you will do. Then stick with your program. Develop a set of guidelines for deciding what exercise to do and when to do it. No single set of guidelines is right for everyone. Does yours fit into your lifestyle and allow for both consistency and flexibility? For example, rather than having a single target, set a range of acceptable types and amount of exercise so you can adjust readily to changes in your schedule and daily demands.

What drives people to exercise too much? Below are some commonly heard reasons and what we recommend to overcome them.

Problem	Solutions
No-pain, no-gain mentality	Try pushing yourself as hard, but fewer times each week.
Fear of losing training benefits	Gradually cut down the amount of training, by a few minutes each day or by dropping one workout a week. Testing will show no effect on strength or conditioning.
Exercise "addict"	Find another pleasure and substitute it for a workout twice a week.
Worry about weight	Try keeping a log of calories consumed and vary your exercise every two to three days. Weigh yourself daily. Find the "energy in—energy out" formula that works best for you.

If you're worried about overexercise, avoid getting fixed in a single exercise routine. There, in particular, the temptation to keep increasing your output is the greatest. Think of your body as a machine that works best when a fuel-efficient engine is developed. Also, when a machine is always in overdrive, the parts wear out more quickly and things break down and go awry. The analogy is really a good one and visualizing yourself as a well-running machine may help the tendency to push yourself too hard. There are many kinds of exercise to try, but two of the most popular currently are aerobic exercise and strength training.

Aerobic Exercise Aerobic activity is important for overall fitness, endurance, and cardiovascular health. There are many types of aerobic exercise, including walking, jogging, and swimming, to name the three most popular. All of these should be done at a pace that increases your heart rate, as described earlier in this chapter. A key here is the word *sustained*. Stopping and starting does not provide the best aerobic workout. But neither do you need to push yourself to the point of exhaustion. A continuous, moderate demand on your body does the trick.

Strength Training Repetition at low resistance is not effective for muscle development. Rather, fewer repetitions at higher resistance—enough to feel real muscle fatigue—is what it takes. The theory is that taxing the muscles by the extreme stress caused by the resistance actually develops microscopic tears in the muscle cells. The body's cells repair these tears by synthesizing new protein, which further builds up the muscle. It is this breaking down and renewal process that builds muscular strength.

Generally, experts recommend a day off in between each strength-training period to allow this muscular repair process to proceed effectively. Here again, not allowing enough time between sessions can be counterproductive—leading to muscle damage, rather than repair.

Cross-Training Cross-training is alternating between at least two types of exercise, each of which has a different goal: for example, aerobic exercise and strength training, or two different types of aerobic exercise, such as running and swimming. The newest view is that cross-training gives a greater return for the effort than one-sport exercise, both physically and psychologically. It is hard to stay at one exercise without pushing oneself to ever-increasing standards. Cross-training reduces the likelihood of this happening, because it reduces the monotony.

There may also be physical benefits of cross-training. Certainly, the muscles have more time to repair themselves from stress and injury due to a given type of exercise. Weights and aerobic cross-training appear to build up both strength and stamina, increasing endurance significantly and perhaps also speed. Cross-training may increase the likelihood that you will get the full benefit of each workout—your body will not adapt to one type of exercise and lead to the diminishing returns I discussed earlier in the chapter.

Adding variety to your workouts will break a fixation on performance and let you use more muscles in different ways. Pay attention to your body's signals: Persistent soreness or fatigue means you're working too hard. Perhaps most important, schedule time to rest; the body needs to repair itself.

To break the fitness trap, you must overcome the notion that how hard you work out is the measure of what kind of person you are. Exercise and fitness are good for you, not because they show your efforts and self-discipline, but because in moderation, they are good for your health and well-being.

— 8 —

The Success Trap

We try to look good and succeed to impress others. And also to impress ourselves. But even people who look as though they have it all sometimes have difficulty allowing themselves to believe that they are what they appear to be.

Does something as hard to achieve as weight loss always lead to a sense of accomplishment? Does becoming better-looking make someone *feel* better, too? Surprisingly, for many the answer is no. Often, people report in intensive interviews that they feel like frauds because of the enormous effort and money it takes to look good. Margie, a thin, perfect-looking young woman, wailed, "Only I know the real me. Fat and ugly. All the time and energy I put into this project. What a terrible hoax I am. If you knew the real me, you would hate her."

We admire and sometimes envy thin and beautiful men and women. Who would believe that many of them live in a private hell? Narcissistic? Sometimes. But more often, they are tormented by uncertainties of who they really are, worried whether people will like the *real* them, insecure that without their looks they would have nothing. Richard, a male model, sums up: "I'm marketing a product and the product happens to be me." It's frightening to know so much depends on that.

Women who describe themselves as "high maintenance" said the biggest risk was that people get used to the way they look—and expect them *always* to look that way. The minute they *stop* maintaining their beauty routine, roots start to show, unwanted hairs start to sprout, nails begin to chip—and it all seems more noticeable because people are used to their well-maintained self! "High maintenance," confessed one Dallas dynamo, "means peaks and valleys. When you look good, you look *terrific*, but when you look bad you look *really* bad." Said another: "Every time I forget to put on lipstick, people at the office ask me if I'm not feeling well."

Many people who work hard to look good feel like frauds, because they believe the process involves so much deception. They keep asking themselves: "Am I attractive enough? Is my body impressing others and winning their approval?" What they feel they have to do to make sure the answer is "yes" reinforces their feelings of insecurity and self-doubt. And, receiving compliments from others does not help them either. "If someone tells me, 'You look stunning', can I enjoy the compliment? No. All I can think of is all the effort it took to look this way and what would have happened if I hadn't put so much effort into my looks," admits Gloria, a part-time model and student. Feeling like a fraud, and the stress and anxiety it engenders, is part of the success trap.

Psychologists have become impressed by how possessed people can be by their sense of fraudulence. To see if this part of the success trap applies to you, answer the questions on pages 228 and 229 as honestly as possible.

There are other aspects of the success trap, too. These are especially related to the effects of weight loss or other major changes in appearance. Most common is the fear of failure, of regaining the weight. Many people have lost and regained so many times, that they have considerable experience with failure. Maria confides, "I'm caught by a self-fulfilling prophecy. I worry so much about failing, which I've done so many times before, that I seem to make it happen again."

Sometimes successful weight loss also carries with it a frightening loss of one's sense of self. Marie, for example, doesn't know the "new" Marie. She worked so hard to get there, but the person who peers out at her from the mirror is

PERCEIVED FRAUDULENCE SCALE

	Almost Never	Sometimes	Often	Almost Always
1. In some situations, I feel like a "great pretender": that is, I'm not as genuine as others think I am.	——	——	——	——
2. I feel there's something false or misleading about me that others don't notice.	——	——	——	——
3. I would describe myself as an "authentic" person.	——	——	——	——
4. I generalize negative feelings about myself which stem from a specific incident or situation to other, sometimes unrelated, situations.	——	——	——	——
5. My true self is something that I keep secret and share with very few people.	——	——	——	——
6. If I receive a great deal of praise and recognition for something I've accomplished, I belittle the significance of what I have done to myself and to others.	——	——	——	——

7. When people praise me for something I've accomplished, I have no doubt that I will be able to live up to their expectations of me in the future.

    _____   _____   _____   _____

The items are scored as follows. Give yourself a 1 for *Almost Never*, a 2 for *Sometimes*, a 3 for *Often*, and a 4 for *Almost Always*, except for statements 3 and 7: These should be scored in reverse order (i.e., 1 = *Almost Always*). Then add up your score. The higher your score, the greater your sense of fraudulence. If your score is 21 or greater, this aspect of the success trap is a problem for you.

a stranger. She worries about how her new looks will change her life. Carol has the opposite problem, but one equally part of the success trap for many people. Carol expected and wished for everything to change. She dreamed of newfound popularity, men following her down the street, her phone constantly ringing. She was brokenhearted when she lost weight and none of her fantasies came true.

To find out what your own expectations are, complete these sentences: "If only I were thinner, I would be——" "If only I were prettier, I would get——" We all dream of how our lives would be transformed if only we were better in some way, and often the fantasy has to do with our bodies. Expectations like these are part of the success trap. They can set us up for unhappiness and failure.

Changed personal relationships also fuel the success trap. Success often affects friendships, marriages, and families in ways that threaten everyone. Sometimes, the people closest to you actively try to sabotage your success. They can undermine you more or less consciously, but the result is the same in either case. Your ability to succeed is compromised by unsupportive others.

With all these possible dire consequences, it's no wonder that so many people fear success. Because the negative consequences tend to be greater for women than men, women are more prey to fear of success. Worrying about what they may lose by being thinner, prettier, or more competent—in terms of family relationships, friendships, and their own sense of self—causes many women to sabotage their own successes.

Features of the Success Trap

The Impostor Syndrome

Women are more likely than men to feel like impostors. Psychologist Kay Deaux, a leading researcher studying the psychology of women at New York University, found that women have lower expectations of success than men. This is true almost regardless of the tasks.

A high sense of fraudulence comes from feelings of inauthenticity and self-doubt. People who feel fraudulent are also quite anxious. They know they are putting on a facade. Therefore, they feel vulnerable to being exposed as an impostor or fake. They are also worried because they feel strongly that there are vast discrepancies between what others think of them and their own self-assessment. They worry about exposing the parts of themselves that they think would evoke disapproval and rejection.

Jennifer viewed herself from the outside in—her looks encapsulated and determined her sense of self, despite her many accomplishments. She fretted and fussed in front of the mirror each morning, tearing herself away only because she was afraid she would be late for work. "I can't stop worrying. I know it's dumb, but I feel like my looks are all I have," she admits. Jennifer felt like a fraud, valued and respected for the wrong reasons. She recounted: "I'm furious at my friends and coworkers because they all envy and look up to me. Can't they see I hate who I am?—a shallow person whose only accomplishment is that I work hard enough to look good."

Others feel so fraudulent that they lose their sense of who they really are. They define themselves by lists of likes and dislikes, rather than through meaningful, core characteristics of their personhood. Elaine is a young woman who is so afraid she will be found unacceptable, she has developed a completely externalized self-image. She wrote the following self-description:

> I'm 5'3", large frame—dark hair and eyes, weight about 120 lbs. "I like" animals, Soho, Bob Dylan, Henry Miller, Kerouac, reading, writing, plants, cooking, time by myself, Allen Ginsberg, Virginia Wolfe, Anaïs Nin, coffee, cigarettes, walking. "I dislike" pseudo-intellectuals who ridicule Andy Warhol in the college café, apathy, girls who dress out of *Cosmopolitan*, weighing myself, talking about myself, feeling I ate too much, lying to people, waking up bloated with gas, constantly losing and gaining weight, Tama Janowitz, MTV, New Wave, *Rolling Stone* magazine, people who say Elizabeth Taylor was horrid when she was heavy, nightmares.

Maintaining a false self puts people like Elaine under chronic and intense stress. Turning to food is one way some cope with these pressures. So they get themselves into a vicious cycle: Weight loss leads to success, success leads to anxiety and stress, anxiety and stress leads to overeating and weight gain.

Women as Frauds As early as grade school, girls differ from boys in their reactions to success. By age ten, many girls discount their high achievements and are laden with self-doubts. Psychologist Deaux and others have identified at least one of the reasons: Girls and women tend to attribute their successes to temporary causes such as luck or great effort. Men and boys are more likely to see their success as the result of ability. The difference is that ability is stable, it belongs to you and you can expect it to be available the next time you need it. Luck and effort are more variable. In this way, a woman's achievements seem illusory and ephemeral. She can never rest on her laurels, if she believes that the success was not really hers to claim.

To make matters worse, men and women have opposite explanations of failure: Women are more likely to explain failure by their lack of ability; men attribute failure to luck or task difficulty. Gloria understood this well. She said, "If I went skiing and broke a leg, I would say, 'I'm so stupid.' The man being carried down on the ski stretcher next to me would be cursing the bad snow conditions." These attitudes make the success trap a major problem for most women. Not able to take credit for their successes and overly willing to blame themselves for failure, they are in a terrible double bind.

How would you answer the question, "Are my achievements due to external factors, such as luck or extreme effort, rather than to my own inherent abilities?" If your answer is *luck*, you may be falling victim to part of the success trap. The inevitable impostor feelings are difficult to overcome. Clearly no amount of success will help if you don't take credit for your achievements. In fact, more success often exacerbates the problem.

A woman who feels like an impostor often shows one (or more) of the following kinds of behaviors when faced with success. First, the fear that she will be discovered makes her work harder and harder to prevent discovery. Elaine, for example, redoubled her effort when she succeeded at a major presentation of her advertising campaign, instead of relaxing and congratulating herself. She was afraid that the next time, someone would surely find out how bad she really was. Many women like Elaine spend a lot of time worrying about being "found out." And it is precisely their success that focuses people's attention on them and intensifies these fears. Such women often develop magical thinking and ritualistic behaviors that help, temporarily, to overcome their anxieties. Elaine would wear the same lucky bracelet to each presentation, so strong was her sense that she had just "lucked out" in being successful.

A second response to success for some women may be ever-increasing phoniness. Feeling like a fraud anyway, they show people only what they think they want to see. This type of woman frequently uses charm to win the approval of others. But once she impresses them, their opinions no longer matter. She derogates them, because they were unable to see through her. Lois, an artist, admitted, "I concentrate all my energies on second-guessing people to know exactly what they want, then when I've figured them out, I think they're complete jerks for not seeing through me. My boss is so shallow, he thinks I'm great because I fawn all over him. It's easy to get promotions when men are so stupid."

Finally, a woman suffering from the impostor syndrome may also become what psychologists call a defensive pessimist. She actively plays through worst-case outcomes and focuses on only the most negative parts of herself. Then she can be fully prepared for the worst, and in this way, protects her fragile sense of self. Candace, a stockbroker whose career was skyrocketing, was always "catastrophizing." She dramatized every possible flaw and imagined, for example, her clients losing large sums of money because she made an inept decision. Her friends would get furious with her because things usually turned out so well for her. It enraged them that she wasted their time with her thoughts of doom and gloom. Little did they know that imagining good outcomes was impossible for her.

Men as Self-Handicappers There are some men who feel like imposters, but they most commonly use different strategies to cope with their fear of success. They won't take credit for their successes, because they fear they will be expected to maintain them under all circumstances. Success incurs a future obligation to keep doing well.

Two Princeton psychologists, Edward Jones and Steven Berglas, have shown that successful men sometimes use "self-handicapping strategies." By finding or creating impediments that make their success less likely the next time, self-handicappers can protect their fragile sense of self-competence. For example, someone might say he did well on a test this time, because it was especially easy. If he does well next time, too, then he looks really smart, but if he does poorly, he already has an excuse. Regardless of the outcome, the self-handicapping strategist feels he cannot lose. The self-handicapper reaches out for impediments, embraces any factor to reduce personal responsibility for mediocrity, and enhances his opportunities to take personal responsibility for success.

Ralph is a partner in a prestigious law firm. By all external criteria, he has achieved enormous success. He was one of only five people made partner in a group of eighteen lawyers who began with him at the firm ten years earlier. He is well liked and respected. But Ralph has really made his mark by taking on cases that no one else wants—the high-risk cases that don't seem to have a chance. Little do they know that Ralph does this to protect his fragile sense of confidence. It's not that he loves the challenge; he needs to put himself in positions that make excuses unnecessary. If he succeeds, he is a hero, but if he doesn't, the fault can be attributed to external factors.

While this is a decidedly male aspect of the success trap, we have seen self-handicapping tendencies arise in some women who are uncertain about how competent they are. These women set up obstacles and stack the cards against themselves. If they do poorly, the source of failure can then be externalized in the impediment. If they do well, they have done so in spite of less than optimum conditions. In this case, their sense of competence can receive a temporary boost.

Fear of Failure

Many women suffer from an intense fear of failure, which exists side-by-side with their fear of success. This is one of the double binds of the success trap. Women find failure more shameful than men, and the increased pressures to compete and succeed today may be setting up more and more women for failure. Cheryl, for example, worried constantly about failing in all the domains in which she competed—school, ice-skating, her music, and now, most painfully, her body. "My inability to lose weight and look good is my worst fear come true," explained Cheryl. "It is visible proof that there is something important that anyone but I can do."

Psychologists Amos Tversky at Stanford University and Daniel Kahneman at Berkeley have noted that people's behavior is very influenced by having a strong, available "snapshot" in memory to guide their actions. Failure snapshots are more vivid, salient, and highly available for most people than success images. They permit people to easily recall graphic instances of past failures, which then guide their current behavior. Cheryl could vividly recall every skating mistake, every B on an exam, every weight gain. Holding on to these images only made a repeated failure more likely.

One of the most serious threats to those who have successfully changed how they look—especially by losing weight—is the regain which often follows quickly. People who have had this experience often develop a considerable fear of failure. Sensing how fragile their newfound success is, they fall into a self-fulfilling prophecy. For these people, failure is almost inevitable. Fear of failure is what brings it on. Studies have shown that fear of failure is greater in people who have lost and regained weight a greater number of times before. This is hardly surprising. They have a great repertoire of failure "snapshots." "Remember the Christmas when I was so thin, I couldn't hold my pants up? It only took till Easter to regain it all back that time." With such clear examples of failure easily conjured up, it is little wonder they feel afraid. Holding on to an image like this only makes a repeated failure more likely.

Loss of One's Self

Weight loss and maintenance can be difficult, but adjusting to a new thinner self can be even more so. After losing weight, many people don't know what their bodies really look like. They still feel fat and think they look fat no matter how many times they read the scale or tape measure. Instead of reveling in their new svelte shape, many continue to feel the same familiar voice of self-criticism.

Studies have tested people who have recently lost weight by taking their pictures and then putting these pictures in a device with a lens that is capable of distortions, the same type

— 235 —

of study I discussed in the Vanity Trap chapter. Many women have a difficult time adjusting the lens exactly right, so that they see their true body size and shape. But those who have just lost weight have the hardest time of all. Many are unable to see themselves as thin. Some weight-loss experts have speculated that the degree of difficulty they have is an important predictor of how likely they are to regain.

Adjusting to a changed self can be difficult for anyone. Often important relationships are affected. Sometimes more is expected of someone; sometimes she feels she should expect more of herself. Inevitably, she worries about what might happen if she regains the weight. Jane, a young career woman, reported:

> The first four or five months of my last diet, I felt great. I kept losing weight at a steady pace. But somewhere around the time I had lost about forty pounds and was down to a size eight, I really started to notice that people responded differently to me. For example, there was this cute guy at work who had never paid any attention to me before and now he always held doors for me, or stopped by to see if I wanted some coffee, and so on. Strangely enough, I found this attention depressing. It sort of proved to me just *how* ugly I must have been before. I also was kind of mad—what, I wondered, would he do if I gained the weight back?

There are several reasons for the bad feelings. For better or worse, the body before weight loss or the face before plastic surgery was theirs and it was familiar. A new-size body or a different-looking face feels strange and unfamiliar, even if it is "better." The person has become stripped of her comfort zone. She doesn't feel like herself, adding to the impostor phenomenon, as well as causing general anxiety and discomfort.

It can be extremely unsettling to be unfamiliar with your own reflection in the mirror. You might like the new you better, although many people cannot even manage that. But you certainly don't know her. Where have *you* gone? This sense of disconnectedness with your past self is a fundamental part of what sets this component of the success trap. Since your sense of self is so strongly identified with your sense of your own body, you lose a little part of yourself when your body changes. No wonder success is scary!

Unrealistic Expectations

Another part of the trap arises for those who expect their lives to change dramatically for the better as a result of their success. Some fail because ultimately, they would rather not take the risk that their hopes and dreams may not come true. Others fail because their lives do not change profoundly once they get thin. People are not lining up outside their doors with new job offers, promotions, or dates.

Society sets and rewards unrealistic physical ideals. For extremely heavy or unattractive people life does change when they lose weight or alter their looks. But people who fall prey to the success trap are those who rely too greatly on others for their own sense of self-worth and importance. The world stops telling them how good they look because it becomes old news. Those people who have come to depend on the praise and support of others often still need it long after it has stopped. This is one of the ironies of success. When you remain successful, you may lose some of the things you have enjoyed the most about success. Success often brings rewards in terms of other people's esteem, but that passes quickly and, in the end, you are left with yourself.

Another variant to this theme is that some people lose not just pounds but the much-relied-on excuse of being fat. Marta, one of our patients, told us:

> When I was fatter, I often excused my poor performance ratings at work as the result of my boss's negative attitudes toward overweight people. I never really admitted to myself that I did not try as hard as I might to do a good job, because I hated the menial tasks I had to do. When I lost all this weight, it hit me one day that I was the one

to blame for my poor performance. I really couldn't face that realization.

Unsupportive Others

Relationships with family and friends can have an unduly large influence on those caught in the success trap. Family-systems theorists believe that every person serves a function for the other members of his family. One of a family's most important tasks, according to Salvador Minuchin, a family therapy expert at the Philadelphia Child Guidance Clinic, is to preserve and protect the status quo. When one member changes dramatically, the whole balance is altered. Looking, and often acting, different you change your long-established role in that group. The family is out of kilter. Unknowingly, those closest to you may try to sabotage your success so that they themselves will not be forced to change.

Laura, a patient of ours, was a binge eater who purged many times a day. Her parents had an unsupportive relationship with one another and no real communication except about Laura's problems. As long as they could focus their attention on her illness, they functioned reasonably well as a family. But as she got better, they fell apart as a couple. Their alliance depended on Laura being sick, and unconsciously, they sabotaged her success in order to bring balance—even a sick balance—back to the family. Successful therapy in Laura's case ultimately required treating the whole family.

Clearly not all relationships are this dysfunctional. But many relationships are destabilized when one person changes and those closest to him or her struggle to bring things back into balance. As they do, they often undermine the person's success.

Sometimes success drives others away. The relationship is so changed that no one involved can cope. Not knowing how to relate to the new you, those closest become hostile, threatened, confused. Marriages may falter, friendships may collapse. The loved one is not jealous of your success. He is threatened by the new you and possibly grieving over the loss of the old you. For that person, you are fundamentally changed and so, potentially, is the nature of your relationship.

Sam, for example, always nagged his wife, Agnes, about her weight. He watched what she ate and reproached her constantly. Finally she lost fifty pounds. Was Sam happy? Hardly. He was miserable. Gone was his old friend. Agnes looked so different, he didn't know who she was. He missed eating ice cream with her while they watched the eleven o'clock news. He missed having to worry about her weight and monitor her eating. In some ways, he liked the power and control it gave him. In other ways, he just mourned the loss of old, familiar ways of behaving. Not surprisingly, Agnes regained all the weight she lost and more besides. The last I saw them, she was still fat and Sam was happily harping at her.

Fear of Success

Fear of success leads to a cascade of self-defeating behaviors. Women who fear success are victims of their own self-protection. Perhaps it is not surprising that many people fear success, since the results are not always positive. Loss of one's old self, shattered dreams, expectations, and changing relationships, all are part of the dark side of success for many people.

Psychologist Matina Horner, the former president of Radcliffe College, pointed out in her work that women fear success in a variety of domains, not just in those related to weight and appearance. Horner argued that in Western culture, being successful is more in keeping with the male than with the female role. In many domains, women's success may bring them negative consequences, such as unpopularity, guilt, abuse, or self-doubt. Horner's contribution was to focus on the ambivalence or anxiety associated with attainment of success, especially for highly capable and achievement-oriented women.

Psychologists have developed an easily administered diagnostic tool to help identify and measure fear of success. Research subjects are given a written cue with the name of the protagonist changed to be the same sex as the subject: "After first-semester finals Anne (John) finds herself (himself) at the top of her (his) medical school class." Subjects are then instructed to write the rest of the story. In most studies that have used this investigative tool, over 60 percent of women show fear of success as compared with somewhere between 9 and 36 percent of the men.

One common theme was conflict between career and family, for example, "She struggles with her emotions and finally decides, as a true woman would, to put her career second." Another theme was questioning the value of success, noting its great costs. For example, many emphasized a fear of social rejection because of success. Some women who showed fear-of-success imagery completely denied Anne's achievement; for example, "Anne is thunderstruck. She was not even aware that she was enrolled in medical school!"

Some psychologists have criticized the lack of scientific rigor in working with this type of projective material. Indeed, the research literature in this area is fraught with contradictory findings. Yet, many women recognize themselves in hearing these stories. Perhaps the problem with the research studies is that they have focused only on competitive, achievement situations with men. But for many women fear of being successful is much more general than that.

Worrying about what they stand to lose by being thinner or prettier—in terms of family relationships, friendships, and their own sense of self—causes many women to sabotage their own successes. For example, they start bringing fattening foods back into the house, or stocking up on snacks for the office. Sometimes people are "punished" by those they care about for being successful. I described above the costs in terms of loss of important relationships, unfulfilled fantasies and expectations, a disconnected sense of self. People who have experienced these very real consequences of success may justifiably come to fear it.

Anne, for example, recalls the painful loss of her friendship with Tally. "I just couldn't figure it out. We were *so* close. Tally was the pretty one and I, well, I was fat. But Tally couldn't handle it when I got thinner. It was as if she needed the fat me to feel good about herself, you know, to feel superior. The thinner I got, the more she tried to tempt me with rich foods."

For other women, fear of success derives more from imagined costs than from real ones. Such people struggle with what they *think* their spouse will do, or their friend will say, or their superior will try. Success takes on an aura of unmanageable difficulties and petty hassles. When the costs of success are thought to outweigh the benefits, people stop trying. By not being successful, they never have a chance to disprove (or deal with, if true) the dire consequences they have so vividly imagined. In the last analysis, external obstacles can be less insidious and destructive than these internalized psychological barriers to success.

Underachievement

Another means of protecting a vital but fragile image of one's competence involves underachievement. If you stop trying, you can attribute your failure to lack of effort. "I would have lost weight if I had tried harder," is a common response. The crucial implication of this kind of statement is that if and when the underachiever *does* try, he or she will succeed, or at least do noticeably better than now.

Princeton psychologists Janet Riggs and Beth Preston, working with Dr. Edward Jones, studied underachievers. They found that underachievers typically underestimate the amount of effort they've expended. One possible explanation for this tendency is that underachievers have been told (or have told themselves) so many times that they were not trying hard enough that they have become confused about how much effort they're actually putting out. Perhaps they've merely learned to accept the fact that it's never enough.

Underachievers were also likely in these studies to stop trying when they believed a task was especially sensitive to the amount of effort expended. They appeared unduly obsessed with their competence image and this took precedence, under some circumstances at least, over doing well. Some people who feel that they would look far better if only they tried harder may not want to test out their belief for fear of being wrong.

We might speculate that these underachievers come out of families whose parents constantly reiterate to them, "Susie, if you only tried harder and took how you look more seriously, you could look much better." Susie is not so sure. She worries that if she obviously applies herself and doesn't wind up gorgeous, she will shatter her parents' expectations and perhaps lose their love. Thus, the underachiever's preoccupations may reflect the fear that success will not be good enough.

Breaking the Success Trap

The success trap is insidious and pervasive. It places many women in a "no win" situation. If they try too hard and succeed, they feel like frauds. But many never get to that point; they fear success too much to try, relegating many women to chronic underachievement. And yet, not trying hard is troubling, too, especially to those who fear failure. These issues do not apply only to appearance, but to all aspects of women's lives. The feeling they engender impacts strongly on how women feel about themselves and their bodies, and for many, affects eating behavior, as well. As with all the traps, eating salves the intense strain.

But the success trap does not have to be a paralyzing problem. Breaking the success trap needs a lot of mental work. Being aware of it and how it affects you is an important first step in loosening its hold. The first step is recognizing that success is often the trigger, rather than the cure, for bad feelings.

If you scored high on the Perceived Fraudulence Scale, your feelings of phoniness are powerfully associated with overt achievement. If you are afraid of being "found out," then try the following.

Try to recall all the people you think you have fooled. Tell them in fantasy how you conned or tricked them. Imagine out loud how each person would respond to you if they saw your true self, instead of your false self. Try practicing. In your mind, risk being yourself and see what happens. As you begin to break the success trap in fantasy, begin also to seek out those people in your real life who will support you in your struggle to be authentic.

Jennifer began to open up to people more, to trust that they would still like her with faults and anxieties about her appearance and other aspects of her life. She was nervous about doing this and we used role playing with her so that she could actually rehearse disclosing her feelings and worries to another person. She worked on making judicious decisions about whom to trust by giving everyone what she called "a tryout." She would say something confidential to see how they reacted. Did they laugh, look away, act dismissive or embarrassed? Did they reciprocate with a confidence of their own? She made some mistakes, confiding in someone she thought was a friend, only to learn that the woman had told several people that Jennifer was incredibly petty and shallow—just what Jennifer was most afraid others would think. But with other friends she developed a sense of support and much-needed intimacy. Gradually, she showed her "true" self to more people.

Next, using mental exercises, give free reign to your most catastrophic fantasies about the consequences of being successful. You may discover that you are frightened that others may find you exhibitionistic, snobbish, or unfriendly. You may get in touch with memories of being punished or teased during childhood for being good or special at something. Katie remembered how her friends would tease her for getting good grades. Other girls in her class would stay away from her, sure she wouldn't want to play with them, since they were not in the "smart" track. "Getting all A's and having the teachers like me was actually quite awful," she realized. "I guess I stopped doing as well to keep my friends." Katie is someone who is especially gifted, scoring high on standard aptitude and IQ tests. Her ability to adjust well to every situation from childhood on had actually, paradoxically, been a barrier. Part of breaking the success trap for Katie was teaching her to be somewhat less adaptable and more focused on her own needs and competencies, even if it meant losing some friends.

Another technique to break the success trap is to keep a record of positive feedback you receive from other people. Then focus on how you keep yourself from accepting this feedback. Do you derogate those who give it to you? Do you dismiss it quickly? Are you angry? Embarrassed? Put out? Experiment with listening to and taking in the positive response. Allow yourself to get as much nourishment as possible out of it, rather than denying it. Feel appreciative of those who praise you. Express that appreciation to them. It's important for you to hear yourself accepting praise. Then, you must control your own internal dialogues in ways that allow you to believe rather than discount it.

To accept successes you need to change how you think about, or explain, your own achievements to yourself. The explanations we give ourselves about why something has happened have a profound effect on our own behavior. During the 1920s, a French psychotherapist named Emil Coué became world-famous as a proponent of auto-suggestion. Millions of Americans followed his teaching by repeating to themselves: "Every day, in every way, I am getting better and better." Like all fads it died out, but Coué had a good point. Modern research confirms that, to a significant degree, you are what you tell yourself because your perceptions and interpretations strongly affect your behavior.

Three thought techniques are especially helpful in this regard. First, develop some illusions about your positive attributes. In a recent book, UCLA psychologist Shelley Taylor argued that small, overly positive illusions about oneself increase our sense of control and improve motivation. Concentrating on your good qualities and believing that you have made good outcomes occur through your own actions are helpful attitudes. Positive illusions enable us to work toward success and feel comfortable with it. This is essential to a healthy sense of self, since our competencies are central ingredients of our core identity and our social selves.

Second, when you feel like a fraud, look for reasons for your successes in internal factors—aspects of yourself that are permanent and belong to you. Don't look for causes in factors like luck or even hard work that may be more fleeting. By contrast, when trying to explain your failures, look for causes in the situations you are facing, rather than yourself.

Jennifer had to learn to attribute her successes to stable, internal factors—features of her own abilities and personality. She kept a diary of her life at work, monitoring the number of hours she worked, the types of independent decisions she made, and the frequency with which coworkers asked her advice and opinions. From that information, she could identify the hours of hard work, the clever, creative ideas, and the dedication that she showed at the office. This enabled her to begin to appreciate herself for what she could do and not merely how she looked. She started forcing herself to hear and accept the compliments she got on her work. To teach her to accept rather than discount her successes, we had her practice statements to herself such as, "I'm pleased that they recognized my effort in this project," rather than her usual "They just say they like what I do because I'm pretty." Subtle changes in the way she interpreted people's responses went a long way to breaking the success trap.

Third, you must change your internal dialogues. These are the things you say to yourself about yourself. It may not be easy at first, but practice will help. When you catch yourself putting yourself down, try instead to say something more helpful to yourself. Then follow up the helpful statement with a plan to actively solidify it. Suppose, for example, you've just received a compliment on your appearance. A negative self-statement would be, "What a jerk. Doesn't he see I'm really a fat pig?" or "Boy, have I fooled him!" Instead, make a positive self-statement: "It feels strange to hear that, but I am looking pretty good today. I think I'll buy myself that new dress." When you make positive self-statements, you go a long way toward accepting responsibility for the good things that happen to you.

Lois stopped discounting positive feedback by using some of the exercises I just described. She began to experience satisfaction, seeing how much psychological nourishment she had been depriving herself of. Satisfaction builds on itself, and success becomes less and less threatening.

Another important task for breaking the success trap, if you are having trouble learning to be you in your new body, is to redo the body image awareness tasks described in the section on Breaking the Vanity Trap in Chapter 2. Spend time in front of the mirror looking at your body, starting with the parts you like. Experience the panic and anxiety of your changed self-image, if it is there. Use systematic relaxation exercises, successively tensing and then relaxing each part of your body to release the feelings. This helps you to use your body, not your mind, to turn these feelings off.

Breaking the success trap is possible, especially once you've learned how it works. When you realize that succeeding causes the problem rather than providing the solution, you've come a long way.

Conclusion

"And now you can see perhaps why, if we solve the mystery beyond the mystery, the glittering image may simply fade away." So learns Susan Howatch's protagonist, a Cambridge clergyman, in the best-selling novel *Glittering Images*. The glittering image is the perfect self, who works hard, looks splendid, engages in self-denial, and aims to please everyone except himself. He's told that he can find the courage to set aside his glittering image only if he restores his belief in his own worth. And he's led on a deep and probing journey—facing insight after insight—toward the self-understanding that will allow him to triumph over the tyranny of the glittering image that has tormented him for so long.

Like Howatch's hero, women are the victims of this era's story, martyrs to their own glittering images. I've tried in this book to uncover the "mystery beyond the mystery," the multiple traps that bind us to feeling vain and ashamed, that make competition, food, and dieting rituals overpower us and that make success the enemy.

What a tragedy that women today live with this great self-consciousness. Television, magazines, and movies present and reinforce the glittering, false image, but we have taken it for our own. Like Atlas reincarnated as a female, it is women who bear this burden, who have the "weight" of society's image on their shoulders. The deep psychological significance of the body has made the effort, while exhausting and painful, seem worthwhile.

The critical message of this book is that carrying the burden of the glittering image is too costly. Body traps have become double and triple binds that limit other aspects of our lives—happiness, friendships, careers, families. For women caught in body traps, each new hope has a flip side of fear. We want to give up these obsessions to free ourselves, but many of us are afraid to, because the social and personal consequences have seemed great. That's why the traps are so pervasive.

While finishing this book, I attended my twenty-fifth college reunion. It was splendid in many ways, as such occasions are, but once again, I was hit with the sheer intensity of women's body traps. My first vivid observation was the striking appearance difference between the women and men. Some of the men looked young and fit, others seemed clearly middle-aged, and some looked old, almost unrecognizable from twenty-five years ago. I guess that is what you'd expect as the genetics of the aging process and the kinds of life-styles we led for the last twenty-five years have increased the differences among us. But the women all looked wonderful. Almost no one was heavy, everyone was beautifully dressed, and very few had any gray hair. We all thought it was remarkable that the women had aged so well.

It wasn't until coming home from the weekend that I realized what to you must be obvious, but took me three days to figure out, because I was so blinded by my own participation in the charade. Quite simply, the women who didn't look good, didn't come. For the men, it wasn't an issue. They wanted to see their old friends and they came with their paunches and their graying hair or balding heads, but the women who had aged poorly or had gotten fat didn't feel comfortable coming back. They, like many women caught by their own body anxieties, were caught. The message of this book is intended for all people—men and women alike—who feel the same way. The case studies I have explored demonstrate that breaking the body traps is clearly possible. It comes in three ways: by changing yourself, changing other people, and changing society. Insight is the critical first step in all three.

Once you have identified your own issues by reading this book, taking the tests, and thinking about yourself, you should be able to find strategies in each chapter to help you make changes in yourself. Go back to the suggested techniques several times. How you use the advice will depend on how far along you are in breaking your own body traps. In fact, at different points in your progress, at each new level of insight and ability, the same strategy will work differently.

Many of the people described here thought and felt in ways far more extreme than anything you may recognize in yourself, while others undoubtedly seem painfully similar. What you have learned from them should be empowering. All of them are now doing better. I only chose examples from those cases where real and positive change ultimately occurred.

One common theme is that these people all felt vain, ashamed, or at least silly about their preoccupations with appearance, eating, and weight. In fact, most body-conscious individuals feel that they should hide these concerns if they want to be taken seriously as a person. In treatment (self-help or therapy), a crucial first step is to take yourself seriously, to be nonjudgmental about your concerns. These are not silly, trivial complaints, but rather personal and often painful experiences that deserve attention.

You are not alone in your body concerns. Your feelings are pervasive. Many women and some men share them. But you have learned to identify where your own body traps lie and how to break them. You can use this newfound knowledge to become more comfortable with and in your own body. But if you still feel stuck, get help. Don't let the shame trap keep you from finding a therapist or some other professional support if you need it.

Success in breaking the body traps is linked to *treating your body with more respect*. When you give your body what it really needs, including moderate exercise, healthful foods, sensual pleasures and relaxation, your body will respond by treating you better. I've seen person after person look healthier, and walk with a lighter, more confident step when they break their body traps.

From the wide variety of stories in this book there comes a common message. Time and time again, people working out their body traps are coming to learn that they have been trying to manipulate, to mold the wrong part of themselves. *Whether we want to value, accept, or change our bodies, we need first to change our minds.* The way we view and understand ourselves—our feelings, motives, and perceived pressures—is the first central element to our success.

But changing yourself is not enough. Your body traps also arise because of other people and society. Don't accept too much of the responsibility. Stay away from environments and people who make you feel bad about yourself. In other words, first try to change what you can, and then try to stay away from those settings and people who cannot readily be changed. Avoid friends who *only* care about looks and appearance, yours or their own. Choose people who are less hampered by their own body traps. Stay away from people who belittle you and make you feel ashamed. Remember that if you hold a negative attitude about yourself, you're too willing to take abuse from others.

How do you recognize people who can create difficulties for you? They are the people who arouse your self-doubts and threaten your confidence. They focus your attention on your body and make you see it as deficient in some way. Sometimes these people are strangers—models in magazines, movie stars, the local aerobics instructor. Rather than motivating you by their example, they make you feel wanting by comparison. If you can't stop comparing, you can stop looking.

Sometimes it is your friends and even relatives who are unhelpful. If you value the relationship, you should of course first try to change them. Assert yourself in those areas where their behavior or comments threaten your own bodily esteem. Perhaps they don't even realize how it is affecting you. Beatrice, for example, felt like a fat pig because she ate her food with gusto while her friend Prish only picked. She felt guilty for enjoying her meal, and ashamed in front of Prish. She finally told Prish to "order less, but eat it." If she hadn't agreed, Beatrice was ready to avoid eating meals with her in the future.

Identify negative environments, too. A classic one for many people is the exercise context. Jennifer recalls joining an aerobics class right after having Sophia. She was determined to get her body back into shape quickly, and looked forward eagerly to her first session. One time was all it took to start her on a slide into self-criticism and despair. Not only was everyone fit and slender, decked out in shiny spandex, but they all knew the "routines." Jennifer felt fat, clumsy, and inept. Not surprisingly, she never went back. But it also took her several weeks to get started again—weeks during which she hated herself more and more.

Choose your activities wisely to avoid those that arouse your body anxieties and insecurities. Make sure you ask yourself whether the choices you make allow the best in you to come out.

We can change some things—in ourselves and other people—and avoid others. But there's a final, crucial step. We should struggle to alleviate everyone's body traps by changing the look that society values to a more inclusive one. I seriously doubt that we can alter the fact that every culture has an established beauty standard and rules for how our bodies should look. Each of us adheres to these norms to different degrees and, as this book has described, many people feel tyrannized by them. But having a beauty standard which is as restricted as ours, and as difficult to achieve, makes most women today feel like deviants. No one wants to feel different, exposed, or unacceptable. So we diet and exercise, surgically alter ourselves, paint our faces, and worry a lot. And often never feel that we either look good enough or have tried hard enough.

A change in social tastes and attitudes is difficult to bring about, but it is possible. The media—television, movies, newspapers, and magazines—play an important role, and they can be influenced, if we are willing to try. Not that long ago blacks in the United States were largely depicted as dumb or lazy—

the childlike Stepin Fetchit characters. Now the Cosby show is consistently in the top five most popular television shows. The characters are bright, verbal, and popular. Such shows indicate the realm of the possible. They affect people's attitudes and reinforce social change.

Some argue that we are beginning to see the same thing with body tolerance. Roseanne Barr Arnold now stars in a leading television show bearing her name. She and her equally overweight sitcom husband live, love, and laugh their way through a variety of escapades that endear them to their friends and viewers. This is one of the first television shows in years to challenge the supremacy of the Cosby show in the ratings. Perhaps it is not accidental that it too features an oppressed minority reaching out for acceptance through comedy.

As the public indicates its tolerance for a larger-size female superstar, other media changes may follow. Perhaps newspapers will stop drawing the figures sketched to advertise clothes with distorted, elongated trunks and legs. A more normal female shape may sell clothes just as well. Then all women, even those who are slim, may feel less discouraged when they look at the ads.

In some cases, organizations are helping to bring about change in social attitudes. Recently, the National Association to Advance Fat Acceptance (NAAFA) persuaded Hallmark to remove offensive items from one of their product lines. They organized a letter-writing campaign complaining about Hallmark's Shoebox line, which had numerous cards, mugs, and other items that were insulting to fat people. For example, a birthday card that said, "There are worse things in life than birthdays. Like you could be wearing shorts and riding on a bus on a hot day, and you're all sweaty and then some fat guy gets on and insists on sharing your seat, for Pete's sake!" Or a mug that depicted an elephant lying in a hammock with the caption "I exercise as much as the next guy (providing the next guy is a fat, lazy slob!)." When the letter-writing campaign was not successful, NAAFA organized a boycott of Hallmark products. Finally, Hallmark gave in and stopped manufacturing the material.

Advocacy and public outcry do make a difference. Our views do count with opinion leaders, businesses, and the media, but we need to empower ourselves to act. If we feel guilty for seeming to care about our bodies or ashamed at calling attention to ourselves, we will never act in our own best interests.

Change is gradual, but it is possible. Have real compassion for the millions of other people struggling with their own body traps, but also for yourself. And the next time you look in the mirror, confront the person you see reflected back with a deeper vision and insight. You have been bearing a terrible burden and you've been through a lot together. You can make her the "you" you value, because you now understand the mystery behind the glittering image.

Notes

INTRODUCTION

Page
11 *His wife is the perfect woman*: Rodney Tyler, "Doctor Vanity," *Special Reports*, January 1990, pp. 19–22.

12 *Egged on by moms*: Suzanne Alexander, "Egged on By Moms, Many Teen-agers Get Plastic Surgery," *The Wall Street Journal*, September 24, 1990, p. 1.

13 *Working women . . . spent over $7,000 a year for their "high maintenance" look*: "What Price Beauty?" *Glamour*, April 1991, p. 297.

18 *"Normal" women show some characteristics*: J. Rodin, L. R. Silberstein and R. H. Striegel-Moore, "Women and Weight: A Normative Discontent," in T. B. Sonderegger, ed., *Psychology and Gender: Nebraska Symposium on Motivation* (Lincoln: University of Nebraska Press, 1985), pp. 267–307.

19 *Men also experience body preoccupation*: L. R. Silberstein, R. H. Striegel-Moore, and J. Rodin, "Feeling Fat: A Woman's Shame," in H. B. Lewis, ed., *The Role of Shame in Symptom Formation* (Hillsdale, NJ: Lawrence Erlbaum, 1984), pp. 89–108.

CHAPTER 1   WHY NOW?

Page

23   *Review of the . . . eighties*: Vida Roberts, "Review of 80's," *Baltimore Evening Sun*, December 23, 1989, p. 24.

24   *Every period of history*: These are not discussed in the book in any detail since there are many fine works analyzing the role of beauty through time. These include: Lois Banner, *American Beauty* (New York: Alfred A. Knopf, 1983); William Bennett and Joel Gurnin, *The Dieter's Dilemma* (New York: Basic Books, 1982); Susan Brownmiller, *Femininity* (New York: Simon and Schuster, 1984); Barbara Ehrenreich and Deirdre English, *For Her Own Good: 150 Years of the Experts' Advice to Women* (Garden City, NY: Anchor Press/Doubleday, 1979); Bruce Haley, *The Healthy Body and American Culture* (Cambridge: Harvard University Press, 1978); William Hogarth, *The Analysis of Beauty, Written With a View of Fixing the Fluctuating Ideas of Taste* (London. J. Reeves, 1753); Steven Marcus, *The Other Victorians* (New York: New American Library, 1966); Hillel Schwartz, *Never Satisfied* (New York: The Free Press, 1986); Carole Smith-Rosenberg, "The Female Animal," *Journal of American History*, 1973, *60*, pp. 332–356.

26–7 *A joint survey . . . (AACS) and . . . (ASLS)*: Linda Troiano, "Reshaping Images: More Men Opt For Plastic Surgery," *American Health*, September 1990, p. 14.

28   *Better starting salary*: Jerry Ross and Kenneth Ferris, "Interpersonal Attraction and Organizational Outcomes: A Field Examination," *Administrative Science Quarterly*, 1981, *26*, pp. 617–632.

27   *Attractive children are more popular*: M. M. Clifford and E. Hatfield Walster, "The Effects of Physical Attractiveness on Teacher Expectations," *Sociology of Education*, 1973, *46*, pp. 248–258.

27   *Accomplished by cosmetic surgery*: S. M. Kalic, "Plastic Surgery, Physical Appearance and Person Perception," Unpublished doctoral dissertation (Cambridge: Harvard University), 1977.

28   *Physically attractive people have a distinct advantage*: P. L. Benson, S. A. Karabenck, and R. M. Lerner, "Pretty Pleases: The Effects of Physical Attractiveness, Race and Sex on Receiving Help," *Journal of Experimental Social Psychology*, 1976, *12*, pp.

409–415; H. Sigall, R. Page, and A. C. Brown, "Effort Expenditure as a Function of Evaluation and Evaluator Attractiveness," *Representative Research in Social Psychology*, 1971, 2, pp. 19–25.

28 *Attractive applicants . . . better chance*: R. L. Dipboye, R. D. Arvey, and D. E. Terpestra, "Sex and Physical Attractiveness of Raters and Applicants as Determinants of Résumé Evaluations," *Journal of Applied Psychology*, 1977, 62, pp. 228–294.

28 *Are found guilty less often*: M. G. Efran, "The Effect of Physical Appearance on the Judgment of Guilt, Interpersonal Attraction, and Severity of Recommended Punishment in a Simulated Jury Task," *Journal of Research in Personality*, 1974, 8, pp. 45–54; C. Stephan and J. C. Tully, "Influence of Physical Attractiveness of a Plaintiff on Decisions of Simulated Jurors," *Journal of Social Psychology*, 1977, 106, pp. 149–150.

28 *Study on the processes by which people get to know one another*: M. Snyder, E. D. Tanke, and E. Berscheid, "Social Perception and Interpersonal Behavior: On the Self-Fulfilling Nature of Social Psychology," *Journal of Personality and Social Psychology*, 1977, 35, pp. 556–566.

30 *Miss America contest*: D. M. Garner, P. E. Garfinkel, D. Schwartz, et al., "Cultural Expectations of Thinness in Women," *Psychological Reports*, 1980, 47, pp. 483–491.

30 *Weight, height and income for men*: Irene H. Frieze, Josephine E. Olson, and Deborah C. Good, "Perceived and Actual Discrimination in the Salaries of Male and Female Managers," *Journal of Applied Social Psychology*, 1990, 20, p. 63.

33 Psychology Today . . . *survey*: T. F. Cash, B. A. Winstead, and L. H. Janda, "The Great American Shape-up," *Psychology Today*, April 1986, pp. 30–37; E. Berscheid, E. Hatfield Walster, and G. Bohrnstedt, "Body Image. The Happy American Body; A Survey Report," *Psychology Today*, November 1973, pp. 119–131.

33 *Survey of teenagers*: Jack J. Sternlieb and Louis Munan, "A Survey of Health Problems, Practices and Needs of Youth," *Pediatrics*, 1972, 49, pp. 177–186.

34 *81 percent of the ten-year-olds . . . had already dieted at least once*: L. M. Mellin, S. Scully, and C. E. Irwin, "Disordered Eating Characteristics in Preadolescent Girls," *Meeting of the American Dietetic Association*, Las Vegas, 1986 (Abstract).

39 *Five traditional archetypes of masculinity*: Mark Gerzon, *A Choice of Heroes* (Boston: Houghton Mifflin, 1982), p. 22.

39 *Designer Lowell Nesbitt*: Elizabeth Snead, "Macho Mannequins Muscle Into Stores," *USA Today*, June 18, 1990, Section D, p. 1.

39 *Over fifty thousand businesses . . . over a billion dollars*: "What Price Beauty?" *Glamour*, April 1991, p. 298.

40 *"Thirtysomething" generation in 1989*: Clifford Adelman, "On the Paper Trail of the Class of '72," *The New York Times*, July 22, 1989, p. 25.

CHAPTER 2   THE VANITY TRAP

Page
43 *The body . . . we came into the world with*: Olivia Vlahos, *Body, The Ultimate Symbol* (New York: Lippincott, 1979), p. 12.

45 *How body image changes*: Fran Weiss, "Body-Image Disturbances Among Obese Adults: Evaluation and Treatment," *American Journal of Psychotherapy*, 1986, *40*, pp. 522–527.

46 *The private or the public areas of the self*: Michael F. Scheier and Charles S. Carver, "Private and Public Aspects of the Self," in L. Wheeler, ed., *Review of Personality and Social Psychology*, Vol. 2 (Beverly Hills, CA: Sage, 1981), pp. 189–216.

47 *Public Self-Consciousness Scale*: Allen Fenigstein, Michael F. Scheier, and Arnold H. Buss, "Public and Private Self-Consciousness: Assessment and Theory," *Journal of Consulting and Clinical Psychology*, 1975, *43*, pp. 522–527.

49 *Body image is a subjective experience*: Seymour Fisher, *Development and Structure of the Body Image*, Vol. 1 (Hillsdale, NJ: Lawrence Erlbaum, 1986), pp. 169–171.

50 *The centrality of body image to self-concept*: H. Markus and J. Smith, "The Influence of Self-Schemata on the Perception of Others," in N. Cantor and J. F. Kihlstrom, eds., *Personality, Cognition, and Social Interaction* (Hillsdale, NJ: Lawrence Erlbaum, 1981), pp. 233–262.

50 *Experiments where people are given a mirror*: Michael F. Scheier and Charles S. Carver, "Self-Focused Attention and the Experience of Emotion: Attraction, Repulsion, Elation, and Depression," *Journal of Personality and Social Psychology*, 1979, *35*, pp. 625–626.

50 *Self-focus as a prescription for becoming more attractive*: George Masters, *The Masters Way to Beauty*, (New York: Signet, 1977), p. 21.

50 *Body awareness actually* lowers *self-esteem*: Seymour Fisher, *Body Experience in Fantasy and Behavior* (New York: Appleton-Century-Crofts, 1970), pp. 1–57.

51 *Intensified self-awareness also leads to greater conformity*: Michael F. Scheier and Charles S. Carver, "Self-directed Attention, Awareness of Bodily States and Suggestibility," *Journal of Personality and Social Psychology*, 1979, 37, pp. 1576–1588.

51 *Twenty things that you are most aware of right now*: This exercise is adapted from the Body Focus Questionnaire in Fisher, *Development and Structure of the Body Image*, Vol. 2, pp. 673–680.

51 *Dava Sobel*: "Face to Face with the New Me," *The New York Times Magazine*, April 9, 1989, pp. 26–28.

52 *Women's consistent exaggeration of their body*: A. E. Fallon and P. Rozin, "Sex Differences in Perceptions of Desirable Body Shape," *Journal of Abnormal Psychology*, 94, 1985, pp. 102–105: E. J. Button, F. Fransella, and P. D. Slade, "A Reappraisal of Body Perception Disturbance in Anorexia Nervosa," *Psychological Medicine*, 7, 1977, pp. 235–243; R. C. Casper, K. A. Halmi, B. C. Goldberg, et al., "Disturbances in Body Image Estimation as Related to Their Characteristics and Outcome of Anorexia Nervosa," *British Journal of Psychiatry*, 134, 1979, pp. 60–69; D. M. Garner, P. E. Garfinkel, H. C. Stuncor, et al., "Body Image Disturbances in Anorexia Nervosa and Obesity," *Psychosomatic Medicine*, 1976, 38, pp. 327–336

55 *Testing "normal" women*: J. Kevin Thompson, "Larger Than Life," *Psychology Today*, April 1986, p. 42.

53 *Establishing their own boundaries*: Over the years there have been numerous books and studies examining field dependency in children and adults. Overprotectiveness of parents has often been discussed in these works, which include the following. H. A. Witkin, H. B. Lewis, M. Hertzman, et al., *Personality Through Perception* (New York: Harper, 1954); J. Kagen and H. A. Moss, *Birth to Maturity* (New York: Wiley, 1962); R. L. Levine, "Patterns of Perceived Mothering and its Relation to Body Image, Guilt, and Feminine Values in College Women," Unpublished doctoral dissertation, Adelphi University, 1976; Fisher, *Body Experience in Fantasy and Behavior*, pp. 1–57.

54 *Excellent book on body image*: Fisher, *Development and Structure of the Body Image*, Vol. 1.

54 *In a chunk of space that is "mine . . . "*: Fisher, ibid., pp. 79–80.

54 *Daily rituals . . . can serve to maintain a comforting sense*: Seymour Fisher quoted by Daniel Goleman, "Dislike of Own Body Found Common Among Women," *The New York Times*, March 19, 1986, section C, p. 3.

54 *Greater self-confidence and sociability*: T. F. Cash, J. Rissi, and R. Chapman, "Not Just Another Pretty Face: Sex Roles, Sense of Control, and Cosmetics Use," *Personality and Social Psychology Bulletin*, 1985, *11*, pp. 253–255.

54 *Body is a suspicious thing*: Fisher, *Development and Structure of the Body Image*, Vol. 1, p. 84.

55 *Anxiety associated with the body is widespread*: S. Kern, *Anatomy and Destiny: A Cultural History of the Human Body* (New York: Bobbs-Merrill, 1975); Vlahos, op. cit., p. 27.

55 *Bolster some essential body fictions*: Fisher, *Development and Structure of the Body Image*, Vol. 1, p. 84.

57 *Mildly depressed evaluate their bodies*: S. W. Noles, T. F. Cash, and B. A. Winstead, "Body Image, Physical Attractiveness, and Depression," *Journal of Consulting and Clinical Psychology*, 1985, *53*, 88–94.

58 *65 percent of babies recognize*: Fisher, *Development and Structure of the Body Image*, Vol. 1, pp. 85–93.

59 *Body build and self-esteem are strongly related for girls*: G. W. Guyot, L. Fairchild, and M. Hill, "Physical Fitness, Sport Participation, Body Build and Self-Concept of Elementary School Children," *International Journal of Sports Psychology*, 1981, *12*, pp. 105–116; S. W. Davis, D. L. Best, and R. C. Hawkins, Jr., "Sex Stereotypes" (Abstract), *Society for Research in Child Development*, 1981.

59 *Nonobese girls. . .express more worries. . .than obese and nonobese boys*: R. D. Hammer, V. A. Cambell, N. L. Moores, et al., "An Interdisciplinary Study of Adolescent Obesity," *Journal of Pediatrics*, 1972, *80*, pp. 373–382; M. H. Tobin-Richards, A. M. Boxer, and A. C. Peterson, "The Psychological Significance of Pubertal Change and Differences in Perceptions of Self During Adolescence," in J. Brooks-Gunn and A. C. Petersen, eds., *Girls of Puberty* (New York: Plenum, 1983), pp. 127–154.

59 *After puberty girls have 20 to 30 percent more fat*: D. D. Marine

and J. C. King, "Nutritional Concerns During Adolescence," *Pediatric Clinics of North America*, 1980, *27*, pp. 125–139.

60 *Girls . . . want to be thinner*: James Scanlon, "Self-Reported Health Behavior and Attitudes of Youths 12–17 Years," *National Center for Health Statistics*, 1, 1978.

60 *Adolescents, in all Westernized countries*: S. M. Dornbusch, J. M. Carlsmith, P. D. Duncan, et al., "Sexual Motivation, Social Caste, and the Desire to be Thin Among the Adolescent Females," *Developmental and Behavioral Pediatrics*, 1984, *5*, pp. 308–314.

60 *In a study of 195 female high school juniors and seniors*: C. Jakobovits, P. Halstead, L. Kelley, et al., "Eating Habits and Nutrient Intakes of College Women Over a Thirty-Year Period," *Journal of the American Dietetic Association*, 1977, *71*, pp. 405–411.

60 *Five hundred local adolescents*: L. Cohn, N. Adler, D. Irwin, Jr., et al., "Body-Figure Preferences in Male and Female Adolescents," *Journal of Abnormal Psychology*, 1987, *3*, pp. 276–279.

61 *Judged themselves more harshly . . . than their peers*: K. E. Musa and M. E. Roach, "Adolescent Appearance and Self-Concept," *Adolescence*, 1973, *8*, pp. 385–394.

61 *Three primary tasks*: J. Rodin, L. R. Silberstein, and R. H. Striegel-Moore, "Women and Weight: A Normative Discontent," in T. B. Sondernegger, ed., *Psychology and Gender: Nebraska Symposium on Motivation* (Lincoln: University of Nebraska Press, 1985), pp. 267–307.

61 *Virginia psychologists*: J. P. Hill and M. E. Lynch, "The Intensification of Gender-Related Role Expectations During Early Adolescence," in J. Brooks-Gunn and A. C. Petersen, eds., *Girls at Puberty* (New York: Plenum, 1983), pp. 201–228.

62 *Girls . . . rank popularity as more important*: R. G. Simmons and F. Rosenberg, "Sex, Sex Roles and Self-Image," *Journal of Youth and Adolescence*, 1975, *4*, p. 229.

62 *Adolescent tasks of separation and individuation*: Carol Gilligan, *In A Different Voice: Psychological Theory and Women's Development* (Cambridge: Harvard University Press, 1982), pp. 155–157.

64 *Never regain their old figure*: D. F. Williamson, H. S. Kahn, P. L. Remington, et al., "The 10-Year Incidence of Overweight and Major Weight Gain in U.S. Adults," *Archives of Internal Medicine*, 1990, *150*, pp. 665–672.

64 *Most people get fatter in old age*: J. Brozek, Changes of Body Composition in Man During Maturity and Their Nutritional Implications, *Federal Procedure*, 1952, *11*, pp. 784–793.

65 *Elderly people are very self-conscious of their body appearance*: M. Ross, R. C. Tait, G. T. Grossberg, et al., "Age Differences in Body Consciousness," *Journal of Gerontology*, 1989, *44*, pp. 23–24.

CHAPTER 3 THE SHAME TRAP

Page
71 *"The temptation to blame everything on excess tonnage"*: W. Wasserstein, "To Live and Diet," *New York Woman*, February 1988, pp. 24–27.

72 *Darwin's work on emotions*: C. R. Darwin, *The Expression of the Emotions in Man and Animals* (New York: D. Appleton, 1899).

72 *Shame involves "implosion" of the self*: R. D. Laing cited in H. B. Lewis, *Shame and Guilt in Neurosis* (New York: International Universities Press, 1971), p. 101.

72 *Sunny Griffen . . . for Collagen Corporation in* Vogue *magazine*: Collagen Corporation Advertisement in *Vogue*, February 1988, p. 23.

73 *Shame involves feeling bad about who you are*: Lewis, op. cit., p. 101.

74 *Shame arises from a felt gap*: L. R. Silberstein, R. H. Striegel-Moore, and J. Rodin, "Feeling Fat: A Woman's Shame," in H. B. Lewis, ed., *The Role of Shame in Symptom Formation* (Hillsdale, NJ: Lawrence Erlbaum, 1987), pp. 89–108.

74 *Body Shame test*: R. H. Striegel-Moore, L. R. Silberstein, P. Frensch, et al., "A Prospective Study of Disordered Eating Among College Students," *International Journal of Eating Disorders*, 1989, *89*, pp. 489–509.

76 *Self-Ideal Discrepancy test*: A. E. Fallon and P. Rozin, "Sex Differences in Perceptions of Desirable Body Shape," *Journal of Abnormal Psychology*, 1985, *94*, pp. 102–105.

76 *Reactions to a Kinsey survey*: A. Kinsey, W. Pomeroy, C. Martin, et al., *Sexual Behavior in the Human Female* (Philadelphia: W. B. Saunders, 1953), p. 58.

76 *Ashamed of being ashamed*: H. B. Lewis, *Shame and Guilt in Neurosis*, p. 399.

79 *Women . . . feel shame . . . high on the list:* L. R. Silberstein, R. H. Striegel-Moore, and J. Rodin in H. B. Lewis, *The Role of Shame in Symptom Formation*, pp. 89–108.

79 *Overweight celebrities*: Tom Green, "The Weight of Celebrity," *USA Today*, November 27, 1989, section D, p. 1.

80 *Oprah Winfrey's celebrated weight loss and regain*: Marjorie Rosen, Beth Austin, Magda Krance, et al., "Big Gain, No Pain," *People Weekly*, January 14, 1991, p. 82.

81 *Avoid situations in which they will feel looked at*: S. R. Dyrenforth, O. W. Wooley, and S. C. Wooley, "A Woman's Body in a Man's World: A Review of Findings on Body Image and Weight Control," in Jane Rachel Kaplan, *A Woman's Conflict* (Englewood Cliffs, NJ: Prentice-Hall, 1980), pp. 29–50.

83 *At home, my mother . . . would always watch exactly what we ate*: J. Palmisano, "Hidden Obsessions," *The New Journal*, November 1990, p. 22.

84 *The many layers of shame*: J. Rodin, L. R. Silberstein, and R. H. Striegel-Moore, "Women and Weight: A Normative Discontent," in T. B. Sondernegger, ed., *Psychology and Gender: Nebraska Symposium on Motivation* (Lincoln: University of Nebraska Press, 1985), pp. 267–307.

85 *"When I'd binge . . . "*: Palmisano, op. cit., pp. 23–24.

86 *"I purged after every meal"*: Palmisano, op. cit., p. 22.

87 *The majority of women who purge do so in carefully guarded isolation*: R. H. Striegel-Moore, L. R. Silberstein, and J. Rodin, "Toward an Understanding of Risk Factors for Bulimia," *American Psychologist*, 1986, *41*, pp. 246–263.

87 *A classic example of the difference between men and women*: P. Richmond, "How Do Men Feel About Their Bodies?", *Glamour*, April 1987, p. 312.

88 *"Men who are losing the hair"*: D. Seeley, "Who Him? Worry About His Body?" *Mademoiselle*, April 1989, p. 258.

89 *If shame could cure obesity*: S. Wooley, quoted in C. Sternhell, "We'll Always Be Fat, but Fat Can Be Fit," *Ms.*, May 1985, p. 143.

CHAPTER 4   THE COMPETITION TRAP

Page
95 *Women of the 1980s and 1990s*: L. Rosch, "The Professional Image Report," *Working Woman*, October 1988, p. 109.

95 *Encouraged to contend with each other*: M. Boskind-White and W. C. White, *Bulimarexia: The Binge/Purge Cycle* (New York: W. W. Norton, 1983), pp. 6, 10.

96 *Women to become closer to one another*: J. Rodin, R. H. Striegel-Moore, and L. R. Silberstein, "Vulnerability and Resilience in the Age of Eating Disorders," in J. Rolf, A. Masten, D. Cicchetti, et al., eds., *Risk and Protective Factors in the Development of Psychopathology* (Cambridge: Cambridge University Press, 1990), pp. 366–390.

96 *Mothers and sisters are often the first place . . .* : ibid.

96 *To secure and attract men*: ibid.

97 *They had a snack together*: S. Chaiken and P. Pliner, "Women, but Not Men, Are What They Eat: The Effect of Meal Size and Gender on Perceived Femininity and Masculinity," *Personality and Social Psychology Bulletin*.

97 *With increasingly rigorous standards*: J. Rodin, L. R. Silberstein, and R. H. Striegel-Moore, "Women and Weight: A Normative Discontent," in T. B. Sonderegger, ed., *Psychology and Gender: Nebraska Symposium on Motivation* (Lincoln: University of Nebraska Press, 1985), pp. 267–307.

98 *Achievement Orientation Scale*: R. L. Helmreich and J. Spence, "The Work and Family Orientation Questionnaire: An Objective Instrument to Assess Components of Achievement Motivation and Attitudes Towards Family and Career," *JSAB Catalog of Selected Documents in Psychology*, 1978, *8*, p. 355.

99 *Male child-rearing . . . female child-rearing*: E. E. Maccoby, "Gender Segregation in the Workplace: Continuities and Discontinuities from Childhood to Adulthood," in M. Frankenhaeuser, ed., *Women, Work, and Health*, 1988, pp. 3–16.

99 *According to Marilyn Moats Kennedy*: "What Price Beauty?" *Glamour*, April 1991, p. 302.

99 *Many have excessively high standards*: R. H. Striegel-Moore, L. R. Silberstein, and J. Rodin, "Toward an Understanding of Risk Factors for Bulimia," *American Psychologist*, 1986, 41, pp. 246–263.

100 *Miss America contest in the ratings*: S. D. Stark, "Miss America: For Women the Pageant Never Ends," *The New York Times*, September 16, 1987, section C, p. 14.

101 *Self-Evaluation Scale*: Adapted from the Eating Disorder Inventory (EDI), D. M. Garner, M. P. Olmsted, and J. Polivy, "Development and Validation of a Multidimensional Eating Disorder Inventory for Anorexia Nervosa and Bulimia," *International Journal of Eating Disorders*, 1983, *2*, pp. 15–34.

100 *Boardroom, not the Boardwalk*: ibid.

100 *Executive producer of the Miss Universe contest*: George Hornchar in ibid.

100 *Body-building . . . on the rise*: J. Adler, "You're So Vain," *Newsweek*, April 14, 1986, p. 48.

102 *Schemas about the self*: H. Markus, R. Hamill, and K. P. Sentis, "Thinking Fat: Self-Schemas for Body Weight and the Processing of Weight-Relevant Information," *Journal of Applied Social Psychology*, 1987, *17*, pp. 50–71.

102 *Women who are schematic for weight*: ibid.

104 *Elaine Hatfield at the University of Hawaii*: E. Berscheid and E. Walster (Hatfield), *Interpersonal Attraction* (Reading, PA: Addison-Wesley, 1978); E. Walster, V. Aronson, D. Abrahams, et al., "Importance of Physical Attractiveness in Dating Behavior," *Journal of Personality and Social Psychology*, 1966, *4*(5), pp. 508–516; E. Walster and E. Berscheid, "Adrenaline Makes the Heart Grow Fonder," *Psychology Today*, June 1971, *5*, pp. 46–50, 62.

104 *Men were more likely to reveal personal facts*: M. Snyder, E. D. Tanke, and E. Berscheid, "Social Perception and Interpersonal Behavior: On the Self-Fulfilling Nature of Social Psychology," *Journal of Personality and Social Psychology*, 1977, *35*, pp. 556–666.

104 *Good looks for girls*: B. E. Vaughn and J. H. Langlois, "Physical Attractiveness as a Correlate of Peer Status and Social Competence in Preschool Children," *Developmental Psychology*, 1983, *19*, pp. 561–567.

104 *Beautiful girls interest the highest-status boys*: E. E. Maccoby and C. N. Jacklin, *The Psychology of Sex Differences* (Stanford: Stanford University Press, 1974), pp. 225–348.

104 *Appearance counts in a relationship*: J. S. Coleman, *The Adolescent Society* (New York: Free Press, 1961); E. Douvan and

J. Adelson, *The Adolescent Experience* (New York: John Wiley, 1966).

104 *Mass media, and television in particular*: A. S. Tan, "TV Beauty Ads and Role Expectations of Adolescent Female Viewers," *Journalism Quarterly*, 1979, *56*, pp. 283–288.

105 *Sources of status for men and women*: R. H. Striegel-Moore, et al., "Toward an Understanding of Risk Factors for Bulimia," p. 248.

106 *Combinations of pictures*: D. Bar-Tal and L. Saxe, "Physical Attractiveness and its Relationship to Sex Role Stereotyping," *Sex Roles*, 1976, *2*, pp. 123–133.

106 *Interviewed a cross-section of American couples*: P. Blumstein and P. Schwartz, *American Couples: Money, Work and Sex* (New York: Pocket Books, 1983), p. 247.

107 *Pay for the extra pounds with angry husbands*: M. G. Gage and D. Christensen's study of 454 middle-class white couples. Described in article by Marilyn Elias, "Extra Pounds Weigh Heavy on New Mom," *USA Today*, November 7, 1989, section D, p. 1.

108 *The double standard of aging that distinguishes men from women*: S. Sontag, "The Double Standard of Aging," *Saturday Review*, September 23, 1972, p. 29.

108 *Old women as relatively less attractive than old men*: E. Hatfield and E. Walster, "Physical Attractiveness in Social Interaction," in J. Graham and A. Kligman, eds., *The Psychology of Cosmetic Treatment* (New York: Praeger, 1985), pp. 77–92.

109 *Women wished for a figure that was significantly thinner*: A. E. Fallon and P. Rozin, "Sex Differences in Perceptions of Desirable Body Shape," *Journal of Abnormal Psychology*, 1985, *94*, pp. 102–105.

109 *Adolescents ages ten to fifteen years*: L. D. Cohn, N. E. Adler, C. E. Irwin, Jr., et al., "Body-Figure Preferences in Male and Female Adolescents," *Journal of Abnormal Psychology*, 1987, *96*, pp. 275–279.

109 *Women more likely . . . in full figure*: D. Archer, B. Iritani, D. D. Kimes, et al., "Facism. Five Studies of Sex Differences in Facial Prominence," *Journal of Personality and Social Psychology*, 1983, *45*, pp. 725–735.

110 *Weight and body shape constituted the* central *determinants*: L. R. Silberstein, R. H. Striegel-Moore, C. Timko, et al., "Behavioral and Psychological Implications of Body Dissatisfac-

tion: Do Men and Women Differ?" *Sex Roles*, 1988, *19*, pp. 219–232.

110 *Large-scale survey of* Glamour *magazine readers*: S. Wooley and W. Wooley, "Feeling Fat in a Thin Society," *Glamour*, February 1984, p. 201.

111 *"Breeding grounds" for eating disorders*: S. Squire, *The Slender Balance: Causes and Cures for Bulimia, Anorexia, and the Weight-Loss/Weight-Gain Seesaw* (New York: Putnam, 1983), pp. 68–79.

112 *Studying sororities*: C. Crandall, "The Social Contagion of Binge Eating," *Journal of Personality and Social Psychology*, 1988, *55*, pp. 588–598.

113 *A more restrictive parenting style*: P. R. Costanzo and E. Z. Woody, "Domain-Specific Parenting Styles and Their Impact in the Child's Development of Particular Deviance: The Example of Obesity Proneness," *Journal of Social and Clinical Psychology*, 1985, *3*, pp. 425–445.

113 *Girls of any weight are at risk for developing high anxiety*: Rodin, et al., "Vulnerability and Resilience in the Age of Eating Disorders," pp. 361–383.

113 *Mother's efforts to control her own weight*: ibid.

116 *Torn between their own aspirations and their loyalty*: K. Chernin, *The Hungry Self: Women, Eating, and Identity* (New York: Random House, 1985), p. 81.

116 *The view that women compete with their mothers*: ibid, pp. 91–93.

119 *Unreasonably high standards*: J. Rodin and R. Striegel-Moore, "Predicting Attitudes Toward Body Weight and Food Intake in Women," paper presented at the *14th Congress of European Association of Behavior Therapy*, Brussels, September 1984.

119 *Ideal is phrased in unattainable superlatives*: C. Steiner-Adair, "The Body Politic: Normal Female Adolescent Development and the Development of Eating Disorders," *Journal of the American Academy of Psychoanalysis*, 1986, *14*, pp. 95–114.

120 *As matching her ideal*: S. M. Jourard and P. R. Secord, "Body Cathexis and the Ideal Female Figure," *Journal of Abnormal and Social Psychology*, 1955, *50*, pp. 243–246; C. Timko, R. Striegel-Moore, L. Silberstein, et al., "Femininity/Masculinity and Disordered Eating in Women: How Are They Related?" *International Journal of Eating Disorders*, 1987, *6*, pp. 701–712.

120 *Maintain greater distinctions*: P. W. Linville, "Affective Conse-

quences of Complexity Regarding the Self and Others," in M. S. Clark and S. T. Fiske, eds., *Affect and Cognition; 17th Annual Carnegie Symposium in Cognition* (Hillsdale, NJ: Lawrence Erlbaum, 1989), pp. 79–105.

120 *Spill over and change feelings*: P. W. Linville, ibid.

121 *Self-Complexity Test*: We have used this test, which we developed for our research, in several studies, including L. R. Silberstein, R. H. Striegel-Moore, C. Timko, et al., "Behavioral and Psychological Implications of Body Dissatisfaction: Do Men and Women Differ?" *Sex Roles*, 1988, *19*, pp. 219–232.

122 *Studies by psychologist Patricia Linville at Duke University*: P. W. Linville, "Self-complexity and Affective Extremity: Don't Put All of Your Eggs in One Cognitive Basket," *Social Cognition*, 1988, *3*, pp. 94–120.

124 *"Juggling" may be the best exercise of all*: R. C. Barnett and G. K. Baruch, "Women's Involvement in Multiple Roles and Psychological Distress," *Journal of Personality and Social Psychology*, 1985, *49*, pp. 135–145; B. J. Hirsch and B. D. Rapkin, "Multiple Roles, Social Networks and Women's Well-Being," *Journal of Personality and Social Psychology*, 1986, *81*, pp. 1237–1247.

124 *Extreme perfectionism and weight preoccupation*: For an overview, see J. Rodin, "Women and Weight: A Normative Discontent, " pp. 267–307.

CHAPTER 5   THE FOOD TRAP

Page
128 *"A baked potato"*: L. Shapiro and E. A. Leonard, "Everybody's Got a Hungry Heart," *Newsweek*, May 13, 1991, pp. 58–59; Robert Lang, "Food Preoccupation," *Self*, December 1990, p. 58.

129 *The noted food writer*: M.F.K. Fisher, *The Art of Eating* (New York: Vintage, 1976), p. 353.

130 *Mystical rites, funerals*: Sidney M. Cantor, "Ideals and Realities in Food Systems," in N. Henry Moss and Jean Mayer, eds., *Food and Nutrition in Health and Disease* (New York: Academy of Sciences, 1977), pp. 262–265.

131 *Emotional Eating Test*: "Dutch Eating Behaviour Questionnaire" developed by T. van Strien, J.E.R. Frijters, G.P.A. Bergers, et al., *International Journal of Eating Disorders*, 1986, *5*, pp. 295–315.

132 *Renowned French writer*: Brillat-Savarin in Joanne Koch Potce, "Baking Bread," *Radcliffe College Quarterly*, December 1988, p. 28.

133 *Hyperactivity and even crime*: Matt Clark, "America's Sweet Tooth," *Newsweek*, August 26, 1985, p. 51.

133 *Connection between women and food*: Carole M. Counihan, "An Anthropological View of Western Women's Prodigious Fasting: A Review Essay," *Food and Foodways*, 1989, *4*, pp. 357–375.

134 *Women use eating . . . to assert autonomy and control*: M. Millman, *Such a Pretty Face: Being Fat in America* (New York: W. W. Norton, 1980), p. 10.

135 *"America's Romance with Food"*: Marian Parry, "Spaghetti with Olive Oil, Lemon Sugar Pancakes," *Radcliffe College Quarterly*, December 1988, p. 25.

136 *People use food to provide themselves with psychological nurturance*: A. H. Murray, *Explorations in Personality* (New York: Oxford University Press, 1938), pp. 77–79.

137 *Self-Nurturance Test*: Adapted from Nurturance Rating Task, A. K. Lehman and J. Rodin, "Styles of Self-Nurturance and Disordered Eating," *Journal of Consulting and Clinical Psychology*, 1989, *57*, pp. 117–122.

138 *"The mouth is the focus of a general first approach to life"*: Erik Erikson, *Childhood and Society* (New York: W. W. Norton, 1950), p. 67.

139 *Bulimic women derive a far smaller proportion of their self-nurturance*: A. K. Lehman and J. Rodin, op. cit., pp. 117–122.

139 *In two surveys done for the Weight Watchers organization*: Marilyn Elias, "Why Hubbies Turn Into Chubbies," *USA Today*, March 9, 1989, section D, p. 1.

139 *Women use food if they don't get enough hugs and love*: R. B. Stuart and B. Jacobson, *Weight, Sex and Marriage* (New York: Norton, 1987).

140 *Food-sharing the very definition of who is . . . family*: Counihan, op. cit., pp. 357–375.

140 *Food prohibitions*: Counihan, ibid.

140 *The idea of flies makes the soup disgusting*: Paul Rozin and

Debra Zellner, "The Role of Pavlovian Conditioning in the Acquisition of Food Likes and Dislikes," *Annals of the New York Academy of Sciences*, 1985, *43*, pp. 289–302.

140 *The Hua people of New Guinea*: Anna S. Meigs, *Food, Sex, and Pollution: A New Guinea Religion* (New Brunswick, NJ: Rutgers University Press, 1984).

141 *The heart of his predecessor*: J. Goody, *Cooking, Cuisine and Class: A Study in Comparative Psychology* (New York: Cambridge Press, 1982), p. 77.

142 *From diet books to books about nutrition*: Carole Sugarman, "Want to Boost Your Brain? Help Your Heart? Squelch Your Stress? There Is a Book for You . . .," *Washington Post Health Magazine*, June 16, 1989, p. 12.

142 *Different . . . foods promoted all sorts of functions*: Joel Gurin, "Lobsters for Romance, Salads for Power," *American Health*, October 1989, p. 44.

142 *"Situational nutrition"*: Reported in L. Mikesell, ed., *Food Insight: International Food Information Council*, March/April 1990, pp. 4–5.

142 *The way we ate even twenty years ago*: Ira Mothner, "Our National Food Fight," *American Health*, October 1987, p. 48.

143 *The editor of Gorman's* New Product News: Martin Friedman cited in Molly O'Neill, "Eating to Heal: Mapping Out New Frontiers," *The New York Times*, February 7, 1990, section C, p. 6.

143 *In a study conducted at a local preschool*: S. L. Goldman, D. Whitney-Saltiel, J. Granger, et al., "Children's Representations of 'Everyday' Aspects of Health and Illness," *Journal of Pediatric Psychology*, in press.

143 *Reminisces about the good old days*: Julia Child, "On Writing a Cookbook," *Radcliffe College Quarterly*, December 1988, p. 6.

144 *Oat bran can lower blood cholesterol about 20 percent*: B. P. Kinosian and J. M. Eisenberg, "Cutting Into Cholesterol: Cost-Effective Alternatives for Treating Hypercholesterolemia," *Journal of the American Medical Association*, 1988, *259*, pp. 2249–2254.

144 *Hippocrates observed*: Hippocrates, quoted in David Kritchevsky, "Dietary Fiber: What It Is and What It Does," in N. H. Moss and J. M. Mayer, *Food and Nutrition in Health and Disease, Annals of the New York Academy of Sciences*, 1977, *300*, pp. 284–289.

144 *Amount of fiber currently being recommended*: National Research Council, National Academy of Sciences, *Diet and Health: Implications for Reducing Chronic Disease Risk* (Washington, D.C.: National Academy of Sciences, 1989).

145 *Changing food habits to help fight heart disease*: R. W. Mahley, "The Role of Dietary Fat and Cholesterol in Atherosclerosis and Lipoprotein Metabolism," *Western Journal of Medicine*, 1981, *139*, p. 34.

145 *Omega-three fish oils:* ibid.

172 *Three meals or as seventeen snacks given hourly*: D. Jenkins, T. Wolever, V. Vuskan, et al., "Nibbling Versus Gorging: Metabolic Advantages of Increased Meal Frequency," *New England Journal of Medicine*, 1989, *321*, pp. 929–934.

146 *Fight against cancer*: M. S. Menkes, G. M. Comstock, J. P. Vuilleumier, et al., "Serum Beta-Carotene, Vitamins A and E, Selenium, and the Risk of Lung Cancer," *New England Journal of Medicine*, 1985, *315*, pp. 1250–1254.

146 *New studies from the Framingham Heart Project*: T. A. Manolio, D. Levy, R. J. Garrison, et al., "Relationship of Alcohol Intake to Left Ventricular Mass: The Framingham Study," *Journal of the American College of Cardiology*, in press.

147 *Increasing scientific evidence*: J. Rodin and J. R. Ickovics, "Women's Health: Review and Research Agenda as We Approach the 21st Century," *American Psychologist*, 1990, *45*, pp. 1018–1034.

147 *Fluoride in our drinking water*: E. Marshall, "The Fluoride Debate: One More Time," *Science*, 1990, *247*, pp. 276–277.

148 *The best estimate of nutrition needs*: G. A. Leveille, "Human Nutrition Norms," *Annals of the New York Academy of Sciences*, 1977, *300*, pp. 259–261.

148 *With new legislation likely*: M. Bloom, "The Flap Over Food Labeling," *Washington Post Health Magazine*, February 6, 1990, p. 17.

149 *"Sugar buzz" to "sugar blues"*: S. Chollar, "Food for Thought," *Psychology Today*, April 1988, p. 30.

149 *Such theories are now widely discussed*: G. E. Gray, "Diet, Crime and Delinquency: A Critique," *Nutrition Reviews*, 1986, *44*, pp. 89–94.

149 *Dan White murder trial*: M. Clark, S. Katz, and M. Muger, "America's Sweet Tooth," *Newsweek*, August 26, 1985, p. 52.

149 *Little . . . evidence that dietary factors have any role in antisocial behavior*: Gray, op. cit., pp. 89–94.

150 *"Halloween effect"*: H. B. Ferguson, C. Stoddard, and J. G. Simeon, "Double-Blind Challenge Studies Behavioral and Cognitive Effects of Sucrose-Aspartame Ingestion in Normal Children," *Nutrition Review Supplement*, 1986, *44*, pp. 144–150.

150 *Methodologically rigorous studies*: ibid.

151 *Merely because of hypoglycemia*: B. Spring, O. Miller, R. J. Wurtman, et al., "Effects of Protein and Carbohydrate Meals on Mood and Performance: Interactions With Sex and Age," *Journal of Psychiatric Research*, 1982, *17*, pp. 155–167.

151 *Brain is sensitive to the specific dietary constituents*: J. D. Fernstrom and R. J. Wurtman, "Brain Serotonin Content: Increase Following Ingestion of Carbohydrate Diet," *Science*, 1971, *174*, pp. 1023–1024; J. D. Fernstrom and R. J. Wurtman, "Brain Serotonin Content: Physiological Regulation by Plasma Neutral Amino Acids," *Science*, 1972, *178*, pp. 414–416.

152 *Both major classes of antidepressant drugs. . .increase. . .serotonin*: R. J. Wurtman and J. J. Wurtman, "Carbohydrate Craving, Obesity and Brain Serotonin," *Appetite*, 1986, *7*, pp. 99–103.

152 *Links carbohydrate consumption to the release of brain serotonin*: J. J. Wurtman, R. J. Wurtman, J. H. Growdon, et al., "Carbohydrate Craving in Obese People: Suppression by Treatments Affecting Serotoninergic Transmission," *International Journal of Eating Disorders*, 1981, *1*, pp. 2–15.

153 *To test this question*: Spring, et al., op. cit.

153 *Stirred up physiologically by the caffeine actually felt hungrier*: J. Rodin, "Stress-Induced Eating: Implications for Diabetes," in P. McCabe, T. Field, and N. Schneiderman, eds., *Stress and Coping* (Hillsdale, NJ: Lawrence Erlbaum, 1990), pp. 135–146.

154 *Doesn't treat all calories as equal*: J. Rodin, "Effects of Food Choice on Amount of Food Eaten in a Subsequent Meal: Implications for Weight Gain," in B. J. Hirsch and T. B. Van Itallie, eds., *Recent Advances in Obesity Research IV* (London: John Libbey, 1985), pp. 101–112.

155 *Vermont state penitentiary*: E.Λ.H. Sims, R. Goldman, C. Gluck, et al., "Experimental Obesity in a Man," *Transcriptions of the Association of American Physicians*, 1968, *81*, pp. 153–170.

155 *Foods high in fat . . . make you eat more*: A. Trembley, G. Plourde, J. Despces, et al., "Impact of Dietary Fat Content and Fat Oxidation on Energy Intake in Humans," *American Journal of Clinical Nutrition*, 1989, *49*, pp. 799–805.

155 *Gain in body fat associated with high fat consumption*: C. Bouchard, "The Response to Long-Term Overfeeding in Identical Twins," *New England Journal of Medicine*, 1990, *322*, pp. 1477–1482.

156 *Greater risk of cardiovascular disease*: M. Krotkiewski, P. Bjorntorp, L. Sjostrom, et al., "Impact of Obesity on Metabolism in Men and Women: Importance of Regional Adipose Tissue Distribution," *Journal of Clinical Investigation*, 1983, *72*, pp. 1150–1162; L. Lapidus, C. Bengtsson, B. Larsson, et al., "Distribution of Adipose Tissue and Risk of Cardiovascular Disease and Death: A 12-Year Follow-up of Participants in the Population Study of Women in Gothenburg, Sweden," *British Journal of Medicine*, 1984, *289*, pp. 1257–1261; A. H. Kissebah, A. Peiris, and D. J. Evans, "Mechanisms Associating Body Fat Distribution with the Abnormal Metabolic Profiles in Obesity," in E. Berry, et al., eds., *Recent Advances in Obesity Research* (John Libbey, 1986), pp. 54–59; G. Enzi, M. Gasparo, P. Biondetti, et al., "Subcutaneous and Visceral Fat Distribution According to Sex, Age and Overweight Evaluated by Computed Tomography," *American Journal of Clinical Nutrition*, 1986, *44*, pp. 739–746; S. Fujioka, Y. Matsuzawa, K. Tokunaga, et al., "Contribution of Intraabdominal Fat Accumulation to the Impairment of Glucose and Lipid Metabolism in Human Obesity," *Metabolism*, 1987, *36*, pp. 54–59.

156 *Different types of sugar*: J. Rodin, "Stress-Induced Eating: Implications for Diabetes," chapter 9.

156 *Diet rich in fiber had 25 percent less body fat*: Kritchevsky, op. cit., pp. 284–289.

156 *Effect is due to fiber's coarseness*: A. S. Levine, J. R. Tallman, M. K. Grace, et al., "Effects of Breakfast Cereals on Short-Term Food Intake," *American Journal of Clinical Nutrition*, 1989, *50*, pp. 1303–1307.

157 *Lose their appetite . . . because of taste adaptation*: E. T. Rolls, B. J. Rolls, and E. A. Rowe, "Sensory-Specific and Motivation-Specific Satiety for the Sight and Taste of Food and Water in Man," *Physiology and Behavior*, 1983, *30*, pp. 185–192; B. J.

Rolls, P. M. van Duijvenvoorde, and E. T. Rolls, "Pleasantness Changes and Food Intake in a Varied Four-Course Meal," *Appetite*, 1984, *5*, pp. 337–348; B. J. Rolls, "Sweetness and Satiety," in J. Dobbing, ed., *Sweetness* (London: Springer-Verlag, 1987), pp. 161–172.

CHAPTER 6   THE DIETING RITUALS TRAP

Page
165 *Television fans will remember*: Marjorie Rosen, Beth Austin, Magda Krance, et al., "Big Gain, No Pain," *People Weekly*, January 14, 1991, p. 82.

165 *Pulitzer Prize–winning author admits to feeling*: W. Wasserstein, "To Live and Diet," *New York Woman*, February 1988, pp. 24–27.

166 *Even very slender women believe*: C. Steinhell, "We'll Always Be Fat, but Fat Can Be Fit," *Ms.*, May 1985, p. 68.

166 *Thirty-three billion dollars on diets*: A. Miller, "Diets Incorporated," *Newsweek*, September 11, 1989, p. 56.

166 *In 1978, a Nielsen survey*: A. C. Nielsen, *Who is Dieting and Why?* (Chicago: A. C. Nielsen, 1979), p. 12.

167 *Number may now be dropping in the early 1990s*: "Fat Americans Eschew Battling the Bulge," from news service and staff reports, *The Washington Post*, August 8, 1989, p. 5.

167 *Weight-loss business is at an all-time high*: Miller, op. cit.

167 *Middle-age spread*: ibid.

167 *"McDonaldize weight loss"*: ibid.

167 *From almost any form of cancer*: K. D. Brownell, "Obesity: Understanding and Treating a Serious, Prevalent and Refractory Disorder," *Journal of Consulting and Clinical Psychology*, 1982, *50*, pp. 820–840.

167 Stringent *dieting . . . may be one of the major causes*: J. Rodin, L. R. Silberstein, and R. H. Striegel-Moore, "Women and Weight: A Normative Discontent," in T. B. Sonderegger, ed., *Psychology and Gender: Nebraska Symposium on Motivation* (Lincoln: University of Nebraska Press, 1985), pp. 267–307; G. L. Blackburn, G. T. Wilson, B. S. Kanders, et al., "Weight Cycling: The Experience of Human Dieters," *American Journal of Clinical Nutrition*, 1989, *49*, pp. 1105–1109.

168 *Genes play a major role*: C. Bouchard, "The Response to Long-Term Overfeeding in Identical Twins," *New England Journal of Medicine*, 1990, *322*, pp. 1477–1482.

168 *Eating disorders . . . after a period of strenuous dieting*: C. P. Herman and J. Polivy, "Dieting and Binging: A Causal Analysis," *American Psychologist*, 1985, *40*, pp. 193–201.

168 *Pursuit of better health*: Joel Gurin, "Leaner, Not Lighter," *Psychology Today*, June 1989, pp. 20–36.

169 *Your diet history*: K. D. Brownell, J. Rodin, and J. Wilmore, "National Runner's Survey on Dieting and Eating," *Runner's World*, April 1987, p. 27.

170 *50% more overweight teenagers . . . than there were 10 years ago*: Miller, op. cit.

170 *Using highly addictive crack and cocaine to lose weight*: "Cocaine Used as 'Diet Aid,'" *NAAFA Newsletter*, November–December 1990, p. 1.

172 *Jane Fonda . . . Oprah Winfrey*: Sternhell, op. cit., p. 66.

172 *11 percent of women feel more guilty*: Survey commissioned by Continental Baking Co. reported in the *Pittsburgh Press*, April 18, 1990: Section B, p. 1.

173 Glamour *magazine survey*: S. Wooley and O. Wooley, "Feeling Fat in a Thin Society," *Glamour*, February 1984, p. 200.

173 *Transformed if only they were thin*: W. C. White and M. Boskind-White, "An Experimental Behavioral Approach to the Treatment of Bulimarexia," *Journal of Psychotherapy: Theory, Research and Practice*, 1981, *18*, pp. 501–507.

173 *"Boils down to body size"*: Sternhell, op. cit., p. 68.

174 Elizabeth Takes Off: Elizabeth Taylor quoted in A. Harmetz "Liz Taylor at 55: Thin Again, and Wiser," *The New York Times*, January 20, 1990, section C, p. 1.

175 *When identical twins overeat*: Bouchard op. cit., pp. 1477–1482.

175 *Match the extremely thin ideal*: J. Rodin, et al., op. cit., pp. 267–307.

175 *Weights were stable over several years*: G. A. Rose and R. T. Williams, "Metabolic Studies of Large and Small Eaters," *British Journal of Nutrition*, 1961, *15*, pp. 1–9.

176 *Inherit their rate of metabolism*: E. Ravussin, S. Lillioja, W. C. Knowler, et al., "Reduced Rate of Energy Expenditure as a Risk Factor for Body Weight Gain," *New England Journal of Medicine*, 1988, *318*, pp. 467–472; S. B. Roberts, J. Savage, W. A. Coward, et al., "Energy Expenditure and Intake in In-

fants Born to Lean and Overweight Mothers," *New England Journal of Medicine*, 1988, *318*, pp. 461–466.

176 *Babies born to thin or obese women*: S. B. Roberts in G. Kolata, "Two New Studies Point Strongly to Low Metabolism Rate as Cause of Obesity," *The New York Times*, February 25, 1988, section B, p. 5.

176 *Lower basal metabolic rates than males*: J. Garrow, "The Regulation of Energy Expenditure," in G. A. Bray, ed., *Recent Advances in Obesity Research*, vol. 2 (London: Newman, 1978), pp. 200–210.

177 *Increases her fat-making capacity*: J. Rodin, et al., op. cit., pp. 267–307.

178 *When diets are less than 1,000 calories a day*: P. Nicholas and J. Dwyer, "Diets for Weight Reduction: Nutrition and Considerations," in K. D. Brownell and J. P. Foreyt, eds., *Handbook of Eating Disorders* (New York: Basic Books, 1986), pp. 122–144.

178 *Inadequate nutrition during weight reduction . . . fatal consequences*: ibid.

179 *High carbohydrate regimes*: ibid.

179 *Metabolic rate by an astounding 15 to 30 percent:* Garner, W. Rockert, M. P. Olmsted, et al., "Psychoeducational Principles in the Treatment of Bulimia and Anorexia Nervosa," in D. M. Garner and P. E. Garfinkel, eds., *Handbook of Psychotherapy for Anorexia Nervosa and Bulimia* (New York: Guilford Press, 1985), pp. 513–572; T. A. Wadden, T. B. Van Itallie, and G. L. Blackburn, "Responsible and Irresponsible Use of Very Low Caloric Diets in the Treatment of Obesity," *Journal of the American Medical Association*, 1990, *262*, pp. 83–85.

180 *The slowing of metabolic rate induced by dieting*: D. M. Garner, et al., op. cit.

180 *They made a group of rats obese*: K. D. Brownell, M.R.C. Greenwood, E. Stellar, et al., "The Effects of Repeated Cycles of Weight Loss and Regain in Rats," *Physiology and Behavior*, 1986, *38*, pp. 459–464.

181 *Animals chose more fat and less protein*: D. Reed, R. Contreras, C. Maggio, et al., "Weight Cycling in Female Rats Increases Dietary Fat Selection and Adiposity," *Physiology and Behavior*, 1988, *42*, pp. 389–395.

181 *Less biologically able to cope with overeating*: K. D. Brownell and L. J. Stein, "Metabolic and Behavioral Effects of Weight

Loss and Regain: A Review of the Animal and Human Literature," in A. J. Stunkard and A. Baum, eds., *Eating, Sleep and
Sexual Behavior* (Hillsdale, NJ: Erlbaum, 1989), pp. 39–50.

181 *More fashion- and weight-conscious*: Miller, op. cit.

182 *Conscientious Objectors*: A. Keys, J. Brozek, A. Henschel, et al.,
The Biology of Human Starvation (Minneapolis: University of
Minnesota Press, 1950), pp. 63–78.

182 *Causes of the high incidence of depression in women*: Rodin, et
al., op. cit.

183 *20 to 40 percent nationwide*: R. H. Striegel-Moore, L. R. Silberstein, and J. Rodin, "Toward an Understanding of Risk
Factors for Bulimia," *American Psychologist*, 1986, *41*, pp.
246–263.

183 *Weekend splurges . . . between 8,000 and 10,000 calories*: A. Keys,
op. cit.

185 *83 percent of the bulimics*: C. Fairburn, "A Cognitive Behavioral
Approach to the Treatment of Bulimia," *Psychological Medicine*, 1981, *11*, pp. 707–711.

186 *Risk of early death increased only at the extremes*: A. Keys,
G. Azavanis, H. Blackburn, et al., "Coronary Heart Disease:
Weight as Risk Factor," *Annals of Internal Medicine*, 1972, *77*,
pp. 15–27.

187 *Weight cycling also contributes to risk of heart disease*: L. Liss-
ner, P. M. Odell, R. B. D'Agostino, et al., "Variability in Body
Weight and Health Outcomes in the Framingham Population,"
New England Journal of Medicine, in press.

187 *Fat cells in the abdomen are metabolically different*: R. L. Liebel,
N. K. Edens, and S. K. Fried, "Physiological Basis for the Con-
trol of Body Fat Distribution in Humans," *Annual Review of
Nutrition*, 1989, *9*, pp. 417–444; E. Presta, R. L. Liebel, and
J. Hirsch, "Regional Changes in Adrenergic Receptor Status
During Hypochloric Intake Do Not Predict Changes in Adipose
Size or Body Shape," *Journal of Metabolism*, 1990, *39*, pp.
307–315.

187 *Abdominal fat and risk*: M. Krotkiewski, P. Bjorntorp, L. Sjo-
strom, et al., "Impact of Obesity on Metabolism in Men and
Women: Importance of Regional Adipose Tissue Distribution,"
Journal of Clinical Investigation, 1983, *72*, pp. 1150–1162;
L. Lapidus, C. Bengtsson, B. Larsson, et al., "Distribution of
Adipose Tissue and Risk of Cardiovascular Disease and Death:

A 12-Year Follow-up of Participants in the Population Study of Women in Gothenburg, Sweden," *British Journal of Medicine*, 1984, *289*, pp. 1257–1261; A. H. Kissebah, A. Peiris, and D. J. Evans, "Mechanisms Associating Body Fat Distribution with the Abnormal Metabolic Profiles in Obesity," in E. Berry, et al., eds., *Recent Advances in Obesity Research* (New York: John Libbey, 1986), pp. 54–59; G. Enzi, M. Gasparo, P. Biondetti, et al., "Subcutaneous and Visceral Fat Distribution According to Sex, Age and Overweight Evaluated by Computed Tomography," *American Journal of Clinical Nutrition*, 1986, *44*, pp. 739–746; S. Fujioka, Y. Matsuzawa, K. Tokunaga, et al., "Contribution of Intraabdominal Fat Accumulation to the Impairment of Glucose and Lipid Metabolism in Human Obesity," *Metabolism*, 1987, *36*, pp. 54–59.

187 *Men are at greater risk for heart disease*: ibid.

187 *Waist-to-hip ratio of 1.0 or more*: ibid.

193 *Highest fiber content in their breakfast meal*: A. S. Levine, J. R. Tallman, M. K. Grace, et al., "Effect of Breakfast Cereals on Short-Term Food Intake," *American Journal of Clinical Nutrition*," 1989, *50*, pp. 1303–1307.

194 *Don't trust your memory*: A. F. Smith cited in T. DeAngelis, "On a Diet? Don't Trust Your Memory?" *Psychology Today*, October 1989, p. 12.

CHAPTER 7　THE FITNESS TRAP

Page

196 *A man says to me*: Robert Lipsyte, "What Price Fitness?," *The New York Times Magazine*, February 16, 1986, p. 32.

197 *The fitness boom . . . is "a cyclical phenomenon"*: ibid.

198 *Moderate exercise benefits most people*: D. C. Neiman, "Exercise: How Much Is Enough? How Much Is Too Much?" *Women's Sports and Fitness*, June 1989, p. 31.

198 *As much as 30 percent*: D. L. Costill, M. G. Flynn, J. P. Kirwan, et al., "Effects of Repeated Days of Intensified Training on Muscle Glycogen and Swimming Performance," *Medicine and Science in Sports and Exercise*, 1988, *20*, pp. 249–254.

199 *45 percent of our body mass*: W. L. Haskell, "Exercise as a Means of Maximizing Human Physical Performance and Pro-

ductivity," in R. S. Williams and A. G. Wallace, eds., *Effects of Physical Activity*, HKP Sport Science Monograph Series, 1989, *2*, pp. 115–126.

200 *Exercise History*: Adapted from the "National Runner's Survey on Dieting and Eating," K. D. Brownell, J. Rodin, and J. Wilmore, *Runner's World*, April 1987, p. 27.

202 *Exercise has potential preventive or therapeutic benefits*: Nieman, op. cit.

202 *Relate the effects of exercise and biological changes*: Nieman, op. cit.; Haskell, op. cit.

202 *An increase in aerobic power*: Haskell, op. cit.

203 *Building muscles may be essential in preventing injury to bones*: Nieman, op. cit.

203 *Older women who have osteoporosis . . . can partially reverse this problem*: Nieman, op. cit.

203 GET OFF YOUR DUFF: D. Sperling, "Try 'Human Power,' Live Longer," *USA Today*, November 3, 1989, section D, p. 1; S. N. Blair, M. W. Kohl III, R. S. Paffenbarger, et al., "Physical Fitness and All-Cause Mortality: A Prospective Study of Healthy Men and Women," *Journal of the American Medical Association*, 1989, *262*, pp. 2395–2401.

204 *Two-year increase in life expectancy*: R. S. Paffenbarger, R. T. Hyde, A. L. Wing, et al., "Physical Activity, All-Cause Mortality and Longevity of College Alumni," *New England Journal of Medicine*, 1986, *314*, pp. 605–613.

204 *Capacity of a person twelve to forty years younger*: Nieman, op. cit.

204 GET FAT? OR GET MOVING?: P. Wood, "The No-Diet Diet," *New Woman*, May 1987, p. 155.

204 *Dieting combined with exercise stimulates energy expenditure*: P. A. Mole, J. S. Stern, C. L. Schultz, et al., "Exercise Reverses Depressed Metabolic Rate Produced by Severe Caloric Restriction," *Medicine and Science in Sports and Exercise*, 1989, *21*, pp. 29–35.

205 *"Gorge yourself with impunity"*: D. B. Greenspan, "Fitness," *Ms.*, November 1989, p. 21.

205 *Successful maintainers exercised*: S. Kayman, W. Bruwold, and J. S. Stern, "Maintenance and Relapse After Weight Loss in Women," *American Journal of Clinical Nutrition*, in press.

206 *Feel better right after . . . strenuous physical activity*: J. Rodin and T. G. Plante, "The Psychological Effects of Exercise," in R. S.

Williams and A. Wallace, eds., *Biological Effects of Physical Activity* (Champaign, IL: Human Kinetics Books, 1989), pp. 127–137.

206 *The highly acclaimed Perrier Survey*: L. Harris and Associates, Inc., *Fitness in America: The Perrier Study: A Natural Research Report of Behavior, Knowledge and Opinions Concerning the Taking Up of Sports and Exercise* (New York: Garland Publishing, 1984).

207 *Higher self-esteem and perceived competence*: G. W. Guyot, L. Fairchild, and M. Hill, "Physical Fitness, Sport Participation, Body Build and Self-Concept of Elementary School Children," *International Journal of Sports Psychology*, 1981, *12*, pp. 105–116.

207 *Athletic competition may provide a structure*: M. J. Mallick, T. W. Shipple, and E. Huerta, "Behavioral and Psychological Traits of Weight-Conscious Teenagers: A Comparison of Eating-Disordered Patients and High- and Low-Risk Groups," *Adolescence*, 1987, *22*, pp. 156–168.

207 *Endogenous opioids*: S. Amir, Z. W. Brown, and Z. Amit, "The Role of Endorphins in Stress: Evidence and Speculations," *Neuroscience Biology and Behavior Review*, 1979, *4*, pp. 77–86.

208 *"Euphoria" during a run*: R. K. Dishman, "Medical Psychology in Exercise and Sports," Symposium on Medical Aspects of Exercise, *Medical Clinics of North America*, January 1985, *69*, pp. 128–143.

208 *Muscle electrical tension*: L. Fehmi in R. Flippin, "Beyond Endorphins: The Latest Research on Runner's High," *American Health*, October 1989, *82*, pp. 78–83; Dishman, op. cit.

209 *Activities that require jumping and running . . . promote the most injury*: B. Kevles, "When You Haven't Got Time for the Pain," *Women's Sports and Fitness*, July/August 1989, p. 12.

209 *Excessive exercise . . . may depress the immune system*: Nieman, op. cit.

210 *Risk of heat injury*: K. Rosenberg and G. Perlman, "Allergic to Exercise," *American Health*, March 1987, p. 42.

210 *"Runner's Anemia"*: L. F. McMahon, M. J. Ryan, D. Larsson, et al., "Occult Gastrointestinal Blood Loss in Marathon Runners," *Annals of Internal Medicine*, 1984, *100*, pp. 846–847.

210 *Delayed menarche . . . related to the age of initiating training*: R. E. Frisch, A. V. Gotz-Welbergen, J. W. McArthur, et al., "De-

layed Menarche and Amenorrhea of College Athletes in Relation to Age of Onset of Training," *Journal of American Medical Association*, 1981, *246*, pp. 1559–1563.

211 *Decreased bone mineral density*: G. W. Barrow and S. Saha, "Menstrual Irregularity and Stress Fractures in Collegiate Female Distance Runners," *American Journal of Sports Medicine*, 1988, *16*, pp. 209–215.

211 *Soda drinkers*: G. Wyshak, R. E. Frisch, T. E. Albright, et al., "Bone Fractures Among Former College Compared with Nonathletes in the Menopausal and Postmenopausal Years," *Obstetrics and Gynecology*, 1987, *69*, pp. 121–126.

212 *Animals on an exercise program*: J. S. Stern and E. A. Applegate, "Exercise Termination Effects on Food Intake, Plasma Insulin, and Adipose Tissue Lipoprotein Lipase Activity in the Osborne-Mendel Rat," *Metabolism*, 1987, *36*, pp. 709–714; P. Lowney, V. M. Lee, R. J. Hansen, et al., "The Effects of Exercise, Detraining, Starvation and Refeeding on the Lipogenic Capacity of the Osborne-Mendel Rat," *American Journal of Physiology*, 1988, *254*, pp. 648–654.

212 *Cycles of stopping and starting exercise*: K. D. Brownell, S. N. Steen, and J. M. Wilmore, "Weight Regulation Practices in Athletes: Analysis of Metabolic and Health Effects," *Medicine and Science in Sports and Exercise*, 1987, *19*, pp. 552–560.

213 *Most restrictive often gain the most weight*: K. D. Brownell, J. Rodin, and J. Wilmore, "National Runner's Survey on Dieting and Stress," *Runner's World*, August 1988, p. 32.

214 *4,542 readers of* Runner's World: ibid.

215 Three studies of female runners: S. M. Short and W. R. Short, "Four-Year Study of University Athletes' Dietary Intake," *Journal of the American Dietetic Association*, 1989, *82*, pp. 632–645; B. L. Drinkwater, K. Nilson, C. M. Chestnut, et al., "Bone Mineral Content of Amenorrheic and Eumenorrheic Athletes," *New England Journal of Medicine*, 1984, *311*, pp. 277–281; R. Marcus, C. Cann, P. Madvig, et al., "Menstrual Function and Bone Mass in Elite Women Distance Runners," *Annals of Internal Medicine*, 1985, *102*, pp. 158–163.

216 *Women who had stopped menstruating*: Marcus, et al., ibid.

216 *Survey showed 38 percent of female and 23 percent of male runners*: K. D. Brownell, et al., "National Runner's Survey on Dieting and Stress," p. 32.

217 *Instances of anorexia were in national . . . companies*: J. Brooks-Gunn, L. Hamilton, and M. P. Warren, "Sociocultural Influences on Eating Disorders in Professional Female Ballet Dancers," *International Journal of Eating Disorders*, 1985, *4*, pp. 465–477.

217 *"Exercise addiction"*: J. Crossman, J. Jameson, and L. Henderson, "Responses of Competitive Athletes to Lay-Off in Training: Exercise Addiction or Psychological Relief?" *Journal of Sports Behavior*, 1987, *10*, pp. 28–38.

218 *Overtraining can cause depression*: J. S. Raglin and W. P. Morgan, "Influence of Vigorous Exercise on Mood State," *The Behavior Therapist*, 1985, *8*, pp. 179–183.

219 *Family or other social problems*: S. Colorado in K. Cobb: "When Is Too Much of a Good Thing Bad?" *American Health*, October 1989, p. 83.

219 *Use of anabolic steroids . . . has increased*: R. E. Windsor and D. Dumitru, "Anabolic Steroid Use by Athletes," *Postgraduate Medicine*, 1988, *84*, pp. 37–49.

220 *Black market anabolic steroids*: K. B. Kashkin and H. D. Kleber, "Hooked on Hormones? An Anabolic Steroid Addiction Hypothesis," *Journal of the American Medical Association*, 1989, *262*, pp. 3166–3170.

220 *Girls are doing it to cut their body fat*: C. Andringa, cited in M. Elias: "Steroid Use Is on Increase Among Teens," *USA Today*, May 2, 1990, section D, p. 1.

220 *Use of anabolic steroids may also be addictive*: Kashkin and Kleber, op. cit.

220 *Abstinence leads to severe depression*: Windsor and Dumitru, op. cit.

220 *Exercise-induced anaphylaxis*: Rosenberg and Perlman, op. cit.

221 *From sexual impotence*: L. Schroepfer, *American Health*, October 1989, p. 83.

221 *Each leaf raked contributes*: R. S. Paffenbarger, cited in Carol Krucoff, *The Washington Post Health Section*, January 30, 1980, p. 27.

CHAPTER 8   THE SUCCESS TRAP

Page

226 *Women who describe themselves as "high maintenance"*: "What Price Beauty?" *Glamour*, April 1991, p. 297.

228 *Perceived Fraudulence Scale*: J. Kolligian and R. J. Sternberg, "Perceived Fraudulence in Young Adults: Is There an Imposter Syndrome?" *Journal of Personality Assessment*, in press.

230 *Women are more prey to fear of success*: G. C. Leder, "Successful Females: Print Media Profiles and Their Implications," *Journal of Psychology*, 1986, *120*, pp. 239–248.

230 *Women . . . feel like imposters*: K. Deaux and M. E. Kite, "Thinking About Gender," in B. B. Hess and M. M. Feree, eds., *Analyzing Gender: A Handbook of Social Science Research* (Newbury Park, CA: Sage, 1987), pp. 92–119.

231 *By age ten*: ibid.

231 *Girls and women tend to attribute their successes*: C. S. Carver and M. F. Scheier, "Outcome Expectancy, Locus of Attribution for Expectancy, and Self-directed Attention as Determinants of Evaluation and Performances," *Journal of Experimental Social Psychology*, 1982, *18*, pp. 184–200.

233 *What psychologists call a defensive pessimist*: J. K. Norem and N. Cantor, "Anticipatory and Post-Hoc Cushioning Strategies: Optimism and Defensive Pessimism in 'Risky' Situations," *Cognitive Therapy and Research*, 1986(a), *10*(3), pp. 347–362; J. K. Norem and N. Cantor, "Defensive Pessimism: 'Harnessing' Anxiety as Motivation," *Journal of Personality and Social Psychology*, 1986(b), *51*(6), pp. 1208–1217.

233 *"Self-handicapping strategies"*: E. E. Jones and S. Berglas, "Drug Choice as a Self-Handicapping Strategy in Response to Non-Contingent Success," *Journal of Personality and Social Psychology*, 1978, *36*, pp. 405–417.

235 *Strong, available "snapshot" in memory*: A. Tversky and D. Kahneman, "Availability: A Heuristic for Judging Frequency and Probability," *Cognitive Psychology*, 1973, *5*, pp. 207–232.

236 *Women have a difficult time adjusting the lens exactly right*: J. Kevin Thompson, *Psychology Today*, April 1986, p. 42.

238 *One of a family's most important tasks*: S. Minuchin, B. L. Rosman, and L. Baker, *Psychosomatic Families* (Cambridge: Harvard University Press, 1978), pp. 35–38.

239 *Women who fear success*: M. S. Horner, "Toward an Understanding of Achievement-Related Conflicts in Women," *Journal of Social Issues*, 1972, *28*, pp. 157–175.

240 *In most studies that have used this investigative tool*: D. M. Pedersen and T. Conlin, "Shifts in Fear of Success in Men and Women from 1968 to 1987," *Psychological Reports*, 1987, *61*, pp. 36–38.

241 *Princeton psychologists . . . studied underachievers*: E. A. Preston, "The Framing of Competence," *Personality and Social Psychology Bulletin*, December 1989, *15*, pp. 477–492; J. M. Riggs, "The Effect of Performance Attributions on Choice of Achievement Strategy," unpublished doctoral dissertation (Princeton University, 1982); E. A. Preston, "The Role of Effort Expenditure in Academic Achievement," unpublished doctoral dissertation (Princeton University, 1983).

244 *Small, overly positive illusions*: S. E. Taylor, *Positive Illusions* (New York: Basic Books, 1989), pp. 46–85.

Index

Permissions